a hidden madness

A HIDDEN MADNESS

James T. R. Jones

Professor of Law
Louis D. Brandeis School of Law
University of Louisville

Foreword By

Elyn R. Saks

New York Times Bestselling Author of
The Center Cannot Hold: My Journey Through Madness
and Winner, 2009 MacArthur Foundation "Genius Grant"

ISBN-13: 978-0615571546 (James T.R. Jones)
ISBN-10: 0615571549

Book design by Rebecca J. Burke

Cover photograph by Kathleen Murphy Jones

for Kathi

Cogito ergo sum
I think, therefore I am
—RENÉ DESCARTES, *Principles of Philosophy*

Foreword

by

Elyn R. Saks

Author of *New York Times* Bestseller
The Center Cannot Hold: My Journey Through Madness
Winner, 2009 MacArthur Foundation "Genius Grant"
Orrin B. Evans Professor of Law, Psychology, and Psychiatry
and the Behavioral Sciences, University of Southern California
Gould School of Law
Adjunct Professor, University of California,
San Diego Department of Psychiatry
Assistant Faculty, New Center for Psychoanalysis

I am pulling into the driveway of the Omni Hotel in downtown Los Angeles to meet a man with whom I have had extensive phone and e-mail contact. The man is Jim Jones, and he had contacted me a year earlier when he learned that I had an interest in mental health in the academy. He identified himself as having bipolar disorder. I called us "fellow travelers," and identified myself as having schizophrenia. Jim was coming to LA to give a talk before my law school, the University of Southern California Gould School of Law, and for the first time I met him in person, as well as his wonderful wife who was accompanying him. I didn't know what to expect, but Jim was tall and very thin, with kindness in his eyes and a sharp wit. His talk went beautifully and his presence cemented what was already a deep relationship.

I was therefore thrilled when Jim enthusiastically said "yes" to my offer to write the Foreword to his memoir about his bipolar illness. Jim's book is extremely important, beautifully written, and very compelling. He masterfully conveys what it feels like to be in a psychotic mania or a psychotic depression—gives a window into the mind of someone suffering in this way. He also discusses what he sees as a childhood that helped lead to his becoming ill—a childhood full of being bullied and tormented. And he talks about what has helped him thrive as an accomplished academic in the face of what can be a crippling mental illness. Jim's is a success story in the case of an illness that often leads to ruin and despair.

Jim's story in a way is similar to mine, and in a way it is not. First, my illness has only rarely affected my mood, and his has only rarely led to disorganized and confused thinking. Second, Jim immediately accepted the need to take medication, which took me a decade. Third, Jim found his hospitalizations benign and helpful, while I found mine traumatic. Fourth, while I have made extensive use of therapy—four to five times a week for years, and continuing—Jim sees a therapist only once every other week. Our differences help paint the landscape of how mental illness affects different people and what treatments may help and what hurt.

Indeed, Jim and I are the only current academics in law who have "come out" with our mental illnesses. Despite differences in our stories, for me, meeting Jim made me feel less alone. I could identify with many aspects of his story, and we have shared many experiences. No one without a psychotic illness can understand as well as another sufferer.

In light of this, it is my hope that Jim's and my stories serve for others what our stories have served for each other: that they help people feel less alone and less defective. Given the differences in our stories, adding another voice will give more people scope to identify. Indeed, we hope that our stories will encourage others to come forward if they can do so without great risk to themselves. Putting a human face on these illnesses should help sufferers feel more hopeful, and should help others in the community understand mental illness more and stigmatize it less. Less stigma will mean many things, but perhaps most important, it may mean that fewer will be deterred from getting treatment. Mental illnesses are illnesses like any other; most of them are treatable. People shouldn't have to suffer, but when stigma leads them to avoid care they likely will. We must seek to encourage people to get the treatment they need.

—Elyn R. Saks

1

In 2004 I could no longer take the drug lithium that for twenty-one years had held the manic-depressive illness from which I suffer in check. Consequently, I endured a major mental breakdown. I had to take a medical leave from teaching at the Louis D. Brandeis School of Law at the University of Louisville where I was a professor. Of necessity I told a few colleagues, in confidence, of the disease that I had kept secret for over eighteen years.

Now I began to ponder whether to go public with my condition. This was a core issue for me: the desirability, and wisdom, of relating my story to the legal academic world, and thereby ultimately to society at large. I knew that Dr. Kay Redfield Jamison had written *An Unquiet Mind* about her life as a successful psychiatry professor at Johns Hopkins University Medical School despite suffering for many years from, and being the world's primary expert on, bipolar disorder. She, however, was a mental health professional, part of a community poised to understand. No law professor had made a similar disclosure about that or any other severe mental illness.

I thought it was important for the legal academic profession to recognize that people with severe mental illness are among the roughly 8,500 law professors in the United States. This knowledge would be vital both to help destigmatize mental illness in my profession and to let those in it with psychiatric conditions learn that they are not alone. It would also be cathartic for me to write my story and thus let everyone know what I had experienced in the past and very well might encounter in the future.

I decided I should write an article particularly tailored for the *Journal of Legal Education*, a law review that goes to all law professors in the nation. I could think of no better way to put my story before my desired audience than having it appear in the *JLE*. With an appropriately catchy title it would grab the eyes of my colleagues both at the Law School and elsewhere.

Clearly, the decision to write such a work is not reached lightly. It particularly troubled me considering my fear of stigma and discrimination that had made me go to great lengths to keep my secret. How would my colleagues, students, and others react when they learned that I was "insane?" Would I be marginalized by legal academia or have students fear to take my courses or give me bad teaching evaluations in light of my disclosure? Would the University support me? Would the taxpayers of Kentucky protest having someone with my diagnosis teaching in one of their professional schools? I knew that once I opened Pandora's Box I could never close it again—for the rest of my life I would be known as "the bipolar law professor." Did I want to bear such a label?

Stigma and discrimination are nothing new. They have followed mental illness throughout history. It has been viewed as internally generated and the product of poor character. Indeed, people in the twenty-first century stigmatize those with psychiatric conditions, *the* most stigmatized group today, even more than their ancestors did fifty years ago. Sadly, while most people no longer use racial and ethnic slurs that once were common, ridicule of those with mental disorders endures. The late Senator Jesse Helms stigmatized when he equated transvestites and kleptomaniacs with people with bipolar disorder. The Democratic Party stigmatized when it forced Senator Thomas Eagleton off its 1972 presidential ticket as running mate with Senator George McGovern when it learned he had been hospitalized three times for depression and treated with electroconvulsive therapy years before. Apparently that group has not changed its views since 1972: then-Indiana Senator Evan Bayh reported that in 2008 when he was "vetted" as the possible vice-presidential running mate for Barack Obama he was asked such questions as had he ever seen a psychiatrist, taken an anti-depressant medication, or talked with any doctor about any mental or emotional issue. Indeed, even today political experts agree a psychiatric history is the kiss of death for anyone with political aspirations. Clinton Administration official Vincent Foster's concern over stigma and the possible loss of his White House security clearance if he saw a psychiatrist, which he did not do, may have led to his suicide.

Many families of those with mental illness are so embarrassed by their loved one's disease that they are afraid to acknowledge their condition. Indeed, advocacy group leaders report donors who condition gifts to help those with mental illness on keeping the donations anonymous. The donors do so because they fear if their generosity becomes public people will think they or someone close to them has a psychiatric condition. Job applicants hide hospitalizations or gaps in employment from mental illness as they fear they will not be hired if they disclose their condition; attorneys are particularly unlikely to be tolerant. To this day those who take the bar examination in many states must reveal if they have ever seen a psychiatrist or been treated for any mental disease.

Insurance companies traditionally have stigmatized relentlessly against those with mental conditions. For example, health insurers long have distinguished between those with "physical" and "mental" ailments to the severe detriment of the latter. Before the effective date of the 2008 federal mental health insurance parity law many Americans were treated differently depending on their type of illness. Insurers put limits on coverage for psychiatric conditions that were much higher than those for other illnesses. They restricted hospital inpatient days and outpatient visits for mental health treatment when they did not do so for those with cancer, heart disease, diabetes, or other "respectable" sicknesses. Deductibles and co-pays were higher. For some, disparity in treatment persists.

Employers that provide long-term disability insurance to their employees frequently discriminate by covering the "physically" disabled to age sixty-five but the "mentally" incapacitated for a period of only a few years. This leaves those unfortunate people to depend on meager Social Security disability benefits for support.

Perhaps one of the greatest problems with stigma is that you never really know what will happen if you go public with your mental illness, whether voluntarily or not. Almost all fear the unknown, those with psychiatric conditions perhaps more than the majority of society. Thus, we keep our condition in the shadows, safe from prying eyes.

I successfully had kept my story a secret for twenty-four years. I was ashamed to have a mental illness, even though I had it through no fault of my own, could not make it go away no matter how hard I tried, and had done all I could to keep it under control. Although I was no different than anyone with a chronic, incurable, but treatable disease, I felt I had disgraced my family since my disorder was psychiatric. Rather than seek support from friends, colleagues, and others I believed I had to keep my condition from practically everyone I knew.

It is incredibly difficult, demeaning, and stressful to have to keep a crucial aspect of your life a secret, but in current society you must do so. How much I would have benefited from encouragement from others over the years! To have just one friend at work with whom I could confide about my concerns and feelings as those with other problems are able to do! I got no such help throughout most of my life coping with a mental disorder because I simply, but justifiably, was afraid to ask for it. As a result I was out in the dark, a marginal figure in the world. Effectively the only ones to whom I could open my heart were the doctors and therapists I paid to listen to me.

The level of my terror of disclosure is demonstrated by the fact I once changed psychiatrists just because the psychiatrist wife of a junior colleague joined the group of doctors with whom my then-psychiatrist practiced. I was afraid if I kept going to my psychiatrist I might be recognized by my colleague's wife and then somehow word about my condition might get back to my employer. My concern showed both paranoia and, sadly, an accurate perception of reality.

The stigma of mental illness is evil and unwarranted, but it is still very real and all-encompassing. I know many people who are petrified that those in the "normal" world will learn they have depression or schizophrenia or bipolar disorder. What is so truly sad about the situation is that mental illness affects millions of Americans during their lifetimes. It is the leading reason for disability for those between ages fifteen and forty-four and accounts for over fifteen percent of the disease burden in the United States, a higher percentage than that of all cancers. A history of a psychiatric disorder is not a moral failing and, contrary to popular belief, many like me have never had problems with alcohol or illegal drugs despite having a severe mental disease. Most with serious mental illness pose no threat of harm to anyone, other than perhaps themselves. Indeed, they frequently become crime victims because they often live at the margins of society subject to homelessness and related conditions.

Still, societal stereotypes, often reinforced by selective media reporting of incidents such as the Virginia Tech University shootings, unduly link violence with psychiatric disorders. A report of the United States Surgeon General emphasizes that the vast majority of those with mental illness are not violent and that the portion of the violence attributable to those so afflicted is very small. Psychiatric disorders are diseases just like any other chronic sickness. People like me with severe mental illness can be successful members of society in high-level and often stressful professional jobs despite having a psychiatric condition.

Nevertheless, in 2004, stigma was particularly an issue by virtue of the way I intended to tell my story. I hoped to use the *JLE*, the most esteemed peer reviewed journal in law, to reach my colleagues in legal academia, and I had no idea how they would react to having one of their own reveal that he has a mental illness. I knew my fear of stigma would haunt me during the entire writing of the article.

During the years after 2004 I periodically mulled over how to proceed. I frequently discussed the matter with my wife Kathi, who encouraged me to go forward but said she totally supported whatever I wanted to do. Both my psychiatrist Dr. Deborah Quinton and my therapist John Turner could see advantages, both for society at large and me, from telling my story, but agreed it was a serious question to be approached cautiously. My friend and colleague Sam Marcosson, who is gay and had come out of the closet years before, strongly suggested that I do the same. I engaged in a cost benefit analysis as I debated the proper course. Finally, I fell back on the conclusion of Dr. Jamison in her memoir: "I have no idea what the long-term effects of discussing my illness so openly will be on my personal and professional life, but, whatever the consequences, they are bound to be better than continuing to be silent. I am tired of hiding, tired of misspent and knotted energies, tired of the hypocrisy, and tired of acting as if I have something to hide. One is who one is."

Thus, by the fall of 2006 I started down the road of recalling the high and low points of my life with my disease and putting them on paper. Gradually doing so became a compulsion that captured my spare time, hampered my sleep, and helped worsen the mania that was increasing exponentially since my cessation of lithium. Some parts of the article were very difficult to write, but I forced myself to address them. I carefully researched bipolar disorder, buying a number of books on the subject and talking with Dr. Quinton and John Turner about it, to enable me accurately and dispassionately to report on it.

When I actually began to compose my story I had no guarantee the *JLE* would accept the piece, and at times hoped it would not. As I worked on it I was careful to take the newly prescribed medication Seroquel exactly as Dr. Quinton recommended. Unlike many with my disorder, I am compliant with doctor's orders and take the drugs that allow me to function at a high level. Unfortunately, despite doing so my manic symptoms grew worse and worse. In a search for the right amount Dr. Quinton kept doubling and redoubling the dose of Seroquel to control my symptoms, but it was not working.

By spring 2007 my life was spiraling out of control. Despite all Dr. Quinton's efforts, I now was increasingly manic. I was teaching demanding courses: Torts, the law of personal injury and related civil wrongs, and Decedents' Estates, the law of wills and other ways people dispose of their property when they die. My students had to put up with my bizarre classroom behavior as I exhibited the theatricality, amusing irrelevancy, racing thoughts, and tangential thinking common in one gripped by the mad ecstasy of florid mania.

What exactly is mania? According to such authorities as the National Institute of Mental Health, along with the conduct listed above, the manic phase of bipolar disorder features behaviors like increased energy or restlessness; euphoria, despondency, or both in rapid succession; extreme irritability, volatility, and impatience; rapid speech that cannot be interrupted; distractibility and inability to concentrate or distinguish whether thoughts are relevant;

inability to or lack of need for sleep; poor judgment; spending sprees; denial that anything is wrong; provocative, obnoxious, or aggressive conduct, including angry tirades; drug or alcohol abuse; and diminished impulse control that can lead to demanding and self-centered actions and sexual misbehavior. Forty percent of those with my condition are arrested at some point during their lifetimes. Fortunately, many people with bipolar disorder, including me, do not suffer from all these symptoms, although I have had many of them at one time or another.

Racing irrelevant thoughts, those I had in abundance. One evening in Decedents' Estates I discussed challenges to wills on the basis the testator was unduly influenced by a beneficiary to leave some or all his or her property to the "undue influencer."

"Kentucky courts look for a number of 'badges' of undue influence," I said. Before listing them, however, I blurted out "Badges? We don't need no stinking badges!," my favorite line from Mel Brooks' classic comedy film *Blazing Saddles*. "*Blazing Saddles* is one of my favorite movies."

A student piped up "I think *Blazing Saddles* is very good, but I prefer Brooks' *Young Frankenstein*."

"Oh, that's a great movie too, and I love the song 'Oh, sweet mystery of life at last I found you!' from it." On a roll, I then sang part of it in my best baritone voice. Some students seemed a little confused over what this had to do with the course, but were too polite to ask if it would be on the exam.

I also demonstrated my singing prowess when I was talking about the disposition of famed singer James Brown's body after his death. I launched exuberantly into "I feel good, I knew that I would" accompanied by an air guitar riff. Finally, in Torts Aretha Franklin came up and I warbled "R-E-S-P-E-C-T, Find out what it means to me, R-E-S-P-E-C-T, Take care . . ." to the considerable amusement of the class. On each occasion, the mania left me exhilarated, overjoyed to have the floor and perform in front of a receptive audience.

Things really got out of hand when I fell prey in Decedents' Estates to my longstanding fascination over the fate of the ocean liner RMS *Titanic*. My discussion was relevant at the outset. I was explaining the rule that a husband may provide in his will that if his wife remarries after he dies she will forfeit the money he leaves in a trust for her. The widow of millionaire Colonel John Jacob Astor IV lost her life income interest in a five million dollar trust when she remarried a few years after he went down with *Titanic*. I could not, however, leave it at that. Instead, I talked extensively and elatedly about the Astors.

"When Colonel Astor divorced his wife of many years, the scandal was the talk of an enraged New York City high society. Things got even worse when two years later Astor married an eighteen year old who was younger than Astor's son. To get away and allow New York blueblood outrage to die down the newlyweds took an extended honeymoon trip to Europe. When they learned Mrs. Astor was pregnant they decided to return to New York. The Astors, their two servants, and their pet Airedale Kitty all got on *Titanic* in Cherbourg, France. Two of the four (and Kitty) went down with the ship."

I then noted that "Colonel Astor was crushed to death by a falling smokestack. His body later was identified from his initials on his shirt collar, and he eventually was buried in Trinity Church Cemetery in New York City."

I even focused on the actor who looked like and portrayed Astor in the 1997 blockbuster film *Titanic*. "Hans Gudegast made his first splash as the German officer in the 1960s World War II television series *The Rat Patrol*. It told the story of a small U.S. unit that drove around North Africa in two jeeps and wrecked havoc on any Germans who got in its way. Starting in 1980 Gudegast, now using the name Eric Braeden, took the role of Victor Newman on the television soap opera *The Young and the Restless.* He's been there ever since."

My ability to recall useless trivia like this makes me an excellent *Jeopardy* player. Indeed, I amazed even myself when I could recite the early career of a soap opera actor whose show I had never watched, much less the breed and name of the Astor family dog. At the time I realized on some level that I had gone beyond the pale, but at that moment mania, in the form of a single-minded euphoria and enthusiasm, ruled over all reason.

Perhaps my most tangential episode of the semester was in both Torts and Decedents' Estates after I saw the 2007 movie *300*. It reminded me of my love of ancient history in general and the Battle of Thermopylae in particular. I talked for some time about the battle between the Greeks and Persians as it was portrayed in the film. I then focused on the writings of the ancient Greek historian Herodotus.

"One of the great moments in Herodotus was when he quoted the Spartan officer Dienekes [or Διηνέκης, as I wrote on the board since I know classical Greek]. When told there were so many Persian archers that their arrows would blot out the sun, he responded 'Good, then we'll fight in the shade.' After the Persians killed all the Spartans and some time had passed, the Greeks placed a marker atop their burial mound. It reads: 'Ὦ ξεῖν', ἀγγέλλειν Λακεδαιμονίοις ὅτι τῇδε κείμεθα, τοῖς κείνων ῥήμασι πειθόμενοι.' That translates as 'Go tell the Spartans, you who passest by, That here, obedient to their laws, we lie.'"

It escapes me today what any of this, especially the ancient Greek, had to do with Torts or Decedents' Estates, but it somehow seemed appropriate in my then state of mind.

I certainly enjoyed the semester, and the mania that helped fuel it. At least some students, however, indicated in their course evaluations that they thought I was eccentric and wasting their time. Their understandable irritation, if not outright anger, could gravely damage my career. When I focused upon it I seriously wondered whether I was making a huge blunder in planning to publish the story of my mental illness. Was I recklessly about to expose myself to the stigma from which I successfully had hidden for so long? What if the completed article, submitted to the *JLE*, was rejected, but because I had exposed it, word of my situation leaked back to Louisville, especially all my colleagues in the Law School? I was in a conundrum of my own making, and was unsure what to do next. I saw danger all around me: student uprising, the wrath of my dean, loss of tenure, unemployment, insolvency, bankruptcy, homelessness, addiction, sexually transmitted disease, divorce, imprisonment, insanity, and death through malnutrition, disease, violence, or suicide.

2

Many children are targeted by others for bullying and torment and are greatly affected by it. In my case, however, my parents perceived my reaction presaged worse problems. As a result of my psychophysiological warning signs, including severe gastric symptoms and budding depression, my mother wanted to take me for mental health counseling. My father, however, would not hear of it. "He was afraid a psychiatric history would haunt you later in life," she subsequently recalled. In other words, both my parents realized I was so broken that I needed professional help while still in my mid-teens. Society in the late 1960s and early 1970s viewed any sort of mental health care so negatively that my father may have been right about his concern. Still, the benefit to me of early psychological treatment may have outweighed the burden of stigma. I will always wonder if I would have turned out differently had I gotten some help early in my life. Regardless, I learned early the stigma of "being different" and the need to hide that status at all costs.

I was born in 1953 in Richmond, Virginia. My father was a certified public accountant who helped manage the business matters of a hospital and a group of physicians who practiced there. My mother was a typical 1950s homemaker who was always there when I came home from school.

My childhood on the surface was normal. For me, however, it was a nightmare. I was different from the mainstream in various ways, including physical appearance, high grades, dress, and personality quirks. As a consequence, other children verbally tormented me brutally and relentlessly.

In the late 1950s and early 1960s, my most formative years, Richmond, the former capital of the Confederacy, was rife with the bigotry and intolerance that were so characteristic of the Old South. To children of that time and place the worst thing they could think of to say to or about someone was to categorize him with a persecuted minority. They would do this whether or not he actually belonged to the targeted group. With me they constantly did so using words and terms that were, and were intended to be, so offensive that they should not be repeated. Indeed, my contemporaries effectively totally excluded me from conventional society. I, who wanted nothing more than for others to accept me, got the unmistakable message that my classmates would not do so under any circumstances. I truly was a pariah.

In 1964 we moved to Jacksonville, Florida. The abuse continued. Over much of my youth I had nothing and no one to help me absorb the cruelty that others directed at me. This mistreatment made me a loner who dealt with stress by vomiting every day when I came home from grade school. Throughout elementary and high school I was bullied unmercifully.

My mother later noted that, unlike my brother Rick, my only sibling, five years older than I, I never misbehaved. Instead, she suspected the truth: I fixated on being a perfect child in order to gain parental approval in an unsuccessful effort to compensate for the peer abuse.

Although I know in his own way my father loved me, he was not one to express his feelings. My desire for paternal appreciation motivated my academic success that, in turn, further alienated me from my classmates.

Even though my behavior and grades were exemplary, I missed considerable time from the hell at school by claiming real or imagined physical ailments. I was clever enough to hold a thermometer next to a light bulb to generate a fake fever so my mother would think I was sick and keep me home.

My principal pleasures were collecting comic books, which may have been the first manic spending episode in my life, and listening to the Atlanta Braves major league baseball team on the radio. I eventually also became a huge fan of the Miami Dolphins National Football League team. It was good that I enjoyed these things that I could do alone, as I had practically no friends.

I entered Jacksonville Episcopal High School in the eighth grade and stayed there until I graduated in 1972. I won an award every year for my grades, and earned a semester of college credit through taking advanced placement courses. History was my focus, and my lifelong love of that topic dates to my years at Episcopal. Ultimately, I was selected for the National Honor Society, was a National Merit finalist, and was on the school's television quiz show *It's Academic!* team. At graduation I finished third in my class.

My parents were both extremely conservative Republicans. It is thus not surprising that they strongly opposed the dress and hairstyles of the late 1960s. Hence, I had to wear my hair short and was forbidden to wear jeans and other styles of the time. Although I inwardly was angry that I was forced to look starkly different from my classmates, I wore what I was told to wear. I also made regular trips to the barber.

I deeply resented my parents for the ridicule I constantly endured for being different. I felt helpless, yet chronically enraged, over my lot in life.

Rather than avoiding those who tormented me, I stubbornly thrust myself among them. For example, I served as student manager for the baseball, basketball, and football teams. The stress I felt dealing with abusive peers helped cause me to develop severe duodenal ulcers by the age of fifteen. My condition greatly surprised my gastroenterologist, who had never seen such severe disease in one so young.

Because I was such a loner I was socially backward, and developed an acute inferiority complex. I did not date in high school for fear that no one would go out with me. I did not even attend my senior prom.

A look at my high school yearbook shows me stooped over a tray in the lunchroom in a mocking candid photograph. It was as if someone on the yearbook staff said "let's put in a funny picture of the lonely nerd." That sort of thing really hurt. It all made me feel down much of the time.

Despite my loner status, I had two special friends. The first was Andy Baker, whom I met shortly after we moved to Jacksonville and who remains a good friend today. Several spring vacations we camped out at his family's lake property for the week and spent our time fishing, boating, and talking about our experiences with adolescence for those who were not part of the "in" crowd. We would have a contest to see who would catch the most fish, and it was usually a neck-and-neck experience. We ate what we caught, with me doing the cooking over a camp stove. Once there was great excitement when I caught a huge largemouth bass. It fed my entire family for two meals! As we grew closer and closer, Andy always accepted me for who I am, and was always there for me. This helped me handle the torment I generally endured.

My other special friend was Sue-Sue, a/k/a/ Susie, a solidly-built black and tan female miniature dachshund. She was sweet, beautiful (I adore the appearance of all dachshunds), and the source of unquestioned love. She never cared what I looked like, what clothes I wore, or anything else.

Susie was highly intelligent. Indeed, she was scary smart. She almost seemed to be able to read your mind, and would react based on what she seemingly perceived. Her deep brown eyes and wagging tail conveyed her own emotion, which generally was extreme happiness. She indicated it by various expressions of affection, including lots of doggy kisses. Appropriately enough for my dog, however, she had her own psychological issues. She could not stand to be left alone: when we built her a lovely doghouse with a picket fence around it she promptly dug down several feet through hard clay and proudly escaped to meet us triumphantly when we returned home. She would destroy any room in which we confined her. Indeed, I always thought she was part beaver, as she would eat through woodwork, dry wall, or a two by four, in addition to raising a tremendous ruckus, during her single-minded pursuit of freedom. I found her sheer spunk lovable and endearing.

Susie shared my days, slept in my bed, and demonstrated to me what many professionals say, that pets provide much comfort and support to those who have mental illnesses. I dearly loved Susie, and wonder in retrospect if I would have survived adolescence had I not had the blessed few like my friend Andy Baker and my dog Sue-Sue.

My parents were strong Presbyterians. They force-fed that creed to me. At Episcopal I had to study religion and attend regular chapel services. Between the Presbyterian and Episcopalian indoctrinations I developed a strong aversion to organized religion that continues to this day. For once, I acted on my feelings of rebellion against my parents and their surrogates.

By the time I was eighteen I had done very well in school. Indeed, as someone once remarked: "You're the only person I know who always speaks in complete sentences." Still, I was an outcast and a loner, deeply traumatized by years of taunting and bullying. According to authorities on bipolar disorder, environmental conditions like this early in life often are found in those who eventually develop the disease. I had strong feelings of anxiety, inferiority and depression. I had a severe physiological reaction to stress in the form of my gastrointestinal concerns; my current psychiatrist attributes this problem to burgeoning mental illness that definitely merited psychiatric treatment had my father allowed it. I had difficulties with irritability and volatility, classic symptoms of bipolar disorder, and frequently lashed out at others, including Susie, when upset. Indeed, it would have almost been miraculous had my mental health not been severely compromised by my being the principal target of peer abuse during my most formative years. As the "untouchable" in high school, I was not in a particularly propitious mental state as I headed off for college.

3

As a proud native Virginian I wanted to attend college there. My parents and I visited Washington and Lee University, Hampden-Sydney College, and the University of Virginia. I was particularly impressed by Mr. Jefferson's University, or the "University," in Charlottesville. It oozed history everywhere. For example, Edgar Allen Poe's room was a mini-museum. The University had a beautiful neo-classical architectural core designed by Jefferson himself from his home in nearby Monticello. Despite being a state university it had only gone co-educational a few years before, thereby demonstrating its overall conservative slant. The anti-Vietnam War demonstrations and other concerns that swept many college campuses around this time were pretty much non-issues at Virginia.

My ego got a much needed boost when my application to Virginia was accepted in November 1971. Things got even better when I was invited to join the Echols Scholar program. Only about 120 students per year were Echols Scholars, and we had our own dormitory. All the normal academic requirements were waived for us. We could take any courses we wanted either on the undergraduate or graduate level, and we did not have to declare a major. Still, I ultimately majored in ancient—mainly Greco-Roman—and modern English history. Over eighty of my 120 credits were in history or history-related courses. Because each Echols Scholar was a bit eccentric in his or her own individual

19

way, I undoubtedly fit in better with the other Scholars than I would have with the normal University population.

In August 1972 my parents delivered me to Charlottesville. As my stomach was doing reasonably well, I was able to discover alcohol. I consumed it in large quantities like most of my fellow students. In those days the University had a much deserved reputation as one of the premier party schools in the nation. I maintained a mini-bar in my room and became adept at mixing drinks, although the standard beverage was Virginia Gentleman bourbon whiskey and Coke. I also tried beer, which I enjoyed to excess. I will never forget my last experience with it. I drank somewhere between fifteen and twenty-one large cups at a keg party, and proceeded to be so violently ill that I have been unable to stomach any sort of beer since then.

I began to try to date, but was generally unsuccessful in that regard. Like many survivors of bullying, who have serious self-esteem problems, I was very much afraid that doing so would only lead to rejection.

Fraternities were still a major force at the University, and I went through rush like many of the students. Although most fraternities were not interested in the nerdy Echols Scholars, some liked to take them as members in order to raise the fraternity grade point average. I was particularly interested in one very conservative chapter. I apparently would have been accepted into membership had I not been so overeager that I telephoned someone to check on my status and was black-balled as a result. Once again, I was enough of an outcast to be rejected by mainstream University society. Incidents like this reinforced my feelings of insecurity and inadequacy and led to periods of depression that hampered my ability to function and damaged my digestive health.

I did continue the family tradition by joining the College Republican Club. As a member I volunteered as a poll watcher at a rural precinct on behalf of President Richard M. Nixon. I was proud that, due at least in small part to my efforts, Nixon prevailed there. Like my parents, I have almost always favored Republican presidential candidates.

I also became a member of the University Guide Service, a volunteer student organization whose members gave tours to visitors from all over the world. This was a further expression of my love of history, and gave me considerable pleasure.

Like many of the "preppy" students at the University, my standard attire for class during my first year was blue blazer, khaki slacks, button-down shirt, tie, and penny loafers or Sperry Top-Siders. While I did "dress down" for my other two years at the University, I always wore khaki slacks and Top-Siders. To this day, I have never owned or worn a pair of blue jeans. I was finally able to grow my hair long enough to fit in, at least appearance-wise, with the preppy crowd.

Maintaining my outsider status, in January 1973 I particularly enjoyed watching Super Bowl VII. Then, in a television room surrounded by rabid Washington Redskins fans, I saw my beloved Miami Dolphins, whose stocking cap I proudly wore, win fourteen to seven. Needless to say, my vocal cheering for the Dolphins did not increase my popularity.

My biggest social, escapist, and nerdy activity was one I shared with many of the Echols Scholars, among others, war gaming. As an illustration of my competitive streak, and vivid imagination, I joined the Historical Simulation Society, a/k/a the War Games Club. We met every Friday in the wardroom at the Navy R.O.T.C. building. While I played a variety of war games, my most famous in the local gaming community was a recreation of the World War II Battle of Midway, which turned the tide of the War in the Pacific. As U.S. commander I had an unusual approach. At the start of the game I would send out long range scout planes to locate the main Japanese aircraft carriers. Once they did so, I waited for the carriers to reach the maximum range for the attack planes on my carriers and Midway Island. As soon as they did, I launched all planes for a surprise attack. When they reached the enemy carriers I could visualize the Japanese with fully fueled and armed planes, as well as stacks of bombs and gallons of fuel, just sitting on their decks ready to explode. My torpedo planes and dive bombers would have a field day, often sinking all four major enemy carriers. With that done, my fleet would just hide from the Japanese battleships for the rest of the game, which I would win on points.

Of course, this strategy would have been problematic in real life: I had made kamikazes of all the U.S. pilots since they lacked the fuel to return home after the attack. Their family members would not have looked kindly on such a tactic. An illustration of how a war gamer can do things in a contest that would never actually be attempted. I played to win, any way I could. That approach later would serve me poorly.

In my third year I discovered the brand new and wildly popular role-playing game, Dungeons and Dragons. I became totally immersed in its imaginary world. In those early days of D & D there were no prepackaged game scenarios or miniature figures as are available today. Instead, all was left to the imagination of the players and the game leader, or dungeon master. He (few women played D & D) would create a dungeon and have events occur at designated spots or randomly depending on a roll of various polyhedral game dice.

In the game, a make-believe party of heroes would make their way through a maze in search of treasure and experience. The characters were recurring, which meant that you might play with the same persona for many game sessions. In the process, he would become increasingly rich and powerful. You would get extremely attached to, and empathize with, him. It would be disastrous to have him die in battle, so you tried to avoid that at all costs. The dungeon master, on the other hand, wanted to make the game challenging. Thus, he would create situations that would greatly tax, or even kill off some of, the characters. Individual game sessions often lasted for many hours, with all totally immersed in what they imagined was happening based on what the dice, and the dungeon master, said.

After each battle or skirmish the surviving group members would head on in search of more wealth, power, and glory for their characters and, indirectly, they themselves who controlled, and identified with, them. All this let you and the other players escape for a time into another universe, avoiding the travails of the real world, *par excellence*. We might not date, or interact well with others, in the planet at large, where we were deemed weird at best, but we felt our D & D exploits made us important people in our own, special realm.

I participated in another somewhat unusual activity, the Society for Creative Anachronism. I role-played in costume as a medieval archer (I liked archery). I went to SCA tournaments and observed the jousts the more athletic members fought. The pseudo-medieval banquets were always a highlight of each event. I was renowned for my mulled wine recipe. I even met a very nice University undergraduate female SCA member who clearly wanted to start a relationship with me. As usual, however, I was not comfortable doing so and accordingly missed a golden opportunity for romance.

I did partake in more traditional University events, such as attending football games. In those days the University had a lousy football team, but that did not really matter much to the crowd at home contests. Pretty much everyone, including me, dressed up for the occasion in his or her finest attire. Almost all also brought a flask of Virginia Gentleman to the contest. Each time the University scored we would all sing the University anthem, "The Good Old Song," to the tune of "Auld Lang Syne" and have a bourbon and Coke to celebrate.

Despite all these activities, my grades were high even though I took mostly graduate level history courses. I won numerous academic awards. Most important, I was inducted into the Phi Beta Kappa Society, the oldest and most selective honor society in the United States, during my third (and last) year. I thus joined my father, who became a Phi Beta Kappa when a student at the University of North Carolina at Chapel Hill.

As I am quite superstitious—for example, I have a severe case of triskaidekaphobia, an irrational fear of the number thirteen—I developed a mantra I would recite to myself for luck before each exam. I continued using that formula in law school, and even today employ it for its soothing effect when I am in times of extreme stress.

My mantra consists of three parts: First, despite my anti-religion feelings, I state the first verse of the Gospel of John in its original Greek, "ἐν ἀρχῇ ἦν ὁ λόγος, καὶ ὁ λόγος ἦν πρὸς τὸν θεόν, καὶ θεὸς ἦν ὁ λόγος." Then I recite the opening Greek words of Homer's epic poem the *Iliad*, "Μῆνιν ἄειδε θεὰ Πηληϊάδεω Ἀχιλῆος οὐλομένην." Finally, I again go against the grain and cross myself repeatedly while saying the Latin "*in nomine Patris, et Filii, et Spiritūs Sancti.*"

I did have serious health difficulties. They, as when I was at Episcopal, evidenced stress on my part and, as noted, were precursors of mental illness. My ulcer problem recurred by my third year, and in the spring semester I suffered a near-fatal gastrointestinal bleed. After I passed a large quantity of bright red blood, I walked over to the Student Health office for aid. I tried to avoid hospitalization. "If you don't get treatment right now," the Student Health doctor stated, "you'll probably bleed to death. I won't be responsible for what happens if you don't go into the hospital." At that, I reluctantly followed his advice.

I stayed in the hospital for a week, and nearly had to have

emergency surgery. After I returned to my apartment things continued to be touch-and-go. A month later I was back in the hospital for intractable pain. I convinced my doctor to give me a pass so I could enter my special world by playing D & D for a few hours.

I had to withdraw from several courses, but obstinately refused to take a medical leave of absence in view of my planned enrollment in law school that fall. My illness postponed my graduation until August, and over my final year my GPA fell from a 3.95 to a 3.85. I took my degree, with highest distinction, on the same day I started law school.

I underwent the then-recommended surgical treatment for severe duodenal ulcer disease after the spring semester. There was no good non-surgical alternative treatment since the medications now used to control this condition were not yet available. The numerous complications of the surgery have afflicted me ever since.

While in general I still did not make friends easily, I hit the mother lode with another Echols Scholar, Thomas L. Ramey. Tom, who was a pre-med student, was the son of a professor in the University's Engineering School. In addition to having an exceptional mind, he was a wonderful friend, as close as or closer to me than Andy Baker. We hung out together a great deal.

Tom's grandfather had been a high-level administrator at Duke University, so Duke was where Tom wanted to go for medical school. Like me, Tom took his degree from the University in three years, and he was inducted into the Phi Beta Kappa Society along with me.

Tom is a great lover of classical music, especially opera, and he passed that passion over to me. I started to collect classical records, today cds, sometimes at a near manic level. Indeed, I have spent many thousands of dollars on them over the years. I listen to them constantly. For example, as I write this, I am enjoying a recording of Mozart dances. I mainly enjoy pre-

Beethoven works. Classical music became my escape from the travails and disappointments of the real world. Like Martin Luther, I used music as a remedy for my often depressed, or melancholy, nature. To this day it is my principal means of both relaxation and release. It also gives me a way to show I am an intellectual and different from the vast majority of society that rejects me. I have never really listened to popular music.

I stayed close to my family in nearby Henderson, North Carolina. I spent every Thanksgiving from 1972 to 1977 with my Aunt Bet, my father's only sibling. I loved her dearly, and she was my favorite relative.

During the fall 1974 semester I started to ponder my future. I wanted to attend graduate school in history, earn my Ph.D., and become a college history professor since college was where I felt most comfortable. However, when I talked with my English history professor he laid it on the line.

"You'd make an excellent history professor," he said. "But let me tell you something. Last year ninety-six students earned Ph.D.s in English history in the United States. There were jobs for three of them."

I reflected on this sobering statistic and reassessed my plans.

"Where can a bright young man with a B.A. in ancient and modern English history study to have a promising career?," I thought. The answer was clear: "Law school!" I could always try to become a law professor at some point.

With my career choice made, I signed up for the LSAT, on which I did well. Considering my regional preference I decided to apply to law school at the University, Washington and Lee, Chapel Hill, and Duke. I hurried up my applications, especially to Duke, when I learned Tom Ramey was going there for medical school. Still, I really wanted to stay at the University. Indeed, I applied for and won the right to stay in one of the original Jeffersonian student rooms there. The only problem was that I had to get into the University's Law School to use it.

Despite my high grades and solid LSAT score, the Law School put me on its waiting list. Meanwhile, Duke, which like Virginia was a top-ten ranked law school, immediately accepted me and made it very clear I was welcome. Washington and Lee and Chapel Hill each also offered me a place, but I did not consider them as I had gotten into Duke.

All spring and summer of 1975 I waited to hear from the University, but the good word never came. Hence, I decided to attend Duke where I would already have a close friend in Tom Ramey. I was very bitter over the University's treatment of me, and here my tendency to hold grudges has evidenced itself: while I was very loyal to Virginia while I was there, I have ignored it since I took my degree. Instead, I regularly have supported Duke University School of Law and Jacksonville Episcopal High School.

College certainly went better than my years before it. I did well academically, thereby furthering my goal of achieving parental approval. I encountered others with my outlook on the world, especially many other nerdy Echols Scholars and the gamers with whom I appropriately could demonstrate my competitive streak. I made a wonderful friend in Tom Ramey. I found a world, higher academics, where I was reasonably comfortable and could foresee having a career. I discovered the healing power of classical music. Still, I battled depression and saw my gastrointestinal problems, with their prescience of mental illness, lead to near loss of life. I persisted in having a limited social life. Various reasons may have resulted in my continuing failure to date even when I had a viable chance to do so, including possible fear of the opposite sex given my own experience with a very strong mother and the aforementioned self-esteem upshot of the bullying in my pre-college life. I was less of an outcast than I had been at Episcopal, but I still did not fit in with much of mainstream society, as represented by the fraternity crowd. I was deeply hurt and disappointed by my rejection by the Law School. Still, I stubbornly moved ahead, ready for the next great period of my life: Duke Law School.

4

When I entered Duke University School of Law in August 1975 my health was still precarious on account of my recent ulcer surgery. I lived in a furnished apartment Duke provided for graduate students. I generally was unable to make friends with whom I might have resided and Tom Ramey wanted to live alone. Therefore, I stayed in the same complex for all my time at Duke with randomly assigned apartment-mates each year.

My first semester featured the typical problems incident to adjusting to law school. These were magnified by my usual feelings of depression, anxiety, inadequacy, inferiority, and social awkwardness.

In keeping with my history, I studied alone and did not outline or join a study group with other students although most of my colleagues did both. I was so used to being an outcast that it never occurred to me that others might want to help me.

Like everyone else in the class, I had no idea how I was doing. This did not help my mental status. I preserved my sanity through various methods. One was occasional visits to Henderson to see Aunt Bet. Another was constantly listening to classical music. A third entailed spending considerable time with Tom Ramey, with whom I went on frequent classical record buying jaunts. Fourth, I discovered a D & D game and spent as much time playing it as possible. Finally, I attended a few Society for Creative Anachronism jousts and related events;

once again, my mulled wine was a hit at the feasts. As usual, I did not date. Retiring into the fantasy world of D & D and the SCA let me avoid interacting with mainstream individuals.

By the end of the semester I was in a pretty sorry state thanks to severe anxiety and depression. I cannot say, however, I was much worse off than many of my classmates. I studied, alone, incessantly for exams, poring repeatedly over my encyclopedic notes. I hoped my good short-term memory would serve me well. I somehow made it through finals and then headed home for the Christmas break. My father had arranged an interview for a summer job for me with the law firm that represented the group of doctors whose practice he managed. I was lucky enough to land a position for the grand sum of $600 per month.

When I returned to school in January, classes resumed. The big question in each first year student's mind was the burning one of how he or she had done on the all-important fall semester exams. Faculty grades were not due until weeks into the second semester, and anxiety ruled everywhere. I was convinced I had failed my finals. As time passed I grew increasingly desperate to know something. I have never waited, and do not wait, well. This was particularly the case when evaluation of my academic performance, the success to which my fragile ego inextricably was tied, was the issue.

Finally, I went to see the admissions dean, a delightful lady with whom I had bonded. "I can't take the suspense any longer. I'll just drop out now to avoid the shame of public failure."

"Isn't that an overreaction? You may have done fine."

"No, I've made up my mind. I'm too proud to be disgraced in front of my classmates."

"Wait a minute while I check on something in my office." When she emerged a few minutes later, she said "Calm down. You're worrying yourself to death over nothing. You rank third in the class."

Suddenly, I felt immeasurably better!

The rest of the spring semester went fine. I felt good about my performance both for my own sake and as I hoped it engendered pride in my parents and Aunt Bet. The faculty treated me as one of the best students in the class. Indeed, Property Professor Bertel Sparks bestowed upon me his honorific of "judge," calling on me as "Judge Jones" to handle difficult issues.

I was fairly confident about spring exams. As it turned out, I did extremely well. I even got one of the highest grades in the course I thought I understood the least. My class rank continued to be third, a status I maintained until my final year. I was still somewhat depressed, but felt as well as I had since the time at Virginia before my gastric concerns grew severe.

I enjoyed my time during the summer at the firm in Jacksonville. I got considerable experience writing memoranda about torts, the area of the law I would begin teaching a little over a decade later.

Meanwhile, I received, based upon my grades, an invitation to join the Editorial Board of the *Duke Law Journal*. My initial inclination was to demur, as I thought it would interfere with my study time and my yearning to raise my class rank. Wiser people, however, told me "being on law review is a very smart career move." Indeed, someone pointed out that "if you want to become a law professor someday it's an invaluable credential." Hence, I accepted the invitation. I even began to learn the then-essential criteria for a job in legal academia, the place where I thought both that I best would fit in and be most comfortable: having excellent grades at a highly ranked law school; being on law review, and even better, publishing an article, called a Note or Comment in law review lingo, while there; clerking for a federal appellate judge; and practicing at a major law firm, preferably somewhere on Wall Street, for a time. I turned my attention to doing these things.

When I got back to school in August 1976 I started my *Journal* work. I labored on what was published as a Note in the *Journal* in 1977 and was to be a jewel in my crown.

As fall progressed I found myself in the unusual status of a hot commodity. Numerous law firms vied to interview me for a job during the second summer of my law school tenure. The idea was to work for a firm for the summer and then take a permanent position there as an associate, a younger attorney who had not yet earned the status of partner in the firm, upon graduation.

I saw this as an opportunity to return to Richmond, and interviewed with all the major firms there. Several offered me a summer associate position. At the same time, my Uncle Tom, my mother's only sibling, who was a vascular surgeon in New York City, encouraged me to try a Wall Street firm. Trusts and Estates Professor Sparks, who formerly had taught at New York University School of Law and consequently had many New York City connections, pushed me in that same direction. I ended up splitting my summer between one of the premier firms in Richmond and White & Case, a major Wall Street firm. Uncle Tom was kind enough to invite me to stay with him and my Aunt Linnie in their large Fifth Avenue co-op overlooking Central Park during my time in Manhattan. Hence, my summer was set.

One more criterion for my eventual entry into the Shangri-La of legal academics remained to be met: the judicial clerkship. As coincidence would have it, one of Duke Law School's most loyal alumni who frequently hires law clerks from Duke is The Honorable Gerald Bard Tjoflat, then a Circuit Judge on the United States Court of Appeals for the Fifth Circuit. Judge Tjoflat, who is one level below a United States Supreme Court Justice, lives in Jacksonville. He is a former student at the University of Virginia and a founder of Jacksonville Episcopal High School. He also is the great mentor of my life. He has always been there when I have needed him. He came to Duke to interview prospective law clerks and met with me. I had contacted some other federal judges about clerkships, and even had a few other interviews, but I hit it off with Judge Tjoflat. He hired me to start with him in January 1979, as he liked to stagger his clerks so he would not have three rookies at the same time.

At this point, after my first semester angst I loved law school. It witnessed my ultimate triumph in the world of academia. My consistent hard work earned me the highest grade in several classes and for the second year overall. Still, I had continuing digestive problems plus self-esteem issues with which to cope, and there was that nasty tendency for depression with which to deal.

I was still worried about how my parents felt about me, especially the distant father I adored and for whose approval I would give anything. Finally, I spoke with my mother about my concern that my efforts to "earn" paternal approval apparently had been fruitless. She, in turn, prevailed upon my father to write me a letter:

"Your mother tells me you aren't sure how I feel about you. First, I love you very much. Also, both your mother and I are extremely proud over your performance in school. All we have spent on your education from Episcopal to Duke has borne fruit."

Only years later did I learn he really *was* proud of me and used to take my grade reports to his Rotary Club meetings to show off to his fellow members. I very much wish I had known about this during his lifetime, since I often later feared I had let him down in some respect.

So, going into my second summer in 1977, was all well? There actually were some worrisome signs. Many of my interviews both on campus and at law firms had been unsuccessful. Notably, none of the large firms in Jacksonville were interested in me. I perceived some problems in the interviewing process that probably were attributable to some combination of my personality and increasing manifestations of mental illness.

It can be hard to separate your personality from a psychiatric disorder when you have lived with it, knowingly or not, for most of your life. What else would make someone with my outstanding record practically unemployable? You could dress me in a suit and give me excellent credentials, but deep down inside I was still the nerdy little kid almost everyone picked on because he was different and who was stubborn and insecure and socially inept and a perfectionist and anxious and highly competitive and irritable and subject to physiological reactions to stress and who hid in a world of fantasy games, classical music, and compulsive record collecting. It was almost like when I was at Virginia in fraternity rush and was an outcast who did not mesh with society at large. I was rejected for being who I was and what I really could not change. Maybe I *would* only fit into the world of legal academics, where eccentricity is much more the norm than in the great world as a whole.

The second summer proved that all my fears were justified. Although I loved the Richmond firm and wanted to live there, it did not like me. This was perhaps attributable to my clingy, anxious, impatient, irritable, immature, perfectionist, depressed, and moody nature. The harder I tried to do a good job and fit in, the more I seemed to turn off the attorneys there. Like many with bipolar disorder, I need a great deal of reassurance and stroking in light of my fragile ego. Attorneys at large law firms are wont to provide neither. By asking for lots of positive feedback I merely annoyed the attorneys for whom I was working. Much like my telephone call to the fraternity at Virginia, my actions cost me a spot there.

I would never work in Richmond again, as no other firm there wanted sloppy seconds. I could only blame what I deemed my own undesirable self and feel the same sting of rejection that had so tormented me in childhood and adolescence.

I wish I could say New York turned out better, and in some

ways it did, but ultimately the news there was not good either. I enjoyed practice in New York City and took full advantage of being there rent free at a high weekly salary. I went to various Broadway shows (alone), a Yankees game (alone), a number of Mostly Mozart concerts (alone), and bought many records. Uncle Tom and Aunt Linnie were very nice to me, and I was living in the lap of luxury in their very tastefully decorated residence. Indeed, Oscar winning actor Joel Grey lived upstairs from them. They had a huge oceanfront home in fashionable Quogue on Long Island, and we spent several weekends there. During one, I apparently accidentally insulted some other guests of Uncle Tom due to my usual social awkwardness. I also had once answered a question from him in a way he considered flippant, although I was merely inept in my attempt to be humorous. These events led to an unfortunate rift I never could repair in the ensuing years before his death in 2008. This was yet another example of not being able really to get along with the world at large, even when it was close family.

At work, I meshed well with the trusts and estates attorneys and enjoyed that area of law practice very much. Still, ultimately, the news at White & Case was only marginally better than that in Richmond. White & Case did not outright reject me. Once the firm heard about my clerkship with Judge Tjoflat, however, I was informed that firm policy on conflicts of interest precluded me from taking a job there between graduation in May 1978 and the start of my clerkship in January 1979. The firm gave the same reason for not offering me a permanent position. Therefore, at the end of my second summer I had no permanent position lined up for the years after I clerked and nothing remunerative to do for the eight months after I graduated from Duke. As I pondered my situation, I felt the curtain of depression close around me.

Most people feel down at times during their lives. "Blues"

like that, however, are far different from full-fledged bipolar depression, a nascent version of which doubtless already was afflicting me. One with that condition exhibits severe symptoms such as sadness and anxiety; feelings of hopelessness, pessimism, guilt, worthlessness or helplessness; tearfulness; lack of interest in activities one once enjoyed, including sex; decreased energy and fatigue; difficulty concentrating, remembering, or making decisions; irritability; sleep disturbance; unintended weight gain or loss; chronic pain and complaint about symptoms that are not caused by physical illness or injury; and thoughts of death or suicide, or even suicide attempts. The sheer pain of depression, what Sir Winston Churchill, who many believe himself had bipolar disorder, called "the Black Dog," can be overwhelming. This circumstance helps explain why bipolar disorder is the leading cause of suicide in the United States, with twenty-five to thirty-three percent of its sufferers *attempting* it and fifteen to twenty percent of them eventually *completing* it—we do not just try suicide, we get it right. Certainly a frightening statistic both for those with my disorder and their loved ones. Indeed, those with my disease kill themselves twice as often as people with schizophrenia. One of my favorite comments from the many books about the subject I have read is that "bipolar disorder was a mighty but malignant muse" for suicides Ernest Hemingway, Sylvia Plath, and Vincent van Gogh. My present psychiatrist regularly asks during my monthly sessions with her whether I currently am suicidal.

A specific symptom of bipolar depression (and mania as well)—crying—was a particular issue. While society accepts such behavior from women in any number of situations, it views it far differently from men. This is a problem for me since at the best of times my mental health concerns make me emotional, and when suffering from bipolar mania or depression I can quickly dissolve into tears. Over time I have reconciled myself to this result, and the reaction of others to it, but it took me years to understand the reasons underlying, and accept, my response.

When I returned to my third year of law school I did my class work, finished my Note for the *Journal*, and interviewed frantically. Although an editorship on the *Journal* would have been another plum on the résumé of a budding academic, I decided not to run for one. This was the case both as I wanted to raise my grade point average by focusing on my classes and I feared another rejection would await me if I vied for an editorial position. In other words, due in large part to my longstanding inferiority complex I thought I was not popular enough to win the vote despite my strong credentials and writing ability. I later learned I probably *would* have gotten an editorship had I tried for one, but by then it was too late as all the spots were taken.

On the job front, I did not really want to return to the impersonal world of New York City. However, by virtue of my personality issues I felt that no firm in Richmond or Jacksonville would offer me a position. Fortunately, I was the one for whom New York City firms were looking. This was especially the case both by virtue of the fact I was interested in a trusts and estates practice and came recommended by Professor Sparks. I made a number of interview trips to New York City. By now, the typical journey, which featured a morning of interviews with attorneys, a firm tour, and a final lunch with some of the firm's associates before I flew back to Durham, had become incredibly stressful for me due in large part to my desperation over my employment status. Still, I managed to maintain a façade of self-confidence.

I ended up the object of a bidding war between two of the most conservative and famous Wall Street firms, Sullivan & Cromwell and Davis Polk & Wardwell. Both are known in the trade as "white shoe" firms, and today are among the five finest firms in the nation according to the 2011 edition of the *Vault Guide to the Top 100 Law Firms*. Each offered me a job for the time both before and after my clerkship. Conflict of interest did not concern either of them, which made me wonder whether the real problem at White & Case was the stated conflict issue or actually dislike of me or my work. I never found out the answer to this conundrum since I never reapplied to White & Case since both Sullivan & Cromwell and Davis Polk were more prominent firms.

I was most swayed by the atmosphere at Davis Polk and accepted the position there, at the "Tiffany of law firms." Accordingly, I found myself with a permanent job on Wall Street in the loneliest city in the world, far from most family and my few friends. At least I would primarily be working in the most human area of a big firm, the trusts and estates department. It was also the most humane part of a Wall Street firm, from an hours worked perspective. And Davis Polk had a great trusts and estates clientele. Its premier customer was that exceptional handler of very wealthy, typically old-moneyed families, Morgan Guaranty Trust Company. Now known as JPMorgan Private Bank, it currently estimates that about forty percent of the billionaires listed in *Forbes* magazine are its clients. So now I had something to which I could look forward to, and feel anxious about, doing. At least, despite all my foibles, I had a job at a top law firm that would look good on my résumé.

Once my employment status was resolved, the rest of the academic year went along routinely until early 1978. Then, I got the terrible word that my beloved father had lung cancer and needed immediate surgery. I drove home all night at once and spent a week in depressed shock after the operation before my father was well enough for me to return to school. I remember talking with one of the physicians whose practice my father managed and whom I had known for over fifteen years. I noted hopefully that the thoracic surgeon had said "The cancer's adenocarcenoma encapsulated in scar tissue. That's the best type of lung cancer to have."

The doctor replied, truthfully, "There is no good type of cancer."

Somehow I got through the rest of the semester despite my devastation over my father's dire diagnosis. I was thrilled when he recovered from his surgery sufficiently that he, my mother, and Aunt Bet all came to my graduation. I remember learning I had won the award for excellence in property law-related courses. I graduated second in my class and was chosen for the Order of the Coif, which is the Phi Beta Kappa for law schools.

Overall, I was a success at law school, where I positioned myself to achieve my longtime goal of a career as a professor in higher academics. Still, I was not accepted by mainstream society as represented by the attorneys in Jacksonville who would not consider me despite my record. More to the point, those for whom I actually worked at the firm in Richmond and maybe even at White & Case rejected me. I continued to have psychophysiological issues such as my gastrointestinal problems and battled my melancholy, depressed tendencies. My father's lung cancer diagnosis in my final semester was a real blow, but I hung on despite it.

I got through law school on the basis of sheer stubbornness and hard work. I simply was not going to let my problems prevent my achievement. Much as at Virginia, Aunt Bet and Tom Ramey were keys to my success. I could always depend on each of them for a boost when I needed it. Tom in particular was essential. I could not have had a better friend had I created him myself. Insofar as family members were concerned, Aunt Bet was the ideal relative, nonjudgmental and a source of unquestioned love and support.

Depression and my introspective, loner nature meant I still did not date or socialize much. I did develop a severe crush on my Business Associations professor, who is about five years older than I, while I was in her class because in her shy, quiet, studious nature I sensed a kindred spirit. However, I never mentioned this to anyone until 2008. It would be many years after I left Duke before I felt ready to take the risk of any sort of romantic relationship. In any event, I was probably as prepared as I could be for my next big step, life from May until December 1978 in the Big Apple at Davis Polk.

5

After graduation I went home to visit my parents. After a short stay, I went to New York City. Once there, I sublet a furnished studio apartment on the West Side of Manhattan near Lincoln Center. I decided not to take the New York bar examination until I knew whether I was going to settle there permanently. Therefore, I immediately reported to Davis Polk as a junior associate.

Davis Polk's principal office was downtown at One Chase Manhattan Plaza near Wall Street. Most of its trusts and estates attorneys, however, were in midtown where they occupied part of the building that also contained the main office of Morgan Guaranty Trust Company. I had an office downtown that I shared with a very friendly, but, like all Davis Polk associates I met, totally driven junior litigation associate.

I rotated through the various sections of the firm, but spent much of my time in the trusts and estates department. I frequently put in what were, at least to me, long hours. This was especially true when I was doing corporate or litigation work downtown. As I quickly learned, extensive labor had its benefits. If you worked past 7:30 PM you got a free taxi ride home. In addition, if you toiled much past 9 PM you could go to the Wall Street Club at the top of One Chase Manhattan Plaza for dinner and bill it to the client for which you were working. Still, my delicate constitution made stress and long hours difficult for me. I can truly say I never worked harder, or saw others do the same,

41

than I did at Davis Polk. It was not notorious as a "sweatshop" like some big firms. Still, associates who wanted to advance really put in the hours all day, in the evenings, and frequently on weekends. I was not really an outcast there, as all Davis Polk associates were eccentric in their own individual ways, and most worked so hard that they had no time for personal lives. Still, depression was a problem.

I was happy to collect the reward for my labors, the then-unheard of salary of roughly $28,000 per year. After I paid my rent and expenses, I had plenty of extra money to buy Brooks Brothers clothes and classical music records. My record collection grew exponentially while I was in New York City.

I did some interesting work in the trusts and estates unit, which handles most of the "people" problems a Wall Street firm ever addresses. I helped probate estates, prepare wills, and wrote memoranda on various issues. I learned that wealthy individuals face many of the same concerns as everyone else. They can, however, afford to have these issues handled for them by expensive attorneys. And, they can have their money managed by a company like Morgan Guaranty. Many of Morgan Guaranty's trust officers, who were the individuals who administered the client accounts, were former Davis Polk trusts and estates associates. Had I stayed at Davis Polk rather than entering academia I might well have ended up as such a trust officer.

The trusts and estates attorneys also handled the occasional matrimonial case, and here I got my taste of New York litigation practice. A Davis Polk staff member was being represented gratis by Davis Polk in a very nasty divorce case. The downtown trusts and estates partner asked me to work on it with a senior trusts and estates associate. It was my pleasure to do so, as the associate, who today has a flourishing midtown Manhattan family law practice, was an extremely kind and generous teacher.

The divorce proceeding, which was still raging when I left

Davis Polk, really opened my eyes. Neither party would give an inch on anything as the spouses hated one another. Every issue had to be resolved by a judge. Our client had no incentive not to fight, as he had to pay nothing for the hundreds of hours we spent on his case. His wife had family money, so she also could afford to battle on and on. I have never either worked on or seen a more intense case than this one. When I once asked the associate "Is this sort of bloodshed common in New York divorce actions?" he responded "Unfortunately, yes."

In sum, from a professional standpoint, I learned a considerable degree about Wall Street practice, especially in the trusts and estates field, while at Davis Polk. Still, I was desperately lonely, depressed, and unhappy during my months in Manhattan. One reason I worked long hours was I had nothing better to do. "Alone" was the operative description for my time in New York, and loneliness was very bad for my already precarious mental health. My best moments were when I shopped for and later listened to my classical music purchases or attended Broadway shows, classical music concerts or the Metropolitan Opera. Indeed, I felt the music helped keep me going from day to solitary day, and I enjoyed it as often as I could.

During the late fall my parents came for a visit. It meant a lot for me to have a place where they could stay, especially since my father's health clearly was failing. I still remember being devastated when my mother got angry with me after we saw the Rockettes' Christmas show at Radio City Music Hall. I briefly delayed our departure in order to look for a particular record at a store located near there, and she thought this was hard on my father.

By mid-December my time at Davis Polk was over. I had an offer to return after my clerkship. However, I was unsure either whether I would return to New York City or if I would survive if I did so. About that time, I decided I was unlikely to live until age thirty as I probably would commit suicide before then.

My inclination toward ending my life prematurely was furthered by what I witnessed one day. I was in the Seventy-Second Street and Broadway subway station during morning rush hour on the way to work. As usual, the station was crowded and noisy. I was near the edge of the platform where I would be by the rear of the express train when it stopped. I heard the signature rumble of the train close to the station, and looked up to see the headlights illuminate the gloomy tunnel from which it was about to emerge. Suddenly, I detected rapid movement across the platform. Everything seemed to go into slow motion as I saw a man approach the edge. Rather than stopping, I watched him deliberately leap down onto the track and slowly lie across it. I shouted at him to move, but no one could hear me over the roar of the oncoming express. There was a squeal of brakes as the train approached him, but it seemed inexorably to rumble past where I knew the man had lain down. At this point real time seemed to resume. The public address system on the train told everyone to get off as soon as it came to a halt. Few people realized why they were ordered to do so. I, of course, knew I had just witnessed a completed suicide.

I felt exhilarated by what I had observed. Here someone actually had done what I was already contemplating right before my eyes! Seeing it happen made it seem a really viable way to end my increasingly hopeless life. I remember wondering "Will I have the courage someday to do that?" So only what I deemed cowardice was keeping me alive. Many may question my thinking, but it is how it feels to be haunted by the suicidal urges of bipolar depression. By acting, I would be ending what was, right then, the unbearable pain of a depression it seemed would never end. The effect on family or friends would not matter.

I ruminated over the issue for days thereafter. While at that time I took no further steps, I never forgot what I had seen and how I felt about it. Later, when I faced what I considered to be a hopeless situation I knew what I must, and acceptably could, do: I tried, as best I could, to imitate what I saw that day in New York City. It was lucky that at that time Dr. Kay Redfield Jamison had not yet written her masterwork on suicide. Its "how to do it" segments easily might have helped me complete suicide rather than fail at it. Since then, I have had my suicidal periods, and near attempts. My "New York moment" endures.

Based on this experience, I was able to see that New York City was not a healthy place for me to live.

6

In January 1979 I began my clerkship with Judge Tjoflat. It was one of the best periods of my life.

When I started my new job, I planned to take the Florida bar examination in late February since I hoped to stay in Jacksonville after my clerkship. Judge Tjoflat agreed to give me ten days off to do so. I had thought I would study for the test during January and February. However, there was a backlog of cases that required the complete attention of all who worked in his chambers before a court sitting in the Fifth Circuit headquarters in New Orleans in mid-February. By the time everything was done I was in New Orleans with Judge Tjoflat, his two other law clerks, and his stalwart secretary Dot Bradley. Meanwhile, I had not studied for the bar exam for a moment.

Upon returning to Jacksonville I headed off to St. Petersburg, Florida for a ten day bar review course. Some subjects involved Florida law, about which I of course knew nothing since I had not gone to school there. I was rather worried that my lack of study time meant I would be retaking the test in July, to my considerable embarrassment. My anxiety harkened back to my days as a first semester student at Duke and did not help my perpetual state of depression. However, I passed based on what I learned in the review course and remembered from law school before my stint at Davis Polk.

Luckily for me, my bipolar disorder had not yet been diagnosed when I applied for the Florida Bar and, thanks to my father, I had no history of mental health treatment. Thus, I truthfully could deny having any mental illness on my bar application. Even today, unlike in a number of more enlightened states, the Florida Board of Bar Examiners asks a series of broad and intrusive mental health questions on its application questionnaire. Just reading them gave me insight into the stigma those with mental illness endure every day. Among the reasons I have never attempted to get a Kentucky law license is my reluctance to subject myself to the character and fitness committee of the Kentucky Board of Bar Examiners' numerous detailed and inquisitional inquiries about an applicant's psychiatric history. Even if my record of accomplishment insures I ultimately would be admitted the process is sufficiently demeaning to insure I will never apply.

I was sworn into the bars of the State of Florida, the United States District Court for the Middle District of Florida, and the United States Court of Appeals for the Fifth Circuit in front of Judge Tjoflat and my parents in May 1979. One of my most prized possessions is a picture of the four of us taken that day. I joined the bar of the Supreme Court of the United States in 1982. As I recall, no mental status questions appeared on its application.

At the same time my professional career seemed to be going well, my personal life was in turmoil. I was living at home with my parents and consequently daily faced the horrible realization that my father was slowly dying from metastatic lung cancer. He was a real fighter, and he and my mother made frequent trips to M. D. Anderson Cancer Center in Houston for experimental chemotherapy. Ultimately, of course, the chemotherapy merely delayed the inevitable. In the process it made my father miserable from the horrendous side effects of the treatment. My mental status gradually declined as I watched him die a little bit each day. Judge Tjoflat was fully aware of all of this as he had become a close family friend who frequently stopped by to visit with my father on the way home from the office. It meant a great deal to my father, mother, and especially to me to have a federal appellate judge keep close tabs on his health and join him for a drink on the days he could have one.

Judge Tjoflat also knew I was very worried over my post-clerkship employment prospects. I really wanted to stay in Jacksonville near my parents but was having no luck finding a job with any of the firms there. Once again, while my credentials were solid no one wanted to have to work with me and my own, rather unusual, personality and world view. Judge Tjoflat recommended me for a clerkship with then-Chief Justice of the United States Supreme Court Warren E. Burger, whom Judge Tjoflat knew fairly well. Although I made the finalist list, I did not get the job. That probably was just as well, as I do not know how I would have handled such a high stress position even though it would pretty much have guaranteed a good legal academic appointment.

Lest it sound like everything was going badly, I really enjoyed my clerkship. Being in the halls of power is heady stuff, and I got to know several of the Fifth Circuit judges fairly well. I felt like what I did really mattered, as Judge Tjoflat listened to his clerks when deciding cases. He had a very large desk, and when he went over a draft opinion he would have the clerk who wrote it sit next to him as he read. Periodically he would peer over his reading glasses and ask piercing questions of the clerk. I was always pleased when he would nod approvingly at my answers and read on in the draft.

Judge Tjoflat had nicknames for most of his clerks. On account of my conservative orientation, which he shared in many respects, mine was "the wool hat." Unlike some clerks, whose liberal views he would shoot down when reviewing their draft opinions, Judge Tjoflat almost never rejected what I suggested. Indeed, in one criminal appeal he was so shocked when I said reversal of a conviction could not be avoided that he called the other two judges on the case and convinced them to change the result on which they had agreed when it was argued.

One aspect of the job was sheer pleasure, the roughly monthly trips to hear oral arguments in New Orleans. As they say there, "*laissez les bons temps rouller!*" We would always fly over on Sunday afternoon, check into the hotel, and then go to the French Quarter for oysters on the half shell followed by dinner at Galatoire's. Galatoire's has been my favorite restaurant since I first ate there in February 1979.

After dinner Judge Tjoflat would head for the hotel. Some clerks would party through most of the night. My bad stomach insured I merely would escort Dot Bradley back to the hotel. Indeed, Dot and I spent much of our free time in New Orleans together. We dined on Mondays through Wednesdays at some combination of excellent restaurants and became good friends.

At least once each trip Dot and I would enjoy the classic New Orleans jazz at Preservation Hall. I learned to love hearing such immortals as the incomparable "Sweet Emma" Barrett. As I watched her eat soda crackers and pick at the piano while singing "Just a Closer Walk with Thee" I always thought she was ready to make that trip herself. I usually paid the band to play "Closer Walk" and the "Saints" while I was there.

It was pure joy to watch Judge Tjoflat in action, as his intelligence was obvious. His mind was miles ahead of the lawyers appearing before him. Once, in a case that had been awaiting oral argument for several years the attorneys for the parties finally had their moment to shine. When the first one started his argument Judge Tjoflat immediately asked him whether one of the requirements for an appeal had been met. When the attorney replied yes, Judge Tjoflat said he had been through the record in the case and could not find the essential document. The lawyer again responded it was there. Judge Tjoflat said "Show me." He and the lawyer then rummaged through the large box that held the record. When they could not find what was needed Judge Tjoflat advised the attorneys that their appeal was dismissed. They would have to go back to the trial court to get what they lacked and then start the appellate process all over again. I still do not think the lawyers understood what had happened to them. When I teach appellate advocacy, I always tell the students this story to emphasize why all procedural requirements must be satisfied in any appeal.

It was a special privilege to attend an *en banc* sitting of the court, as then all the Fifth Circuit judges sat together as they dealt with especially important cases. I will never forget attending the twenty-six judge *en banc* session in January 1980. Considering the unwieldy size of this court, which looked more like an early session of the United States Senate than a judicial proceeding, Congress split the Fifth Circuit in 1981. Judge Tjoflat then became an original member of what is now known as the United States Court of Appeals for the Eleventh Circuit.

Despite the good times the stress of the job did get to me. This was particularly demonstrated by a special case. One morning I was the first person in the office. As I opened the door I found an express packet slipped under it. When I opened the envelope I discovered a Petition for Writ of Stay of Execution on behalf of one John Arthur Spenkelink. I knew Spenkelink was in imminent danger of execution in Florida's electric chair for a murder he had committed some years before. Exhibit one to the Petition was a copy of the black-bordered Death Warrant signed by the then-Governor of Florida Bob Graham. I immediately realized this was to be a very unusual day, as Spenkelink's would be the first truly "involuntary" execution since the death penalty was reinstituted in the United States in 1976. Gary Gilmore had been shot by a firing squad in Utah in 1977, but he had demanded to be executed rather than opposing his fate.

Once Judge Tjoflat arrived and saw the petition he immediately had the clerks drop everything and go over it thoroughly. He prepared to confer with the other two judges with whom he would decide how to rule on the petition. Spenkelink, with the aid of his attorneys, was fighting his death sentence using every possible argument at his disposal. By the end of the day the court denied the petition. After a few more legal delays Spenkelink was executed.

I did, and still do, believe in the death penalty and I know that Spenkelink's case was handled properly. Still, it greatly bothered me to have a role in an execution, no matter how insignificant my part. Judge Tjoflat saw this. I cannot imagine what it must have been like for him, the person who actually had to cast the vote whether to grant or deny the stay.

As my clerkship proceeded, Judge Tjoflat increasingly focused on how poorly I dealt with my future employment status, my father's health, and the stresses of my job. One day, somewhat out of the blue, he said "Jim, I realize your future isn't working out as you'd like. I think you'd benefit from some career counseling. I know about a local group of clinical psychologists who, among other things, test people to see what sort of job would be best for them. Law practice may not be the ideal fit for you. I've taken the liberty of talking about you with one of the head men over there, and he's expecting your call for an appointment."

"Do you really think that's necessary?"

"Yes, I do. You need to learn some things about yourself before you can really succeed outside of school."

As always, I obeyed Judge Tjoflat so I said "I'll do what you suggest" and placed the call. This had to be a difficult step for Judge Tjoflat, as I now understand what I suspect he really was encouraging me to do. He wanted me evaluated and treated for probable emotional problems, or even outright mental illness. Finally, someone was seeing the complete picture and recognizing that I needed help coping with my life.

I consulted with clinical psychologist Joseph H. Hartman,

Ph.D., who interviewed me and gave me extensive personality and vocational tests. He then wrote an evaluation of me that was a harbinger of future difficulties with mental illness, possibly including bipolar disorder.

Dr. Hartman explained a number of things to me about his report:

"First of all," he said, "you realize how hard you try to avoid change in your life and to maintain your emotional self-control. You know you're prone to physiological responses to stress, such as your gastrointestinal problems, which can interfere with your ability to work. You probably don't recognize how much you lean on others when you're depressed, like you are now. At the same time, you get frustrated and impatient when dealing with them. They probably view you as unduly-sensitive and thin-skinned. You're competitive and status-seeking, but not particularly dollar-motivated. You're uncomfortable around other people, who view you as hard to get to know. Your ambition, interest in achievement, and personal high standards may cause others to mistake your naturally reserved nature for arrogance or aloofness generated by feelings of superiority. Your nature makes you take criticism personally, as you can't readily separate business from private matters. You tend excessively to mull over any negatives in your life to the point that they adversely affect your physical and emotional health."

In summary, Dr. Hartman anticipated a number of the issues in my life including my bouts with depression and its impact on my ability to work, my difficulty getting along with people, my dependence on others, my powerlessness to deal realistically with real-world issues, my inability to handle criticism appropriately, my ruminating over problems, and above all my physiological reaction to life's stressors.

Dr. Hartman had one particularly interesting parting observation: "When you indicated potential long-term career goals, you said you can see yourself 'happily established' as a professor of estates and trusts at a good university. You seem to understand you've been happiest and most comfortable in academic settings in the past." I apparently could foresee where I would be fifteen years later when I first taught Decedents' Estates in Louisville.

I was very impressed with Dr. Hartman's analysis, whose scope was far beyond career counseling and went to the heart of my personality and possible psychiatric concerns. It was almost a relief to hear what he said, which I thought was totally accurate. It helped explain the problems I had had when coping with life and trying to be the sort of person law firms wanted to hire. Clearly, job acquisition and later difficulties in the typical law firm like the one in Richmond or even White & Case could be expected for one with the pathology Dr. Hartman described. Either I needed another career path or help in traversing the law firm one to which I was headed.

Dr. Hartman recommended that I start regular psychotherapy with him in order to help me deal with my psychological issues, which I did. To help with my problem with stress he explained the value of biofeedback. He would leave me in a darkened room and give me the chance to calm down. He was very surprised one day when he found me quietly humming the slow, rhythmically perfect chord progression of the *Canon in D major* of Baroque composer Johann Christoph Pachelbel to relax myself. He later said I was the only client he ever had who used classical music in that way. Yet another example of the importance of music in my life.

Dr. Hartman suggested that I consult a psychiatrist to get medication to deal with my depression, which I also did. I started taking the antidepressant Elavil, which helped me. I have been on psychotropic medication, and regularly have seen a psychiatrist, ever since 1979. I continued as Dr. Hartman's client until my spring 1983 breakdown. As always, I complied with the recommendations of a professional whose credentials and skills I respected. One reason I have done as well as I have over the years is my willingness to follow the advice of my various psychiatrists and therapists.

I still lived with my parents and did not date. As Dr. Hartman put it, "Considering himself a 'confirmed bachelor,' Jim resides with his parents in Jacksonville and leads a very circumscribed social life. Classical music is one leisure outlet for him." It would be several more years before I mustered up the courage to approach the opposite sex.

Meanwhile, I continued with my abiding interest in listening to classical music. I also on occasion would drive over to Valdosta, Georgia to visit Andy Baker, who for several years had managed a multiplex cinema there. We would hang out together as we had done at Episcopal. We went into the country near Valdosta and shot Andy's circa 1919 high caliber Russian sniper's rifle, which kicked like a small bazooka, at targets of opportunity. As was true some years later, the classical music aficionado also liked the rush of discharging heavy munitions.

Judge Tjoflat's last favor to me while I was his law clerk was to convince his old law firm to hire me as an associate. Thus, I could stay in Jacksonville and would not have to go back to New York City. Of course, neither Judge Tjoflat nor I said anything about my mental health issues. I advised Davis Polk that I would not be returning there and prepared to start my new position early in 1980. Little did I know that Judge Tjoflat would do even more for me in the years to come.

7

As a new decade began I entered the mundane world of private law practice. It was a realm for which I was ill-suited.

My first job at the firm was to work on an appeal by a major public utility. It was one of the firm's best clients. It objected to the Florida Public Service Commission's treatment of its most recent rate increase request. As time was of the essence on the case I agreed to report for work immediately upon the end of my clerkship. It was understood that I would get a few weeks off once the brief was finished.

The senior partner in charge of the case was very pleased with my work on the brief. He said it was excellent even though it was in a specialized area of the law in which I had no prior experience and had not even studied in law school. He edited my draft and presented it to the client for its approval. It signed off, and I made certain all was properly filed with the Supreme Court of Florida.

The case illustrated the usual problem that arises for one who works for a large firm. I was well paid to argue for an increase in utility rates that I, as well as everyone else in Florida, would have to pay if the client won. The analogy of the highly paid prostitute comes to mind, although at least no one is directly harmed by his or her actions. Luckily, when I was at Davis Polk I was not really working against others except in the divorce case. There, generally I was merely insuring that clients' estate issues were handled as they wished. Accordingly, it was a no lose scenario.

I dealt with the moral quagmire of the brief by leaving town to go to Richmond to visit Tom Ramey. By now he was a first year intern in internal medicine at the Medical College of Virginia. We went about Richmond when he was off work and did some serious classical music shopping.

Around the time I returned to Jacksonville my mother waited until the evening before I had an appointment with Dr. Hartman. Then, she said "Jimmy, I want you to talk with Dr. Hartman tomorrow about your living arrangements. You're now twenty-seven years old and have a permanent job. It's not like when you were clerking with Judge Tjoflat. You need to get your own apartment. It isn't good for you to be living with Daddy. Seeing his health worsen depresses you. In addition, I'm no longer able to have you here. I'm under a tremendous strain from caring for Daddy, and just can't take the additional burden of looking after you. Finally, you're never going to develop much of a social life when you're living with your parents. Part of being an adult is being independent, and that means living on your own. There are some nice apartments near here so you can be close by, and can still come over for meals or visits."

At this I gulped, and felt dreadfully insecure. Being on my own seemed like a scary thing. Still, as I thought about it, I had been there before. If I could live alone in New York City where I knew no one I certainly should be able to do so in a city where I had lived off and on since 1964 and would be near my parents. My mother undoubtedly was right when she said it certainly was extremely bad for my mental health for me to watch my father die a little more each day.

I said "I'll talk with Dr. Hartman tomorrow and tell you what he says."

When I met with Dr. Hartman, I passed along my mother's words. Being a good therapist, he asked me a question: "How do you feel about this?"

"Well, I have mixed sentiments. One the one hand, I hate to be alone, but on the other I probably will benefit from being on my own. Spending time with my father does upset me, so doing so less frequently will be a good thing overall. I'm pretty sure the lawyers at the firm will have a hard time ever taking me seriously if I'm still living with my parents. In any event, my mother sounds like her mind is made up so I'll have to move out whether I want to or not. I might as well make the best of the situation and focus on the positive. What do you think?"

"I think you've hit the nail on the head. We'll work on getting you ready for the move, which I think will be very good for you."

With that, the issue seemed to be resolved. That evening I said "I've decided it's time for me to move out on my own. I think that will be the best thing for all of us."

My mother immediately said "I agree, and I'll help you all I can."

She was as good as her word. She helped me locate and tastefully furnish a pleasant apartment in a complex in the general vicinity of my parents' home. Even today my wife and I still use various items I bought in 1980 for that residence.

Now that the utility case was handled at least temporarily I went to work with the senior partner who was my permanent supervisor. He had a varied practice, and at that time one other associate worked for him. The partner was very interested in law and economics, then an emerging field of law. He was handling some antitrust, or antimonopoly, cases. The other associate had studied law and economics and worked on the antitrust cases. I labored on the remainder of the work of the partner's many clients. The only exceptions were matters that were so complicated that I could not manage them and the partner lacked the time or inclination to work on himself. He liked to keep the jobs inside his own little group, or "profit center" as it later came to be known, so he had me handle as much as I could myself. I therefore labored in many different areas but developed no real specialty that the firm's partners would value.

My favorite client was a non-profit organization my boss represented at cost and on whose Board of Directors he served. It had a program to reform juvenile delinquents by having them work on maritime projects, and was very successful with a low recidivist rate. One way the charity was funded was by selling expensive yachts whose owners had donated them to it and keeping the proceeds. Many of these sales transactions were highly complex. The partner pretty much left me alone with this, as he much preferred his more profitable and to him far more interesting law and economics activities. I spent hundreds of hours moving from transaction to transaction. Unfortunately, this work mattered little, if at all, to the firm's partners other than my superior since it was not really revenue-generating. Accordingly, my efforts for the charity would count for naught when/if I eventually went up for partnership status myself. This was a sterling example why Dr. Hartman said I am not very dollar-motivated. That characteristic is not appreciated in the capitalistic setting of a large law firm.

I mainly worked for the one senior partner and on occasion for the one for whom I wrote the utility company brief. As general firm "rainmaker" he had no associate of his own. In addition, other attorneys would enlist my aid on complex cases as I had a reputation for doing high quality work. Here, however, my personality issues became a problem. I did not interact well with the University of Florida/FSU Law School ex-fraternity crowd who constituted most of the partners and associates at the firm. Indeed, as Dr. Hartman had predicted, I was dysfunctional in the real, nonacademic world of a large law firm. There, the idea was to work seven years and then become a partner who then would spend the rest of his or her career getting along with clients and colleagues. Those who were not congenial and did not make partner were quickly abandoned by the firm.

When under stress, as Dr. Hartman had observed, I often get very irritable, rushed, brusque, and demanding (i.e., manic). This led to problems with the law firm secretarial corps. As was the case with Dot Bradley, whom I greatly respected, I got along very well with most of the top secretaries at the firm. However, I am a perfectionist by nature and that was bad when dealing with the low paid and relatively unskilled secretaries the Jacksonville firm hired for its associates. An associate had no say in the selection of his or her secretary, who was chosen by a firm administrator. Again as Dr. Hartman pointed out, I would get very frustrated, impatient and irritated when working on a complex project only to have to waste much time correcting typographical or grammatical errors in documents that would then need to be retyped. One good thing about Davis Polk was that it paid its secretaries very well, and thus almost all of them were both diligent and top notch.

An example of the problems I faced: One weekend I was working on an important brief and telephoned my secretary in an effort to obtain some important information.

"Hello?," a male voice answered.

"Hi. Is Susan there?"

"Who's calling?"

"Jim Jones."

"Who are you?"

"I work with Susan."

"What do you want?"

"I need some information about a case we're working on."

"Whoa. You're calling Susan at home on the weekend about work?"

"That's right."

"Where do you get off calling my wife on Saturday?"

"Sorry, but I just have a simple question."

"Let me tell you something, you little shit! Don't you EVER

call Susan about work at home again! Got it?"

"Yeah. Sorry to bother you."

Before I finished that sentence Susan's husband hung up on me. Clearly, I had committed what was viewed as a grievous offense. Another example of my lack of interpersonal skills, or, perhaps, merely an illustration of the conditions under which I had to work.

My supervisor regularly changed secretaries, but that was alright as he was a senior partner and hence not one to be challenged over his work habits. I remember him telling me I had to endeavor to get along with others. I wanted to tell him, first of all, I secretly saw a therapist every week to try to do so, and second, physician, heal thyself. All this makes me much prefer my situation today. I do all my own typing on a computer either at home or in my office at my law school, which effectively has no faculty secretaries. As a result, I depend on myself alone.

As I went along through my first year at the firm I had to cope with more than not getting along very well with colleagues and secretaries. My father was sinking rapidly, as the chemotherapy was not stopping the steady advance of the lung cancer. Indeed, the drugs were tearing him up. He effectively was a human guinea pig since the efficacy of his treatment plan was unknown.

The side effects for my father included terrible mouth ulcers, extreme nausea and vomiting, and horrendous neuropathy. Drugs to try to control the side effects, such as steroids for the neuropathy, often seemed only to make things worse. Despite all this he and my mother made frequent trips to Houston for more and more toxic injections or intravenous infusions. Watching all this did me incalculable harm. I was desperate to do something to deal with, in particular, the incredibly severe nausea from which my father suffered. I knew that THC, the active ingredient in marijuana, helps chemotherapy patients cope with this symptom. I did what I could to make this drug available to him, and eventually was able to enroll him in an FDA-approved study that gave him oral THC for the rest of his life. Overall, the stress of his declining health, added to my work difficulties, made my depression much worse.

Finally, by mid-1980 I was so low that I could not work or otherwise function and I called my mother for help.

"What's the matter?"

"I don't know, but I feel terrible."

"In what way?"

"I can't think clearly, and can barely get out of bed. I don't feel like going to work or anywhere else."

"Are you eating properly?"

"Not really. I can't cope with cooking or going out to eat."

"I'll call you back soon."

She in turn called my psychiatrist, who immediately called in orders admitting me into a regular room in the hospital that was staffed by the doctors with whom my father worked. I spent the next two weeks there.

The doctor prescribed the so-called "Elavil sleep therapy." During it I was injected with sufficiently high doses of intravenous Elavil that I slept for days while the drug level quickly built up in my system to fight the depression. Although my main memory of this experience is being extremely groggy I know my parents visited me numerous times. They were extremely kind, sympathetic, and loving when they saw me.

My father never said anything to indicate he felt anything but concern for me. He certainly never indicated in any way that I had "let him down" through my needing hospital care for my depression. Still, for many years I felt great guilt over what I considered being so "weak" that I needed hospitalization to deal with his illness and my mental disease. Little did I suspect this was to be the first of five psychiatric hospitalizations spread over the next twenty-four years. I did feel better when I headed back to my apartment, as the Elavil held the depression at least temporarily under control.

When I reflected on my situation I was totally devastated at being hospitalized for psychiatric reasons. Although Dr. Hartman explained I had no reason for being ashamed for getting needed medical care, the stigma of mental illness in 1980 was particularly overwhelming. I was terrified my employer would learn the real nature of my illness. When I indicated my hospitalization was attributable to a flare-up of my well-known digestive problems, however, he asked no questions. When I was able I struggled on at work. Still, I had moments that made me question my sanity. For example, when I saw Stanley Kubrick's 1980 classic film *The Shining* I found it profoundly disturbing because I already could see myself falling into a state of madness like that which overwhelmed Jack Torrance in it.

Unfortunately, my father's time was about all used up. Aunt Bet came down for an extended visit about the time he entered the hospice unit at a local hospital. For several weeks he drifted in and out of consciousness, heavily medicated with powerful narcotics to try to handle the pain. My mother, Aunt Bet, and I spent hours by my father's bed, hoping for some sign of awareness while not wanting the consciousness that would be accompanied by severe pain.

Finally, early on the morning of December 7, 1980 I got the call that my father had died. I have always thought it somehow appropriate that he, a World War II Naval officer and veteran of the War in the Pacific, somehow held onto life until that particular morning.

I rushed to the hospital. When my mother and Aunt Bet arrived they found me shaving my father with his electric razor so he would look "presentable" to them. My mother thought this was rather odd behavior, but I suppose each person deals with extreme loss in his or her own way.

They say that at times such as the death of a beloved parent one remembers little of what happens next. To a large extent this was true for me, although I recall that there was a nice article in the Florida *Times-Union* newspaper about my father in addition to his obituary. Many people attended his funeral including all the doctors whose practices he had managed for over fifteen years. I will never forget one person who was there, my friend Dot Bradley. After the service in Jacksonville we traveled to Henderson where there was a graveside ceremony and interment in the family cemetery plot on a cold and blustery December afternoon.

The following days are a blur, but I recall leaving work for several weeks while I went to Richmond to visit Tom Ramey and try to regain my composure. My depression recurred with a vengeance.

I returned to work and stayed on at the firm another two and one-half years. During that time, in addition to my supervisor and the rainmaker partner a litigation partner liked me and my work, and therefore used me on several cases. Among those, the last was by far the most interesting.

As background, in January 1963 a U.S. Army Warrant Officer named Joseph George Helmich was a cryptographer, one who transmits and receives top secret military communications. Helmich was stationed in Paris, and dealt with, among other things, extremely sensitive NATO messages. He became mired in debt, and wrote a number of bad checks. His commanding officer threatened to have him court-martialed and thrown out of the military unless he paid off his debts and made good on his checks. Helmich dealt with this problem by walking into the Soviet embassy in Paris with highly classified documents in his possession. He asked to meet with a GRU representative: the GRU is the Soviet/Russian agency in charge of secret message transmission and interception, its equivalent to the United States National Security Agency. When one appeared Helmich asked for money in exchange for the documents. The GRU agent told Helmich to return the next day. When Helmich did so the agent gave Helmich enough money to clear up all his debts and buy a Minox spy camera. Since the Soviets had secretly filmed Helmich's time at their embassy, they had him hooked. Helmich was not really unhappy over this situation, and collected at least $130,000 from them over the next few years.

As Helmich told the story, during 1963 and 1964 he provided his GRU handler "Claude," a/k/a GRU officer Victor Lyubinov, with numerous critical items. Perhaps most importantly, he sold the Soviets the KL-7, the NSA-invented cryptography machine the military widely used for transmission of highly sensitive data. At one point, Helmich was paid a bonus for agreeing immediately to contact Claude if he ever saw a NATO order to attack the Soviets in Eastern Europe. Had he done so, the Soviets would have launched a preemptive nuclear attack on the United States and its European allies.

When Helmich was transferred to Fort Bragg in North Carolina, he made at least four trips to Paris to meet with Claude and give him top-secret documents Helmich had photographed while on duty. These may have included blueprints for a new cryptographic system then installed at Fort Bragg. When he learned he was going to be sent to Vietnam, where the war against the Communists was heating up, Helmich visited the Soviet embassy in Mexico City for an additional payment for services to be rendered in the future. He was told he had been named a "Hero of the Soviet Union" and that a marker in his honor was secreted on the Kremlin Wall in Red Square in Moscow.

Helmich thought he was smarter than everyone else. Still, he made a fatal error. He threw his money all over the place, doing things like buying a house, expensive cars, and a load of live Maine lobsters he had flown to Fort Bragg for a big party he conducted for his friends. When his superiors asked him where he got the money to pay for such things Helmich claimed he had inherited a large amount from his grandmother and earned much money from good "investments" he had made in France. Mistrust grew when he refused to take a polygraph examination. Although he was sent to Vietnam, he definitely was under suspicion and by late 1966 Helmich resigned from the Army in lieu of being forced out. Since he had blown the money the Soviets paid him he drifted through a series of menial jobs.

By 1980 Helmich and his family were living in upstate New York. U.S. intelligence agents observed him entering the Soviet embassy in Ottawa, Canada where he went to try to collect money Claude allegedly told him was being held in escrow for him. Helmich was of no further value to them, so the Soviets of course denied they had anything for him.

Things got even worse for Helmich, as the FBI picked him up and questioned him extensively about his suspected espionage activities. FBI agents told him they had been investigating him for years and had massive amounts of evidence against him. Eventually they somehow convinced Helmich he would be used as a double agent with the Soviets if he came clean, and he told them his story. They let him go and set about putting together the case against him on which the FBI and NSA actually had been working since 1966 now that they could hang him with his own words.

About this time, Helmich moved to Jacksonville Beach. He was arrested and charged with two counts of espionage and two counts of conspiracy to commit espionage, all of which could be capital offenses. As he was looking at four trips to the electric chair, a Jacksonville federal judge decided the indigent Helmich needed the best possible counsel with large resources at his or her disposal. Rather than having the federal public defender handle the case, the judge appointed the partner who liked working with me to represent Helmich. The partner, in turn, asked me to help him, which I gladly did: although Helmich was a traitor and a total sleazebag, it was the case of a lifetime, and even someone like Helmich was entitled to a competent defense. Ultimately, he got much more than that.

By sheer chance, the firm had just hired an associate who had been an Army cryptographer. The partner immediately enlisted him to work as an expert on the case. The government granted the partner and him top-secret security clearances so they could see the evidence against Helmich, much of which still was highly classified. That was no problem, as the partner had been cleared when an assistant United States attorney and the associate when in the Army. Reclearing them took little effort. Although I was working on the case, I was not involved with the classified material and thus the FBI and NSA were not worried about me.

The partner attempted to reach a plea bargain in the case, but the United States Attorney would only offer Helmich a guilty plea to one of the four counts he faced with the sentence left up to the judge on the case. Since this could translate into a death sentence, we could not agree to such a deal, and a highly publicized trial was necessary.

Unfortunately, Helmich had no decent clothes to wear. As we were about the same size, I "lent" him a three piece navy blue suit I no longer needed and a red, white and blue striped tie. The partner's son provided him with a white shirt. As a consequence, Helmich would be properly attired for his trial.

When the proceeding began, an NSA agent was in the courtroom. He was authorized to have it cleared if anything sensitive were about to come out. The partner and the cryptographer associate sat at counsel table with Helmich, while I sat out in the audience when I was needed or something interesting was going to come up.

I will never forget the first witness for the United States. The prosecutor called his name, and he headed up to the stand. He was a fairly tall, striking man in his mid 60s with an incredibly erect posture and close-cropped grey hair. When the clerk swore him in as a witness, he recited "I, William C. Westmoreland, do solemnly swear to tell the truth, the whole truth, and nothing but the truth, so help me God." When the prosecutor dramatically asked "General Westmoreland, were you in command of all United States forces in Vietnam from 1964 through 1968?" he laconically answered "I was."

The prosecutor elicited testimony that the KL-7 had been used extensively for sensitive communications during field operations in Vietnam. General Westmoreland implied that every time a U.S. covert operations team was ambushed by North Vietnamese or Vietcong forces during the Vietnam War this happened because the enemy knew it was coming. This, he indicated, was thanks to the KL-7 Helmich had sold to the Soviets and they in turn had supplied to their Vietnamese allies. Indeed, years later a KL-7 appeared in a collection of war memorabilia the Vietnamese put on display. At this point, the jurors for the trial were looking daggers at Helmich, whom I think they eagerly would have strung up right in the courtroom had they the opportunity to do so.

Fortunately for Helmich, I had helped the partner prepare documents to argue that he was not eligible for the death penalty. Shortly before General Westmoreland testified, the judge accepted our position and ruled Helmich could not be executed. Now, it was time to play "let's make a deal." The prosecutor eventually agreed to have Helmich plead guilty to one count of conspiracy to commit espionage and let the judge determine the sentence. Since Helmich's visit to the Soviet embassy in Ottawa in 1980 counted as an act in furtherance of the conspiracy, there would be no viable statute of limitations defense to the conspiracy charge.

On sentencing day the partner eloquently argued why

Helmich should not receive the maximum sentence. He noted that Helmich had a wife and son, had been a law abiding citizen since 1964, had been willing to work with the FBI to make amends for his behavior by becoming a double agent, and so forth. The judge made a point of saying to the partner "thank you for all your outstanding work in this case, including the sentencing argument you just made. I am not, however, convinced. The sentence is life. Marshal, take him away." At that, Helmich was dragged from the courtroom and sent off to federal prison to serve his sentence. That was the last time I saw my suit or tie.

The partner's appeal of Helmich's conviction, which was largely based on an obscure criminal conspiracy argument I had brought to the partner's attention, was unsuccessful. Helmich died in federal prison at age 66 after being incarcerated roughly twenty years. From the Helmich prosecution on, the partner was firmly in my corner. At least during this case, I was regarded as part of the team rather than as an outsider. Unfortunately, since the Helmich case, like what I did for the charity with the maritime program for juvenile offenders, was not a revenue generator for the firm, my work counted for little with most of the partners I needed to impress in order to be a success there. Once again, my lack of interest in the mercenary part of running a successful business was problematic.

During my remaining time at the firm it experienced monumental changes. Due mainly to my employer's conservative economic views, which would have made famous economist Adam Smith proud, the firm actually was divided up into "profit centers." The earnings of each profit center were calculated and the compensation of the partner and his or her associates was determined based on the profitability of that little group. This plan encouraged profit centers to hoard work and meant those in my group tried to do everything ourselves, with me still handling the bulk of the non-law and economics based matters.

To show how far this principle stretched, when the rainmaker partner wanted me to help him on a project he would have to "rent" me from my boss. My salary came out of his profit center and he wanted his colleague to reimburse him for my time. All this placed considerable stress on me. This was especially true since my superior depended on me for such non-revenue generating activities as making sure he kept up with billing clients, something he was notoriously tardy in doing. How could I "pay my own way" if I spent my billable hours on matters that would generate no money?

Just as this was happening my depression was worsening. I spent considerable time, especially in the afternoons, in a torpid state. I would close my office door and then stare straight ahead until my head gradually fell forward and I dozed in a sort of depressive stupor. I worried over how to bill for the many hours I spent in this condition since I certainly was not doing client work then. I was distressed over, and ruminated about, this dysfunctional behavior but was at a loss over what to do about it. Neither Dr. Hartman nor my psychiatrist could offer any assistance other than a higher dose of antidepressant. A change of job might have helped a great deal, but at this point I was in no condition to look for one. The depression clearly was getting the better of me, and the medication was not really helping.

Around this time, in an effort to foster morale a firm retreat was ordered. We all went to a well-known expensive and exclusive beachfront resort near Jacksonville for a weekend of tennis, sun, and excellent food. It also featured both forced, and mostly insincere, handholding and Kumbaya singing (figuratively speaking). After dinner, most of those present drank large amounts of alcohol and fired up cigars. I refrained as my gastrointestinal problems were flaring up.

Eventually, someone suggested we play "acey-deucey," a non-poker card gambling game, at something like one dollar a hand.

I had never even heard of acey-deucy but willingly joined the fray. As it is a simple game, I quickly caught on and my old war gamer competitive juices quickly started to flow. Being very smart, and sober, I quickly cleaned up. I won over one hundred dollars before the game ended. As Dr. Hartman knew, I lack common sense, which would have told me not to beat everyone else lest I antagonize them. It was not wise to be the nerdy Dukie who defeated the University of Florida and FSU crowd through the "unfair" method of staying sober.

Throughout my years at the firm I dealt with chronic physical ills attributable to my mental woes. By now, my 1975 ulcer surgery had set off a very painful gastrointestinal condition called bile reflux gastritis that has afflicted me in varying degrees ever since.

As if this were not enough, I had chronic constipation problems from both the ulcer surgery and my gastritis and psychiatric medications. Finally, the psychotropic drugs led to chronic prostate infections, which are very painful. It is hard to have a very positive outlook on the world when your stomach burns, you battle constipation, and your prostate is infected most of the time.

About then I bought a condominium in a recently renovated historic building. Mother and I worked hard on proper decoration and furnishings. I even had a huge built-in glass front wall storage unit for my now enormous record collection. Record collecting and listening to music had become a true, albeit soothing, addiction for me that helped me deal with the vicissitudes of my life. I would listen to records once before placing them in perfect chronological order, rarely to play them again. I also purchased a very expensive stereo system. Had I known more about mental illness I would have recognized these acquisitions as a manic collection compulsion like my childhood one of comic books and my later ones of guns, Civil

War memorabilia, and classical music cds. I do not recall ever discussing this issue with Dr. Hartman or my psychiatrist, but I probably should have done so.

In 1981 I learned of a trip to London. The point of the journey was to have a tax deductible tour there that focused on visiting the major sites of the British legal system. This included, among other things, sitting in on part of a murder trial at the Central Criminal Court in the famous Old Bailey. The real reason for my excursion, however, was that I learned the trip coincided with a Mozart festival at London's Royal Opera House at Covent Garden. Sir Colin Davis, one of my favorite conductors, was leading the three greatest Mozart operas over the period of a few days. I had recordings of these three works conducted by Davis and sung by some of the singers who would be appearing at Covent Garden. This was an irresistible attraction, so I took the law tour, got my tax write-off, and reveled in my beloved Mozart. It was an amazing experience, and I was in heaven.

I did have one good friend at the firm who tried to help me deal with my job. He was a very personable and popular associate, and thus an excellent person with whom to interact. Thanks to his encouragement, and even matchmaking, I finally took the epic step at the age of about twenty-seven of starting to date. I actually found a girlfriend with whom I became extremely close, and marriage even seemed to be a possibility. We took trips together, in particular a lavish one at an historic bed and breakfast in Savannah, and slept over at one or the other's residence on many evenings.

While we were together my girlfriend discovered an abandoned black and tan female miniature dachshund that looked exactly like Susie, although she lacked Susie's strong and distinctive personality (indeed, she was very submissive, and I rather suspected she had been abused by a previous owner). I quickly named her Brünnhilde and adopted her. I bonded with her as I had with Sue-Sue years before. Indeed, my girlfriend quickly regretted giving her to me. I transferred much of my affection from the girlfriend, perhaps a vaguely intimidating figure considering my view of my mother, to the dog who reminded me of the non-threatening Susie of my youth.

After my girlfriend and I had been together for nearly a year I suddenly decided I did not really love her, as if I knew what love was or how it felt, and broke up with her. I honestly cannot say why I came to this conclusion, as we had a happy relationship that easily could have resulted in marriage (had I proposed, I am sure she immediately would have accepted). I think I had a real fear of commitment that grew stronger as I came ever closer to entering into a permanent one. In any event, my girlfriend was heartbroken. I had such a hard time, thanks to my deep and abiding inferiority complex, realizing anyone could care that much about me that I could not fathom her condition. Despite a few brief attempts at reconciliation the romance was over as I had made up my mind on the subject, and once I do so the matter is closed. I dated a bit more after this event but basically retreated to my world of depression, work, classical music, and Brünnhilde. The catastrophic events of mid-1983 might not have occurred had I had an adequate social structure in place at that time.

What may have been most remarkable about this turn of events was that it was not just a case of me getting total love and acceptance from a pet that helped me cope with the mental illness from which I suffered. Here, I chose Brünnhilde, a not terribly memorable pet, over a woman who was eager to spend her life with me. I clearly had serious issues with relationships when I felt safer with an unremarkable dog than a loving human being. Perhaps another illustration of my abiding inferiority complex whereby I feared rejection by any person and sought comfort with a generic animal I believed would stick by me through thick and thin. My fear in this regard would play out for real in the years to come.

Despite my lack of religious feeling, Riverside Presbyterian Church, which my family had joined in 1964, provided an important social and musical opportunity thanks to Andrew L. Clarke and the choir he leads. Andy Clarke is the most outstanding musician I have ever met. He has been organist and choirmaster at Riverside since the 1970s and is a leader in the Jacksonville music community.

I sang as a baritone in Andy's choir and accordingly absorbed and enjoyed the talent of the man I like to refer to "Johann Sebastian Clarke," the modern "descendant" of the great Bach. Periodically Andy stages large-scale choral productions of the masterworks of composers like Handel, Mozart and Bach complete with members of the Jacksonville Symphony as accompanists. The concerts are very popular in the community, and it was a great joy for me to take part in them. Indeed, I still listen with pride to my tape of the two-part performance of the Bach *B Minor Mass* in which I participated in December 1984 and April 1985. My experience with Andy would lead me to use other choirs as social opportunities and classical music outlets even though I was not there for religious reasons.

Back at the firm things were going badly. It had become one of the largest in Florida. It had a big Miami office, a branch in Tallahassee, and many powerful clients. Despite all it had going for it, everything suddenly collapsed like a house of cards. In my opinion this was attributable to the profit center mode of operation that shifted loyalty from the firm as a whole to the individual group in which the attorney worked.

At first, a few profit centers split off from the firm. Then, the flood began. Almost no work was done because the attorneys and staff spent much of their time guessing who would leave next. Both the Miami and Tallahassee offices soon were gone.

While that was unfortunate, at least they were populated by people you rarely saw or thought about. Things really got bad when those in the Jacksonville office headed for the door in droves. The suspense became almost excruciating, as each day one wondered whether another group of colleagues was leaving. It was a totally unpredictable situation that affected the stability of a central element of my life, the job upon which I depended for my livelihood and many of my social relationships.

It is unbearable not knowing if or when your employment will disintegrate around you. It got so bad that national legal publications wrote big stories about the collapse and I got calls from reporters asking for comments about the debacle. Major clients started to sever their ties with the firm as they were uncomfortable being represented by attorneys who could not keep their own house in order. That could lead to the total demise of the firm and generated ever increasing amounts of anxiety and trepidation.

All this was exactly the type of stress Dr. Hartman had noted makes me suffer both severe psychological and physiological problems, and it did both. Those with bipolar disorder take uncertainty and change very poorly, and conditions at the firm generated vast amounts of both. Indeed, it was an emotional disaster, and my depression and gastrointestinal symptoms grew unbearable. I had difficulty sleeping despite taking the sleep medication that generally allowed me to do so, while during the day my bipolar stupor worsened markedly.

My boss and the other firm named partner were constantly in meetings trying to salvage things, but met with little success. Eventually what was left of the Jacksonville office merged with another Jacksonville firm. Consequently, there was still a firm with the old name in existence but it was far different than the one of a few months before.

By the time things stabilized, very few of the over one

hundred attorneys who had started the year with the firm were left there. The Black Death of the fourteenth century did not have that sort of mortality rate! My close friend who arranged my romance saw the handwriting on the wall and moved home to Pennsylvania. Eventually, even the rainmaker partner bailed out to become head inside attorney for a major firm client.

Imagine what it is like to have one of the named partners, someone for whom over time you have done considerable work for important clients that made you valuable to the firm, abandon the place he had led for years. You really focus on the disaster in which you are living when that happens! In my supervisor's own group one of the associates suffered a mental breakdown that led to his departure. This left three or so shell-shocked survivors, including me, to try to carry on and do work rather than focus all our attention, or ruminate as I did, over what was happening around us.

I was forced to have frequent appointments with Dr. Hartman to try and cope, and had to take more medications for the depression and anxiety that were overwhelming me. When I asked Dr. Hartman what to do he responded "You have to learn to handle uncertainty. Life doesn't always go as you want or plan for. Take it one day at a time and hope when the smoke clears you'll still have a job. By working for the most senior partner left in the firm you should have as much job security as is possible there."

I tried to follow Dr. Hartman's advice, although at times the unpredictability was almost debilitating. Then, when it seemed things could not get much worse, all for me really went down the tubes.

By mid-1983 part of my problem was the firm collapse, but I also had an unrequited romantic fixation with which to deal. In late 1982 my boss hired a new secretary, an attractive young divorcée named Audrey. As usual, I had to work closely with her on his business. I quickly grew infatuated with Audrey.

She flirted, harmlessly I am sure she thought, with me. I spent considerable time at her desk talking, joking, and generally, from my perspective, bonding and falling in love with her. She had some financial and other issues, and in my own mind I somehow constructed a scenario where I would be her knight in shining armor. Without telling her I changed my firm life insurance policy to make her my beneficiary. Although I had a few dates with other women while this was going on, so far as I was concerned Audrey was the one for me. Unfortunately, as it later turned out, she did not feel the same.

Right about this time my employer announced, seemingly out of the blue one Wednesday, that he did not think I would make partner in what was left of the firm since many people did not like me. Earlier he had me enroll in a Dale Carnegie course to try to make me more charismatic, but apparently that was too little too late.

He spoke very matter of factly: "I only realized very recently that many of the lawyers in the firm, including most of the partners, dislike you. They think you're arrogant and standoffish, and note you don't have any clients of your own or bring much money into the firm. They also say you're overly sensitive to criticism, and generally not their type of person. The acey-deucy game at the firm retreat turned a lot of them against you, as they say you weren't a good sport. You should have known better than to win all their money. They didn't like losing to you."

"But I thought the object of the game was to win, and that's what I did."

"That's not always smart to do. They'd like you a lot better if you'd managed to lose a few hands so they could have recouped some of their losses. In any event, it's too late now, as their minds are made up. It's time for you to consider working somewhere else, although you can stay here for now."

This conversation left me in a state of shock. Truly what Dr.

Hartman had predicted in 1979 had come true. People viewed me as unduly sensitive, hard to relate to, impractical, one who reacted poorly to criticism, and one whose superiority complex made him arrogant and aloof. Accordingly, they wanted me out of the firm. Indeed, why would they want a partner like that? Now, here I was: severely depressed; fixated on a non-existent romance; and, so far as I was concerned, told my career was ruined. What was I to do next? I had a good idea.

One positive result of the aforementioned merger with an old-line Jacksonville firm was that it brought into the firm a slight, sensitive female partner named Jeanne who was about my brother Rick's age and saw in me a kindred soul. While we never discussed the point, I suspected at some time she had dealt with depression issues herself. I could talk with her about my concerns and feelings without the fear she would hold them against me or report me to the other partners. It was now about time for me to discuss the most sensitive of issues with, and request the greatest of favors from, Jeanne.

On Wednesday evening I pondered my devastating exchange with the firm's most senior partner. I felt a deep sense of disgrace and shame for my failure. I could see no good way out of my situation. I did not believe I would be hired elsewhere since my personality problems would be a roadblock wherever I applied despite my credentials. It was like when the Richmond firm rejected me in 1977, only worse considering the duration and depth of my commitment to the Jacksonville one. Had I been thinking clearly I would have realized that some firm or company somewhere undoubtedly would hire me just as Davis Polk did in 1977, but at this point I was far too upset to be rational. Down the road all I could foresee was unemployment, poverty, homelessness, humiliation, and despair. To me that was totally unacceptable.

I certainly could not discuss things with my mother, and

Brünnhilde was not much of a conversationalist. I was too ashamed to call Dr. Hartman as I should have done. I slowly, but inexorably, realized what I must do.

Coincidentally, a few weeks before on television I saw the 1971 antiwar film *Johnny Got His Gun* about a World War I soldier who had been struck by an artillery shell. It left him limbless, faceless, deaf, dumb and blind, confined to a semi-existence in a hospital back room. He finally managed to communicate with his nurse a stark message: "Kill me. Kill me." At the time I saw the film it touched me, but I did not know why. Now the answer seemed clear. I remember fixating on the phrase "death before dishonor."

As noted, I feel suicide is acceptable and appropriate under the right circumstances. In addition, I believe conditions like those created by my conversation with my superior qualify as such. In what was undoubtedly a period of what laypeople would call insanity I saw it as a desirable way to escape the unbearable mental and emotional pain from which I then was suffering and to which I could see no end. Indeed, it seemed to be the best possible alternative, as I could not stand for life to go on as it was. I would not be acting out of anger or some sort of passive-aggressive behavior. Instead, I would be like the terminal cancer patient who knows a terrible future of unremitting suffering and certain death awaits such that suicide is the only sensible way to avoid that result.

On Thursday I went into work as usual. I wrote a perfectly respectable memorandum regarding a corporate law issue someone had asked me to address. I then drafted a will leaving everything to Audrey and composed a suicide letter. At this point, I had some doubts and went to see Jeanne. I told her how I was thinking, and she, of course, expressed great concern. She asked me to go into the hospital, but when I refused she suggested I go home with her and her husband to weather the storm of the evening. That sounded like a good idea. After a delightful dinner I soon was safely ensconced in her guest bedroom. However, despondency took over and I decided to emulate those about whom I learned so much at Virginia, the Romans.

When a plot against an emperor failed, Roman history records, often the plotters were offered an alternative to disgrace and the forfeiture of family assets. They could lie in a tub of hot water, open a vein, and quietly bleed to death. I decided to follow this pattern, which coincidentally was adopted in the Frankie Pentangeli/ Tom Hagen episode from *The Godfather Part II* with which some may be familiar. I drew a tub of hot water, got in, and slashed at my wrist with a razor blade. Not being knowledgeable about such things, I slashed perpendicular to the arm bone rather than parallel to it. I made a slight incision, but suffered no real blood loss and was left with little scarring. As I later learned from some experts at suicide, the parallel cut is the one that is likely to be fatal. In any event, my act satisfied me. It was as if the small wound at least temporarily had released the pent-up pressure to act that had overcome me since the crushing comments the day before. Much relieved, I went to bed. Was this a suicide attempt, or a suicidal gesture: a cry for help, rather than a real attempt to end life? I have never really known the answer to this question.

The next morning, when Jeanne came to check on me I showed her what I had done, and she was horrified. She almost shouted "you must call your psychiatrist immediately!" I did so and told him what was afoot. He said "go to the hospital *now*."

"I don't think I need to do that, I'll just go home."

"I will not treat a suicidal patient on an outpatient basis. Drive to St. Vincent's at once!"

Being a basically obedient person, I reported as ordered.

Unlike the regular hospital where I had the Elavil sleep therapy in 1980, St. Vincent's Medical Center had a real psychiatric unit. The doors locked behind me when I entered. I would not be free again for some time. I left instructions that no one, including my mother, be told where I was. My first memory of future communication with Jeanne was when I called her over twenty-five years later. At that time I learned both that I never received an encouraging letter she sent me when I was in St. Vincent's and that I had totally forgotten that we spoke by telephone while I later was hospitalized in North Carolina. She remained a true friend and supporter through it all, and we continue to keep in touch today.

8

As I quickly learned at St. Vincent's, being in a locked psychiatric unit is a unique, and unsettling, experience. I can have no "sharps" such as razor, knives, pins, staples, paper clips, nail clippers, matches, lighters, or anything else with which I, or anyone else, can cause harm except when under visual supervision of a hospital employee. Smokers either have to hang around the nurses' station where their lighters are stored or else light their cigarettes from those of their comrades. I have to undergo periodic full-body, i.e. nude, physical inspections to check for self-mutilating acts. I can have no belts or shoelaces, as I can use them to hang myself. If on a suicide watch, I am observed continually, including when sleeping, showering, or even using the restroom.

I was voluntarily admitted to St. Vincent's. I have never been committed to a psychiatric facility. At some level I always have recognized the need for care, and in addition I fear losing my law license if judicial action is taken. Indeed, when, on occasion, I have gotten angry and tried to leave a hospital against medical advice I have been threatened with commitment and cooled off as a consequence of my licensure fears.

I stayed at St. Vincent's for several weeks, but the longer I was there the worse I got. I slept less and less, eventually sleeping no more than one or two hours a night despite taking sleeping medication because I had what anyone should have recognized was acute mania. I fixated on suicide and engaged in self-mutilating behavior about which I learned from other patients. I listened to complete symphonies and operas in my head. Particularly when manic I have always been able to hear them played by full classical music ensembles and sung by master vocalists without the need for any listening equipment. Finally, I fantasized I was like Shakespeare's Hamlet, whose famous soliloquy I considered a justification for suicide. Indeed, I had Tom Ramey send me a copy of *Hamlet* so I could be sure I got the language correctly.

"To die, to sleep; No more; and by a sleep to say we end The heart-ache and the thousand natural shocks That flesh is heir to—'tis a consummation Devoutly to be wish'd."

My psychiatrist often said "I can't understand why you're so determined to commit suicide. You're young and have a lot to live for."

"I don't feel that way."

He paused and then asked "Are you familiar with Forrestal?"

"I've heard of the aircraft carrier, and think it was named for a Secretary of the Navy under FDR."

"James V. Forrestal was not just Secretary of the Navy. He also was the first Secretary of Defense after President Truman appointed him to that position."

"Why do you bring up Forrestal?"

"Like you, he had a fine mind. His ending was as sad as the one you're asking for."

"What do you mean?"

"Forrestal was in Bethesda Naval Hospital for a psychiatric illness much as you're being treated here. He leapt from a window to his death while there. What a terrible loss."

"Oh," I said. Insincerely, I added "how tragic."

My psychiatrist seemed to believe hearing about Forrestal would make me renounce suicide. In truth, his story only made the act seem more defensible. I remember thinking to myself:

"If Secretary Forrestal could commit suicide, and Hemingway,

Plath, van Gogh, and countless others could as well, why can't I?"

St. Vincent's was not a bad place. The food was satisfactory, the staff kind, and the other patients interesting. Like most psychiatric inpatients I have known, they were much easier to get along with and forgiving of the foibles of others than "normal" people in the outside world. However, it clearly was a short-term facility. There were limited opportunities for art or related therapy, and the exercise facilities were pretty inadequate. I saw my doctor for only a brief period each day, as he treated both inpatients and outpatients rather than specializing in inpatients only.

At one point I grew angry over something and called two friends from the law firm to get me out. When they arrived, however, they convinced me I needed to stay where I was. Throughout this time, I was aggressively suicidal and was kept under constant observation.

Eventually I let my psychiatrist tell my mother where I was, and she attended to Brünnhilde by having my former girlfriend take her for the time being. As my condominium sat vacant, others debated my future. Finally, my doctor decided that I needed more than St. Vincent's and Jacksonville had to offer. In truth, he was bewildered over what to do with me. He recommended that I go to Highland Hospital, a well-known private psychiatric facility in Asheville, North Carolina. Ironically enough, until recently it had been run by the Duke University Department of Psychiatry. It had a brochure very much like a private school catalog. I agreed to go; now came the logistical problem.

The doctor said "I can't send you to Asheville on a regular commercial airplane as I'm afraid you'll try to jump out or something."

"Quite possibly, yes."

"In that case, I'm ordering a private air ambulance for you. You may find it an interesting experience."

On the appointed day, an ambulance arrived at St. Vincent's.

Once I was strapped into place so I could not move the ambulance drove me to a hangar at the airport. The ambulance drivers handed me over to the air ambulance crew. They loaded me aboard a private jet for the trip to Asheville. I was unfettered for the trip, but in addition to the flight crew there were several burly attendants aboard to insure I behaved myself. They conveyed to me the basic message that "If you don't start any trouble, there won't be any trouble." Being both outweighed and outnumbered, I decided discretion was the better part of valor and merely engaged in pleasant banter with them about the current professional baseball season. Once we landed in Asheville the crew transferred me to an ambulance where I again was tied down and eventually delivered to Highland for admission.

By the time I reached Highland I was in pretty bad shape. My brain was just not right. I could not focus or concentrate. Reading was a real problem and my memory was almost totally shot. My analogy to my condition when I have had an acute breakdown like the one in 1983 is that it feels as if my brain has short-circuited after a severe electrical shock. It withdraws into itself to recover such that it takes a long time to be restored to normal. I need quiet and rest, as well as much medical treatment, to function in the world again. Luckily, I got these in Asheville.

Highland Hospital was a famous institution, perhaps best known as the site where Zelda Fitzgerald, widow of renowned author F. Scott Fitzgerald, perished along with eight other female patients in a 1948 fire. She had been in Highland a number of times in the 1930s and 1940s while being treated for schizophrenia. On the day of the fire, she had undergone an insulin shock therapy treatment that left her unconscious so she did not escape the conflagration.

Highland was an inviting and beautiful facility where I spent the next six months. It was encircled by the Blue Ridge and Great Smoky Mountains close to the banks of the Swannanoa and French Broad Rivers. It more resembled a college campus than a psychiatric institution. It was almost an idyllic place to recover. Located on Zillacoa Street, it was affectionately known by its denizens, in a bit of gallows humor, as the "Zillacoa Zoo." It had a variety of amenities including a tennis court, a swimming pool, both indoor and outdoor basketball and volleyball facilities, numerous and frequent art and music therapy programs, a weight room, television rooms, and periodic telephone privileges. The food was ample and excellent. The Highland staff was outstanding. I still remember those like Nell Endsell and Hugh Reed with incredible fondness after over twenty-five years.

Highland provided all this for a mere $10,000 per month. After my insurance and personal resources ran out long before I was ready for release, my mother paid the bill to the tune of between $20,000 and $30,000. While she had me sign a promissory note for that amount, she has never attempted to collect on it.

Once a new adult patient like me was evaluated in the locked "acute" unit on the first floor of the main housing edifice and showed he was not a danger to himself or to others he moved upstairs to the unlocked area there. I remember being a real pain to my doctor until she quickly allowed me to leave the acute unit. The area upstairs featured a series of double rooms, each furnished with twin beds, two dressers, and a closet. The bathrooms and showers were located down the hall. The whole facility reminded me of my dormitory when I was a first year student at Virginia. My roommate for most of my stay at Highland was a very pleasant, albeit somewhat larcenous, Talwin addict. My experience with him and his periodic petty thefts of some of the small amounts of cash I had in my possession for doing laundry, purchasing toiletries, or enjoying meals in town have colored my view of the honesty and integrity of substance abusers ever since. My dealings with others at Highland who

87

had drug or alcohol problems only reinforced my perception.

Although upstairs was not a closed facility in the sense that we were not locked into the building, if you tried to "escape" by wandering off the premises the staff would alert the police who quickly would return you. You then undoubtedly would spend some time in the acute unit for your trouble.

As 1983 was long before mandatory smoke-free facilities and since psychiatric patients tend to smoke a great deal, I inhaled a lot of second-hand smoke at Highland in the main gathering area. Those with schizophrenia in particular are heavy smokers because for some reason nicotine helps relieve their symptoms. There was a non-smoking sitting room, with television, available, but hardly anyone ever went there except to do laundry as that was where the pay washers and dryers were located. All the action was in the general smoking lounge/television room. Although I generally am a rabid anti-smoker, at Highland I even tried a few cigarettes myself until I decided this was not a habit for me in that I both did not like it and come from a family with a long history of lung cancer.

Many interesting patients were treated at Highland. These included those suffering from schizophrenia, bipolar disorder, unipolar depression, drug and alcohol addiction, anorexia, and other assorted conditions. Some were extremely wealthy. For example, a scion of a Southern condiment empire was a long-term resident who stayed there as he liked it and for him $120,000 per year was nothing. He apparently had schizophrenia and had been on traditional antipsychotic medications (Haldol, Thorazine, Navane, Stelazine, etc.) for many years. He had a severe case of tardive dyskinesia, which is a chronic, often incurable disorder that is not uncommon in those who have taken antipsychotics for many years. It is characterized by repetitive, involuntary, purposeless movements that may include grimacing; tongue protrusion; lip smacking, puckering and pursing; rapid eye blinking; and speedy movements of the arms, legs, and trunk. This man constantly moved his head in a circular fashion, seemed incessantly to chew with his mouth, and had severe speech problems. He, and others at Highland, also walked in an odd, shambling fashion many refer to as the "Thorazine shuffle." I hoped I never found myself with such problems.

I fit in well with the group, as I finally found many others with whom I could relate. As at St. Vincent's, I liked my fellow inmates, and unlike there I had time to get to know a number of them quite well. Once again, most were extremely warm and caring people despite their current situation. I was proud to consider them my friends.

I learned to play endless games of spades and hearts, and watched plenty of bad television. There could be big battles over which shows to watch, and I was frequently outvoted when I wanted to view more "intellectual" programming in place of other popular shows of the day such as *Dallas*, *Dynasty*, or *The Love Boat*. For example, I liked critics' favorites *Hill Street Blues* and *St. Elsewhere*. Unfortunately they competed with nighttime soap operas *Knots Landing* and *Hotel*. Thus, I missed them.

I particularly remember the night the television movie *The Day After* about the onset of a nuclear war between the United States and the Soviet Union and its aftermath was on. I really wanted to watch the film, and lobbied hard to see it.

"This is a really important movie. We all need to be aware of what can happen if we ever go to war with the Soviets."

"You must be kidding," my compatriots responded. "We don't want to watch something like that. It'll be gross and scary and depressing. Besides, it's on against *The Jeffersons*." Game over.

When I was admitted to Highland I was assigned to Dr. Joanna M. Gaworowski. She was an excellent psychiatrist as well as a very kind and attractive woman in her late thirties or early forties. She was thin, fairly tall, and blonde. Both her strong accent and physical appearance were striking. She liked to drive imported sports cars, which went along with her exotic wardrobe and image. Unlike the doctor in Jacksonville, she specialized in inpatient care and only saw a few outpatients whom she formerly had treated as inpatients. Although she never referred to me as "manic-depressive," she put me on an antidepressant and a special easy-on-the-stomach form of lithium carbonate, the "gold standard" drug for bipolar disorder, and I gradually improved. I could sleep with sleeping medication and gradually approached low level functioning after what a layperson would call a severe nervous breakdown.

Dr. Gaworowski's core group of patients included Kathy D., a stylish Atlanta socialite with unipolar depression who was my best friend; Al M., a middle-aged South Carolinian with unipolar depression who had a tremendous sense of humor and was much fun to be around; Joanne M., an attractive early twenty-ish North Carolinian with borderline personality disorder; Janet R., a twenty-something blue-collar worker from Pennsylvania; and Sam A., who had both schizophrenia and a mean streak. With the notable exception of Sam, we all got along very well together. Al, Kathy, and I especially did so as we were all older (over twenty-five) and college-educated. At one point I developed a "white knight" fantasy towards Joanne somewhat like that I had for Audrey in Jacksonville, but I took it nowhere as far. Janet was a self-mutilator whose arms were a disaster area. She had done things like plug in an automobile cigarette lighter, pull it out when it was red hot, and plunge it into one or the other of them. Given the slightest opportunity, she would take something like a shard of glass and slice herself to ribbons with it. Patients like her are why the hospital had the "no sharps" policy, as she could steal a sharp from another patient and cut herself with it before anyone knew anything had happened.

In addition to Dr. G.'s patients, I also socialized with those of other doctors such as Bill J., a strikingly handsome late adolescent with schizophrenia; Richard J., a physician about my age with a substance abuse problem; Chuck R., an athletic and pleasant young man whose diagnosis I do not recall; and Lynn B., an attractive blonde pharmacist my age with a heroin addiction. We were much like an extended family who liked and cared a great deal about one another; while others passed through the ward, the core individuals stayed together for months at a time.

Weekdays at Highland were predictable. Once I got up I joined the line at the nursing station to get my morning medications. Next, other than during the brief period I attempted to grow a beard I checked out my razor and shaving supplies from an attendant, shaved, and returned them. Then, I went with the group headed over for breakfast at the dining room. After breakfast each doctor met with his or her patients for rounds.

During her rounds Dr. Gaworowski read the chart of each patient, in which the nurses or psychiatric assistants had recorded his or her activities during the previous twenty-four hours, to all her charges. As I tended to hang out principally with my friends who were also Dr. Gaworowski's patients, when she read my chart it showed me interacting with them. For privacy reasons, all charts referred to others only by first name and initial. I was mentioned as "Jim J." She would share the most intimate details with all her patients. For example, on a typical day Dr. G. would relate to everyone something like: "After rounds Jim J. went to art therapy where he worked appropriately on his leatherwork project. Then he went to lunch and ate with Kathy D. and Al M. After lunch he went to weight training where Hugh R. reports he managed to increase the amount he bench-pressed. Following the afternoon group therapy meeting he took his medication and played tennis with Kathy D. until time for dinner. After supper he laughed and joked with Kathy D. and Al M. in the front lounge. He watched television for a time and then played cards with Richard J., Lynn B., Chuck R., and Al M. At one point he grew tearful, but quickly recovered after talking with Nell E. about his prognosis for about thirty minutes. He took his medications at the usual time and went to bed, falling asleep fairly quickly. He woke up once during the night and talked with [night nurse] Amanda S. for a few minutes. He then returned to bed and quickly went back to sleep." The charts of her other patients would mirror mine. If one had a difficult day the chart would reflect this and the group would discuss the situation.

After rounds Dr. G.'s patients headed to a variety of activities. In art therapy we made pottery and fired it in a real kiln, did leatherwork, cross stitched, put together mosaics, and painted. We listened to recordings and live music and sang as best we could in music therapy. In gardening we raised plants and generally benefitted from seeing new life around us. Lunch would always be good.

After lunch, the men could try weight lifting under Hugh's supervision and thereby learn the importance of exercise for those with mental illness. I "pumped a lot of iron" while at Highland, including bench pressing an impressive amount of weight. This gave me a very important sense of accomplishment at a time when my ego was at low ebb.

Several days a week Dr. G. conducted a group therapy session for all her patients. Group therapy is an important part of psychiatric treatment. You learn a great deal about yourself while exploring the issues that affect others. Also, you get very close to others when in a group with them; support from such a body is important for me even today. I was lucky to be one of Dr. Gaworowski's patients, as she was one of the best doctors at Highland and devoted much time to her patients. Later in the day, there would be free time before dinner.

After the always delicious dinner we assembled for the nightly television watching and card playing. Often during the evening

I would have heart to heart conversations with Nell, a wonderful nurse who was incredibly important to me. She was a strong positive influence, and even maternal figure, for me.

Following evening meds we went to bed and, hopefully, slept. Every few hours a staff member shined a flashlight on each patient to make sure he or she was in bed and alright. This always reminded me that whatever I did and wherever I was, a hospital staff member was keeping track of me.

Frequent individual therapy sessions with Dr. G. were a critical element of the treatment plan. We would meet two or three times a week, and she would discuss my condition and what needed to be done to improve it. She recognized the tremendous trauma my brain had suffered, and encouraged me to work to repair the damage and return to my pre-breakdown ability to be a contributing member of society. We talked at times about my future, and realized that law practice may not be the long-term place for me. She worked hard to keep me on a positive road so that I would not wallow in self-pity and my fear that I never would be able to work again. She knew I was mired in the depths of despair and depression and focused on getting me out of the black hole into which I had fallen. Unlike me, she was convinced that, although it would take a significant period of time, I could make it back from the depression through a combination of psychotropic drugs and intensive psychotherapy. Overall, unlike most psychiatrists today, she was a fine therapist in addition to being an accomplished psychopharmacologist.

Saturdays often were special at Highland. Daytime gave opportunities for tennis, basketball, and other tests of one's athletic prowess. Saturday evenings frequently saw a gathering in the recreation hall led by Hugh and other staff members. They would turn on the music and there would be quite a party, complete with refreshments. Despite my strong preference for pre-Beethoven classical music, I would dance with Kathy D., Joanne M., Lynn

93

B., and my other fellow patients to then-current popular music. This included songs from the movie *Flashdance*, country tunes like "Mountain Music" by the band "Alabama," and the hits from the late Michael Jackson's best-selling "Thriller" album. Yes, I could rock up a real storm in time with "Billy Jean" and "Beat It!" as well as anyone. I never knew how much fun dancing could be before these events! For the first time in my life, rather than being an outcast I really fit in socially with those of both sexes. As I recall those days, I was actually popular, something that went a long way towards my recovery with a new sense of self-confidence.

When someone was about to be discharged we would usually have some sort of gathering in his or her honor in the front lounge. I particularly remember when Al M. returned to South Carolina. We were all extremely fond of Al, and the wealthy Kathy D. engineered a big sendoff for him. Kathy really knew how to throw a party. Despite the fun that evening, we all really missed Al after he "graduated" from Highland and left for home.

Despite the imagery of Hollywood, I saw nothing while in Highland like *One Flew Over the Cuckoo's Nest* or *Girl, Interrupted*. Still, daily med routines, sharps checks, and the need to check out a razor or nail clippers always reminded you of where you were. If your condition deteriorated severely there was a trip to the locked acute unit downstairs. I was known for my good behavior and reputation. As a result, even after I got in a fist fight with Sam A., the previously mentioned schizophrenic and local bully, he went to acute while Dr. Gaworowski judged me innocent of any offense.

So long as your mental health permitted, as mine generally did, there were weekly outings to a local shopping mall and restaurants, trips to Mt. Mitchell and the Blue Ridge Parkway, and even one memorable golf excursion. You could get permission to attend a movie, such as when I went to see the latest James Bond film. Birthdays were celebrated with parties. You could have visits from outside friends and relatives. For me that included Aunt Bet, my mother, and Tom Ramey and his parents. You could even go off the hospital grounds with them.

I recall well a trip with the Rameys to the Biltmore House, the Asheville chateau and estate of George Washington Vanderbilt. We took the grand tour of the mansion, which was very impressive. Unknown to the Rameys, I got very uncomfortable when we went out to look off a high balcony. They said "What a lovely view." The suicidal impulses that still plagued me made me think "please don't act like Secretary Forrestal and jump." I then discreetly backed up against the building so I was as far from the edge as possible. To this day, I am very ill at ease when around high places, especially when I am suffering from suicidal feelings. On at least one occasion when climbing up a hillside I have frozen to the ground such that someone has had to come and retrieve me. Imagine how embarrassing that is!

There was one event a little like something from *One Flew Over the Cuckoo's Nest*, our famous golf outing. I had talked for some time about playing golf, and eventually in the fall Dr. G. and her colleagues/employer decided to allow a few patients to do so. Richard J. and I both were golfers, although I play badly, as was Hugh Reed, who played very well. While Chuck R. did not know how to play golf, he was eager to come along just for the sake of a pleasant outing outside the hospital. Hugh loaded us into a Highland vehicle and drove us to a local public course where we rented clubs and two golf carts. Considering that we patients had not driven a vehicle since we arrived at Highland, it was great fun just to operate a cart. Playing golf was an extra bonus. Although the main thing we did was lose golf balls, with Chuck hitting them everywhere but on the fairway, we had a grand time. Hugh forever earned a special place in my heart just for this one event. When you add to this his helping me with weight training, running dances, and being a friend and strong male role model when I really needed one, his place in my firmament was assured.

As you might expect, when there were a large number of young adults living together in a co-ed dormitory, romances would blossom. Hospital rules forbade patients to date, much less have relations with others. Still, violations occurred. In particular, I recall Lynn B. and Bill J. frequently sneaking off together to remote areas of the hospital campus. I never broke the non-fraternization rule, but did have feelings for both Joanne M. and Lynn B.

Despite all the good moments, there were bad times at Highland. One of the worst was one day after I had been there for around three or four months. I received a letter in the mail from my mother. When I opened it I found it included a photograph. Closer examination disclosed a photograph of my father's tombstone. I was immediately struck dumb by this discovery and could not fathom why my mother had sent the picture to me. I quickly fell to pieces and started to sob uncontrollably. When Nell came over and asked "What's wrong?" I started to babble.

"It's like in [the Mozart opera] *Don Giovanni*. There the statue of the Commendatore, whom Don Juan killed, comes into the Don's palace and when he won't repent his ways drags him down to Hell. Now my father's come to get me! He's angry at me for having another breakdown. I've disgraced him by being weak like I was in 1980!"

By now I was really making little sense. There was no reason to think my dead father was after me because I was in Highland. Still, logic had little to do with my then-state of mind.

"I deserve to die for what I've done!"

"Do you think you might hurt yourself?," Nell asked.

"I don't know. I'm a bad person, a total loser, a blot on the family name. Everyone would be better off without me."

"I'm going to call Dr. Gaworowski. You may need to spend

the night downstairs in the acute unit for your own protection."

"But I don't want to go there."

"You're just too upset to stay up here. You won't be safe."

By now a crowd had gathered. "Hang in there Jim." "Go on down to acute for the night, you'll be back here soon." "It's not so bad down there."

Eventually I put on my best martyr's face. "OK, I'll go. My father won't be able to get me there."

Once safely downstairs I was told "Take this to relax you." I did so, and soon went to sleep.

The next morning Dr. G. came to see me before rounds. After she spoke with me for a few moments, and I assured her I was my usual self again, she released me from acute and took with her upstairs to rounds.

It was nice to be up with my friends again. While I was gone, the offending picture had been spirited away, never to be seen by me again. I did not return downstairs after that.

Less bad, but still worth mentioning, was when I imitated Janet's self-mutilating behavior. This led Dr. Gaworowski to limit some of my privileges and order me to submit to regular physical inspections. When I got angry and demanded to leave the hospital against medical advice over this situation, Dr. G. quickly calmed me down by threatening to have me committed if I insisted on leaving. As she observed, "we have a judge who'll always commit anybody who cuts on himself."

In the physical realm, I constantly had to cope with the bile reflux gastritis and constipation issues. Moreover, I had to go at least once to an urologist in a taxi, accompanied by an off-duty Highland psychiatric aide, for treatment of a prostate infection. Of course, I had to pay for both the cab and the attendant's time. Try sometime being a shy, socially backward twenty-nine year old male talking to your attractive female psychiatrist about your prostatitis!

Dr. Gaworowski allowed me to go home over Thanksgiving. The real world already had intruded into my life at Highland, as the partner for whom I worked at the law firm in Jacksonville had called Dr. G. and told her I was not welcome to return there after my discharge. He did agree to keep me on the books as an associate until I found another job so I could maintain my health insurance. This was very fortunate, as it guaranteed I would not have the fatal gap in my work history. That undoubtedly would have raised questions from prospective employers that would have required me to disclose my psychiatric record. Information like this likely would have cost me many employment opportunities.

When I reached Jacksonville, as my mother had arranged, I had to sign a deed in lieu of foreclosure that conveyed my condominium to the mortgage holder. Since I no longer had a substantial salary, I could not make the monthly mortgage payments. I was deeply embarrassed and ashamed to have to do this. It was almost as bad as filing for bankruptcy, which would have been unheard of in my family. Fortunately, the head of the mortgage company was the father of a former girlfriend, and I once had spent a weekend sitting with him to help with his Parkinson's disease so his wife could get a much needed break from nursing him. At least in part in gratitude for my good deed, he instructed his subordinates not to go after me for the deficiency between the value of the condominium and the mortgage amount. Hence, I walked away from the mortgage free and clear with my credit rating still relatively intact.

Before I got home my mother had all my possessions packed up and placed in a storage unit. She even had gone to the law firm and emptied my office of my diplomas and other personal items. Under all the circumstances, it was not a particularly joyous Thanksgiving holiday.

Dr. G. let me drive my car back to Asheville and park it at Highland after Thanksgiving. I had transportation and was getting ready to return to society! By now, Dr. G. began to consider my discharge and what would come thereafter. She wanted to keep me around Asheville for post-release care with her but did not wish me to be part of the hospital's day program as she wanted me to do something more demanding. She also did not desire for me to live in the halfway house, as the Highland "graduates" who stayed there were not functioning at a very high level. Instead, she arranged a semi-volunteer job for me with a local lawyer/minister, Scott E. Jarvis, with the idea that he would try to help retrain me as an attorney.

After some looking I found an inexpensive furnished efficiency apartment and rented it on a month-to-month basis starting in January 1984. While Jarvis occasionally might share a fee with me, I basically would be living on a nominal $1,000 per month payment from the Jacksonville law firm's disability insurer. While I was at the firm it refused to offer me much of a policy since I had a background of depression. Even today I cannot buy individual life or disability insurance coverage in view of my psychiatric record. Others in my position encounter the same problem.

Since I cannot buy long-term disability coverage and have about used up the two years of $1000 per month payments provided for in the policy for which I pay, I am in a dangerous position. I only hope any disability I suffer is not psychiatrically-related so that I will be able to collect benefits until age 65 as my personal policy provides for disability from "physical" ailments up to then. Fortunately, at least for now the reasonably generous ($5,000 per month until age 65) long-term disability coverage supplied by my current employer provides full benefits for those disabled by severe mental illness such as schizophrenia or bipolar disorder. This is true, at least in part, by reason of my own advocacy efforts. Hopefully at some point Congress will address parity of long-term disability insurance benefits.

As December advanced, I went for a few desolate but beautiful drives in the mountains. I was still somewhat depressed but in far better condition than I had been six months before. I said my goodbyes, checked out of Highland, and drove to Jacksonville to spend Christmas with my mother. While there, I inventoried my record collection and sold off parts of it to raise cash. I also conveyed my expensive stereo system at a reasonable price to Andy Clarke for additional much needed money. My Christmas presents that year for my mother, sister-in-law Ramsay, and Aunt Bet were all items I cross stitched for them while in Highland. As I had little money to spend, my main donation was the hours and small degree of talent it took me to produce each gift.

Three days after Christmas, my mother and I celebrated my thirtieth birthday. I had done it! "You know," I said, "I never thought I'd make it to thirty."

"What do you mean?"

"While I was in New York I figured I'd kill myself before then."

"How dare you say such a thing!"

"Because it's the truth. I should be able to say the truth."

"I don't ever want to hear anything like that from you again."

"OK," I thought. "See if I talk with you about my feelings in the future."

Shortly after I turned thirty I reflected on a crucial year of my life. By its mid-point I had fallen into an abyss. Doing so had left me at least temporarily emotionally and mentally destroyed and financially destitute and homeless. Still, I was on the way out of that pit, and by the summer of 1984 I would be working again. As I would relearn in 2004, it takes me several years completely to recover from a breakdown of this magnitude, but after one I always work stubbornly towards the nirvana of normalcy.

One thing I know for certain: I always will look back fondly to Highland Hospital and the wonderful professional caregivers who worked with me there like Hugh, Nell, and Dr. G. It, and they, were there when I most needed them. Knowing how much my time at Highland facilitated my proper treatment and eventual return to society makes me sad for the many individuals who lack the resources for such care.

My time at Highland was almost like being back in college, with my fellow students my good friends Kathy D., Al M., Richard J., Lynn B., Joanne M., Bill J., and so on. Perhaps I had earned a graduate degree in life. Like the other hospital patients I have known, they did not consider me a pariah. Indeed, they accepted me for who I am and even liked me. Again, I find it interesting that psychiatric inmates are far more open to the eccentricities of others and ready to befriend them than those in the world at large. I always understood I safely could share my innermost thoughts, feelings, and fears with them just as they knew they could trust theirs to me.

In later years, my warm feelings for Highland have meant that I, unlike many psychiatric patients, have always been willing to go into the hospital when my medical advisors recommend that I do so. Indeed, I voluntarily have been hospitalized three times since 1983.

9

Scott Jarvis was, as Dr. Gaworowski knew, a kind and caring attorney and spiritual advisor. In early 1984 he took in a depressed and devastated young lawyer fresh from Highland Hospital and gave him the chance to start regaining his legal skills and confidence in his ability to function out in the world again. Upon my return to Asheville I spent weekdays in Scott's office.

I toiled on various matters with Scott. I even made my first, and only, trip to a jail while with him. Scott had gotten a call from a prospective client there and he asked me to go over and meet with him both to get his story and see if he could pay for counsel. My judgment was still sufficiently impaired that I asked the one question an attorney should never pose to a criminal defendant: "What happened?"

"Well, me and my buddy waited outside the K-Mart until the armored car pulled up. When the guard came out with the money bag and started to carry it into the store we pulled out our guns and robbed him."

"OK," I thought, "Thanks for sharing!"

I spoke with him for a few more moments and then reported to Scott what had happened. Since Scott soon ascertained the man was attempting to rob K-Mart as he was destitute other than owning a gun, this was the last I heard of him. As lawyers say, "'Mr. Green' [the fee] never arrived." I had, at least, been reintroduced to the real world.

In addition to working with Scott I had regular appointments with Dr. Gaworowski, who kept up with my progress. I contacted a few of my fellow former Highland patients, most notably Joanne M., who was now attending a local college. She gave me my first real exposure to cannabis. It was also my last, as it made me violently ill. We spent a fair amount of time together, which was good since it insured I had someone with whom I could hold off the loneliness that so often had afflicted me in the years before. My apartment was pretty Spartan, a real step down from my lovely Jacksonville condominium. I could never get enough light into it to ward off the winter demons.

Remembering my experience at Riverside Presbyterian, I joined the choir at a local Presbyterian church and made some acquaintances there. In particular, I met a professor at the local university my age who had an Ivy League education and was waiting to hear from Duke Law School, where she was seeking admission. We got to be fairly friendly, although I think she was a little suspicious why someone with my academic pedigree was in Asheville with no really visible means of support. My stigma fears prevented me from sharing the reason for my presence there. It would have been nice to have been able to reveal the truth. At times the need to keep secrets became particularly oppressive coming so soon, as it did, after the period of candor that was part of the Highland experience. Still, I felt I dared not, and was only open with Scott, Joanne, and (of course) Dr. G.

My days with Scott Jarvis brought back my years of legal training and made it possible for me to resume work as an attorney. Rather than being a foreign language, the law again was the familiar tongue I knew so well. Thanks to lithium, proper treatment, my own hard work, and a modicum of luck it would be over twenty years before my next psychiatric hospitalization. That would only come when one of lithium's side effects forced me to stop taking it. As it was, I had no more manic symptoms because of lithium. It did consistently make me moderately depressed, or dysphoric, over the years I took it. Periodically I would dip down into a more severe depression depending on external circumstances and my own mood cycling.

The most obvious sign I was on a strong psychotropic drug was a slight tremor that got worse when I was under stress or cold, the so-called "lithium shakes." I suffered from them for the next twenty-one years, and they interfered with my golf game, my ability to shoot straight (try to aim a pistol or rifle when your hand is shaking the entire time), and occasionally my efforts to keep my having a mental illness a secret. Indeed, once a now-departed former Dean of my law school caught me out in the hall by the mail room on a cold day. "Why are you shaking like that?"

"Oh [starting to shake even worse out of fear], uh, I didn't realize I was doing so."

"Well, what's the reason?"

"As you know, I have to take a variety of medications to deal with my stomach problems. Some of them affect my nervous system, and on cold days sometimes I tremble."

"Interesting. Hope you feel better."

"Thanks." Inwardly, I breathed a sigh of relief as I had fended off a question for which I had no rehearsed explanation. In the future I would be better prepared.

I stayed in Asheville through the spring. Suddenly, things seemed to close in around me and I decided it was time for me to return to Jacksonville. I saw Dr. G. for the last time. I said goodbye to Scott, cancelled my lease, and drove home to stay with my mother while I decided what to do next.

Upon arrival in Jacksonville I established ties with a new psychiatrist. I was so desperate for help that I even attended a few pastoral counseling sessions with the minister at Riverside Presbyterian. In light of my agnostic feelings about religion, it is not surprising that these visits were not very helpful. Still, they led me to cross stitch a new stole for the clergyman as part of the church's gift for him in honor of his many years as a pastor.

In late spring I felt I was ready to work again and drafted a résumé. I decided to ask Judge Tjoflat for assistance and, as always, he came through. He called a local federal trial judge to see if he knew about any positions for which I might be suited. He, in turn, referred me to The Honorable Howard T. Snyder, a United States Magistrate, today called a Magistrate Judge. Judge Snyder needed a legal assistant, which is the same thing as a law clerk. Judge Snyder met with me, heard my story, and decided to take a chance on me. He employed me for the next year.

Judge Snyder worked on both civil and criminal cases, typically handling matters the federal trial judges, who appointed him, wanted to refer to a subordinate. Like all magistrates, his rulings were subject to the approval of the particular trial judge with whose case he was dealing.

Two particular types of cases were especially important to Judge Snyder, and therefore to me. The first was appeals of denials of Social Security disability benefits. The second was habeas corpus cases, which are suits filed by state or federal prison inmates challenging the lawfulness of their convictions and imprisonment. Trial judges want to stay as far from these two as possible, and accordingly send them down to a magistrate to review. Eventually the magistrate issues a "report and recommendation" to the trial court saying how the action should be resolved. The trial judge then almost invariably adopts the "r&r" as his or her decision.

Social Security disability and habeas corpus cases tended to pile up for two reasons. First, the Social Security Administration was, and still is, notorious for denying meritorious disability claims. Its strategy apparently is to turn down almost all benefit requests in the hope the claimants will give up and consequently forego relief. As a result, many cases end up in federal court for resolution. Second, practically all prisoners think they are wrongly imprisoned and have abundant free time in which to submit habeas corpus petitions. My office was full of the files of pending Social Security and habeas corpus cases, and a large part of my job was to make some headway through them. In addition to these matters, I also helped Judge Snyder with whatever other things on which he asked me to work.

Although it could get tedious, my job also could be quite intriguing. The State of Florida had built a special courtroom inside Florida State Prison in Starke for use by the federal magistrates when hearing claims by state inmates. Judge Snyder went to Starke for court every month or so. On the day in question, he took me with him so I could experience FSP.

Just arriving at FSP was dramatic. When we were cleared to enter I noted the snipers in the guard towers. I also observed the giant multiple rolls of razor wire around the prison perimeter. After I visited the courtroom a corrections official took me on a special tour of the facility. I was struck by its sheer size, as it holds well over 1,000 maximum security inmates. I noted that the convicts wore various colors of jumpsuit, and learned the color indicates the prisoner's status. While I do not recall the significance of most of the colors, I will never forget that orange signified those on death row.

I visited the mental health unit, where inmates with severe psychiatric conditions were housed. The walls were an institutional color faded to a grimy pallor. The "patients" were confined in their cells most of the time. Their cries and howls, as well as the stench, are indescribable. Many were clearly delusional as they had schizophrenia or some related condition. I did not know whether the inmates were unmedicated, and hence symptomatic, because of an indifferent prison medical staff or their own choice. I found the locale very sad and depressing after my own recent experience in a pleasant hospital setting. I can think of nowhere worse to be when suffering from a severe mental illness than in a prison where treatment is haphazard at best and release may only occur after many years, if ever. Indeed, one who regained his sanity would merely be put into the general prison population for so long as he kept it to serve out his sentence. Unfortunately, many prisoners have mental illnesses. In fact, today the largest group of those institutionalized for psychiatric disorders are not in psychiatric hospitals. Instead, they are in jails and prisons. I could hardly wait to leave this area of FSP, and later had nightmares about it. I pray I never end up in such a place, which resembled, as much as anything, one of the lower circles of Dante's *Inferno*.

From the psychiatric wing the tour went to death row. I saw many of the cells located there, including that of notorious serial killer Ted Bundy. I was admitted inside that of a prisoner who had gone for a shower, and noted his television set, books, and stereo system.

At the finale of the death row tour I visited the execution chamber home of "Old Sparky," the Florida electric chair. I was asked if I would like to throw the switch on the chair, which of course was not turned on at the time. I did so, noting in the process that the switch in no way resembled the device portrayed in numerous motion pictures ranging from monster movies like *Frankenstein* to death row films like *The Green Mile*. Instead, it looked to me more like the toggle switch once used in voting machines. My guide offered to let me sit in Old Sparky, but I demurred as I thought it would be really bad karma to do so.

Despite the FSP tour and the often interesting underlying facts of the habeas corpus cases, I was not particularly fond of them. Few of the claims had any merit, and most were very time-consuming. On the other hand, I enjoyed the Social Security disability appeals. I felt I could do justice by helping those who were actually disabled collect the benefits for which they had paid during their years of work. At the time I worked for Judge Snyder the reversal rate of the Social Security denials that made it to federal court was fairly high. Ironically, the year before my own Social Security disability claim had been denied on the basis that I would not be unable to work for at least a year as the law requires before one can collect benefits. This was true, as I was unemployed almost exactly one year.

Away from the job, I got my own attractive apartment. I retrieved my possessions, including my record collection, from storage and resumed a normal life for a person who suffers from chronic anxiety and depression. Although my salary was nothing like what I had earned when I was in private practice, I was reasonably well paid and accordingly could live fairly comfortably. I rejoined Andy Clarke's choir as a social outlet. Andy Baker was back in Jacksonville, and we spent considerable time together. I started to date again, and had several different girlfriends. Coincidentally, one was a former Highland worker with issues of her own. In general, things were much better than in the loneliness of Asheville after I was discharged from Highland.

As an additional recreational activity, I even started a new collecting fixation as I purchased several top-quality handguns and expensive leather shoulder holsters to hold them. These included a Browning Hi-Power nine mm semi-automatic like Eddie Murphy wielded in the then-current film *Beverly Hills Cop* and a Walther PPK .380 semi-automatic such as James Bond carried in most of his movies. Despite the lithium shakes I did some target-shooting at a gun range and also shot outdoors with Andy Baker.

Why, the reader might ask, would someone with my psychiatric history decide to acquire firearms? Like many enthusiasts, I enjoyed target shooting. In addition, I got a kick out of playing with guns while watching police shows like *Miami Vice* or films like *Beverly Hills Cop* or *Goldfinger* on television in my living room (the officers on *Miami Vice* had fantastic shoulder holsters after which some of mine were modeled). But there was a much darker reason for my potentially deadly new hobby. My reasoning was that by owning guns I could prove to myself that my willpower was sufficiently strong that I safely could possess them without using them on myself. Alternatively, I knew that if I again decided suicide was the appropriate course of action I would have the sure way of accomplishing it immediately available. No more need to risk ineffective wrist-slitting or the like, as a bullet through the roof of the mouth would complete the job instantaneously and with an almost one hundred percent rate of success. A win-win scenario if ever there was one. Many may shudder at my peculiar logic here, but there it is.

The biggest problem with my return to Jacksonville was that Judge Snyder and I did not get along very well with one another. Judge Snyder was a workaholic, and expected the same from his legal assistant. As he was relatively new to his job when he hired me, he had only one legal assistant prior to me. This person did nothing but work such that Judge Snyder frequently cited him as the example of the "ideal" legal assistant. I, on the other hand, had to make frequent visits to the psychiatrist during work hours that Judge Snyder seemed to resent. I think he interpreted my depression and difficulties making my brain work to its pre-breakdown capacity as laziness and a lack of motivation. Overall, I was physically unable to work at his pace.

Despite my problems, I still did a very good job. In particular, I made significant progress whittling through the backlog of Social Security and habeas corpus actions. I remember one Social Security appeal in particular. After a great deal of work I drafted a report and recommendation granting benefits to the claimant. Judge Snyder reviewed and signed it after questioning me closely about the case. When it went up to the trial judge, he overturned Judge Snyder's r&r. Judge Snyder, in turn, grew quite upset with me as no judge likes getting reversed. Some months later, I felt exonerated when the Eleventh Circuit reversed the trial judge and ordered benefits "for the reasons set forth in the Magistrate's excellent report and recommendation."

When I accepted the position with Judge Snyder it was with the understanding I would stay with him for two years. Our problems with one another, however, meant I was on the lookout for other opportunities. At one point, the former named partner at my old law firm who had left to be general counsel at a major client was interested in hiring me as his assistant. This was, of course, a potentially good permanent position. Just as I got used to the idea of working for him, however, his secretary told him she loathed me since she remembered my personality foibles and that it was her or me. He chose her.

Later in my time with Judge Snyder I started to look into possible academic jobs. After all, prior to my breakdown I had very strong academic credentials between the high grades, law review, published Note, judicial clerkship, and time on Wall Street. In due course in late 1984 or early 1985 I ran across a listing for a Bigelow Teaching Fellow and Lecturer in Law at the Law School of the University of Chicago that piqued my interest.

Bigelow Fellows teach the first year legal research and writing course at Chicago, one of the top-ten law schools in the United States. It is a one year appointment, and would let me get my foot into the door of legal academia. When I called my mentor at Duke and asked him if he knew anything about the Bigelow program, he responded that "In 1953 I was a Bigelow Fellow before I joined the faculty at Duke." "OK," I thought to myself, "you may be on to something." Apparently, being a Bigelow was an entrée into law teaching as well as an opportunity to discover both whether I liked it and was any good at it. I formally applied for a Bigelow fellowship, was interviewed by telephone, and offered the position. Since I thought Judge Snyder was about to ask me not to stay the second year with him—he may even actually already have done so, I honestly do not recall—it was opportune timing when I advised him I had accepted the Chicago job.

Since I wanted a vacation before I reported to Chicago, I gave my notice and left Judge Snyder's employment early in the summer of 1985. Before I departed, the Legal Aid attorney who represented indigent clients with Social Security disability claims and whose successful appeal to the Eleventh Circuit had exonerated my advice to Judge Snyder invited me out to lunch. She did so in recognition of my helping Judge Snyder move through much of the previously backlogged Social Security docket. She, at least, appreciated both the quality and quantity of my work on behalf of some of America's most vulnerable citizens.

I fully recognized what Judge Snyder had done a year before. He had taken a chance on me when he knew all about my 1983 breakdown. For this he deserves great credit, and won my eternal gratitude despite our ultimate difficulties working together. In mid-1984 it took a special person to disregard the stigma of mental illness. Judge Snyder is such an individual. Even today, those like him are few and far between.

Before I headed for the "Second City" I emptied my apartment and put most of my things back into storage. I then loaded up my car and started the two day drive to Hyde Park and the University of Chicago. I was finally ready to undertake that for which I had yearned ever since my years at Duke Law School nearly a decade before, a law teaching opportunity.

10

When I reached Chicago I soon found a cozy furnished apartment in Hyde Park near the Law School and settled in for the next nine months. I almost immediately contacted the University of Chicago Hospital and was referred to a psychiatrist there who took exceptional care of me.

As noted, the six Bigelow fellows taught the first year students legal research and writing. We were left pretty much unsupervised. My group of Bigelows was diverse in nature, and I got along well with them.

I had an enjoyable year in Chicago, which I found much more livable than New York City. This time, I took the initiative and made an effort to socialize. While I did not date while I was in Chicago I was not alone all the time. I joined both the choir of a Hyde Park church and the "alumni" branch of the famous Chicago Children's Choir. I was especially active with the latter group. I remember well going to sing at the funeral of a Chicago civil rights leader only to have to wait for the service to begin for an unexplained reason. The mystery was solved when Chicago Mayor Harold Washington arrived to deliver the eulogy and sat down near me. When I saw him, I thought to myself: "What an imposing figure of a man." After his address I could see why he had risen to the post of mayor, as he was an extraordinarily eloquent and inspiring speaker.

Coincidentally, somehow I learned Audrey, the secretary with whom I had been infatuated in Jacksonville, had returned to her native city. I met with her and discussed the events of the spring of 1983.

"I was crazy in love with you, and was sure you loved me too."

"You're kidding, right?"

"I'm deadly serious. I knew you had money problems, so I made you the beneficiary of the life insurance the firm provided and left you all that I had in my will. I then planned to kill myself so you'd get everything right away."

"Really? That's totally crazy."

"Yes, really."

"I had no idea you did that. All I ever heard was that you had some sort of mental illness and left the firm as a result."

"Were you in love with me?"

"I don't want to be brutal, but absolutely not. I thought you were a nice guy, although a little nerdy, but that was it. You were just a friend at work."

"So you had no feelings for me."

"If you thought that I did, you were in fantasy land. In fact, I secretly was seeing another lawyer at the firm most of the time I was there."

"You were having an affair with someone else?"

"I was involved with someone, yes."

"Who?"

"That's not relevant."

So that was it. After a few pleasantries we parted company, and I have never contacted her since.

A few years earlier Audrey's bluntness would have devastated me. Now, however, I was much stronger emotionally. I already realized the irrationality of my behavior in the spring of 1983. I now had heard what I needed to learn from my chance encounter with Audrey. With that closure I would just go on from there. If I could survive my time in Highland and the events since then,

I certainly could continue to get along without the Audrey I already had essentially forgotten.

I took full advantage of what Chicago had to offer. I enjoyed its wonderful museums, stores, and sports teams—highlights were Cubs games at Wrigley Field and Bulls games at the Stadium.

As the year went along, I got to know my extremely bright and motivated flock of students. Various projects focused on honing their overall excellent writing skills to the exacting and sometimes arcane requirements of the legal branch of that art. In addition, I briefly taught them how to perform legal research. I used what I had learned from as long ago as when I studied at Episcopal, and more recently when serving on the *Duke Law Journal* and clerking for Judges Tjoflat and Snyder. I based several of my assignments on actual cases on which I had worked.

While I am certain I was neither the best nor the worst Bigelow in the over fifty year history of that program, I seemed to be reasonably popular with my students. As I have learned over the years, you can never satisfy all in a class but if you cover the required material in an appropriate fashion and get decent teaching evaluations from most of them you have done your job. Still, I got anonymous comments that hearkened back to Dr. Hartman's evaluation, as some perceived me as arrogant or aloof. Amusing when one considers that my credentials paled in comparison with those of most in my class and that I often felt intellectually inferior to, if not downright afraid of, them.

One aspect of teaching was a real eye-opener. For most of my life, like many people with a severe mental illness I had been petrified of any sort of public speaking. At Duke, my two worst experiences were my first year appellate oral argument in my legal writing class and my mock trial in my trial practice course. I was totally convinced I never wanted to do litigation in large part because I did not want to have to speak in court. Among my various reasons for wanting to practice in the trusts and estates area, a big one was that such attorneys almost never have to go there (few probate cases are tried, and when they are often a litigator is brought in to handle the actual trial work on behalf of the trusts and estates attorney). Now, I successfully was speaking publicly to my class on a regular basis. Perhaps the difference was that school was not an adversarial process, and also as the instructor I was pretty much in control of what occurred. In any event, I could talk in an open setting after all, and actually did a good job of it.

I met regularly for both medication and psychotherapy with my psychiatrist, as in my experience anyone with bipolar disorder needs both. I was very glad to have a good doctor, as the combined stress of teaching for the first time and searching for a permanent academic position was magnified by my usual anxiety and depression issues. I mailed out numerous teaching applications via the Association of American Law Schools (AALS) employment registry with which I indicated a preference for schools in the Southeast. I landed over thirty interviews at the November 1985 AALS Faculty Recruitment Conference at which all law schools in the United States did their annual recruiting. Luckily for me, it was held in Chicago.

The interviews in Chicago generated five or six callback interviews somewhat like the law firm ones when I was at Duke. The school I was visiting would host a dinner with selected professors followed by a full day of meetings with its entire faculty accompanied with a campus and city tour. As time dragged on I still had no job offer in hand. I grew increasingly desperate as I feared that, as when I interviewed with law firms, negative traits attributable to my disorder were sufficiently evident to account for an ultimate lack of success. Finally, I decided to throw caution to the wind and call Professor Russell Weaver, the head of the faculty recruitment committee at the Louis D. Brandeis School of Law. I had not heard from him since the Chicago interview, and I wanted both to see where I stood and remind him I was still available. He spoke with me politely and said he would let me know something in a few days. I sat by, feeling quite helpless, until he called and invited me to Louisville a few weeks later.

I really liked Louisville. The Brandeis School of Law was in a comfortable building, the faculty seemed pleasant enough, and the countryside around the city was enchanting. It reminded me very much of the area outside Charlottesville. This seemed like a place where I could be happy, and indeed made me think in some ways of Richmond. Hence, I quickly decided I wanted this job. I returned to Chicago where I waited anxiously to hear from the Brandeis Dean.

As I waited, Professor Weaver called and asked if I could give him the name of someone on the Chicago faculty who would serve as a reference. One professor in particular had been kind to me all year, and therefore I asked him if he would be willing to serve as my reference. He agreed to do so, spoke with a few of my students, and then called Professor Weaver. I later learned that he was very complimentary of me.

A few days after my reference spoke with Professor Weaver, my office telephone rang and I found myself speaking with the Dean at Louisville. She explained she was calling to offer me a tenure-track position as an Assistant Professor of Law. As I had discussed with the faculty during my visit to Louisville (the Dean apparently was not advised about these conversations—she did not meet with me in Louisville as she was sick on the day of my interview), I would teach legal writing as one-half of my teaching load and a not yet determined doctrinal course as the other half. Slightly in shock, I thanked her for her call. She named a salary that was nearly double what I was making as a Bigelow and asked me to give her my answer in short order. I said I definitely would do so, thanked her again, and hung up. I recall calling my mother and sharing the news with her, as well

117

as with fellow Bigelows and my Chicago mentor.

The offer was not perfect, as it entailed teaching legal writing half the time and legal writing is pretty much at the bottom of the food chain in legal academia. Still, it was a tenure-track job, which is the Holy Grail for academics. Everyone agreed that, since no other offers were on the table, this was the proverbial bird in the hand and that I should grab it. I soon returned the Dean's call and told her I was overjoyed to accept her offer. She said she was glad to have me on board, and that she would look for me roughly August 1.

As by now it was April, the rest of my academic year in Chicago sped by. Once again, I found myself reflecting on events. This time, I had worked successfully at one of the top law schools in the nation. I could celebrate attaining that for which I had striven for so long, a potentially permanent legal academic position. It was almost like when I was back in school myself, racking up awards and other indicia of academic success. My mental health had stayed good despite not only the uncertainties of a new type of work and the academic job search but also the stress of being alone in another big city. I could scarcely believe that only three years before I had been a totally debilitated patient at Highland Hospital. I was very proud when I informed Dr. Gaworowski about the propitious turn my fate had taken, and asked her to refer me to a psychiatrist in Louisville.

In late July I entered the next phase of my life by returning to Louisville, ready to start work on August 1, 1986. I felt as if the world were at my feet. At least for now, I was winning the battle with the disorder that had me on the ropes a mere three years before.

11

Much as when I moved to Chicago, one of my first acts in Louisville was to seek out a psychiatrist. Dr. Gaworowski referred me to Dr. John P. Bell. Dr. G. did not know Dr. Bell personally. He had, however, sent several patients to Highland over the years. As a result, his name was familiar to her. That turned out to be very fortunate for me, as Dr. Bell was an outstanding physician.

Dr. Bell was on the faculty of the University of Louisville's Department of Psychiatry. Those in the know considered him to be probably the finest both there and in the region overall. In fact, over the years he won a number of awards from the Louisville mental health community. Much like Dr. Gaworowski, he was old school. Hence, he both prescribed medication and did psychotherapy for his patients. I saw him several times a month for an hour each visit in his office in the U. of L. Medical School. As it turned out, we worked together for the next decade. He got me through many monumental life changes.

I was rather nervous as I readied to see Dr. Bell for the first time. I recognized that he was, after all, presumably the person who would care for me for many years. During that time I would undertake the stress of a "real" academic job. It could give rise to tenure, and thus essentially guaranteed employment for an entire academic career. In particular, Dr. Bell probably would be my mental health provider for my crucial first six years in Louisville. Over that period I would have to earn tenure.

Accordingly, it was essential that he be someone with whom I could work effectively to minimize the impact of my disorder on my work duties.

Finally the big day arrived. When I met Dr. Bell I saw a slightly rumpled-looking man of about seventy who clearly was a confirmed academic. He was dressed in a comfortable sports coat with patches on the elbows, button-down shirt, tie, slacks, and somewhat scuffed, well broken-in shoes. I saw no indicia of his medical status (indeed, all but a few of the psychiatrists who have treated me over the years have worn typical informal business or smart casual attire rather than a white coat). He was of medium height and solidly built. He looked friendly and approachable, with a warm smile and a grandfatherly demeanor.

We exchanged greetings, and I noted his firm handshake. Clearly, he really was a man at the top of his game. I summarized my psychiatric history to him as he took careful notes.

"So how long do you think you've had manic-depressive illness?"

"Well, no one has ever told me that's what I have."

"Your story clearly points to it. It sounds like you were depressed for years, and then had a manic breakdown in 1983. That would explain the sleep issues, fixation on suicide, and lack of response to the anti-depressants you took in Jacksonville. Once you got to Asheville Dr. Gaworowski put you on lithium and you responded well to it. That translates into manic-depression to me."

"But why didn't Dr. Gaworowski tell me I had that?"

"I can't say for certain, but I imagine she wasn't completely sure about your diagnosis. Also, she probably didn't want to scare you by saying you're manic-depressive. After all, that's one of the most severe forms of mental illness. Incidentally, the historian in you might like to know it's also one of the oldest. It was described in the Old Testament and recognized since the time of Hippocrates in 400 BC. By virtue of your positive reaction to lithium, your condition seems pretty clear. It's only a label, anyway. Your disorder is treatable, although not curable—it'll never go away, but you can handle it like any other chronic disease like diabetes. Let's focus on keeping it under control, and just not worry about what to call it."

"OK. To answer your question, as you say, I was depressed for many years. I'd get irritable at times, and had problems getting along with other people. The catastrophe in 1983 knocked me out for some time, but my year in Chicago seems to show I'm now able to function well once again. Do you think I'll be able to make it through the stress of my duties at the Law School?"

"Absolutely. My job is seeing that you do so, and I know of no reason why you can't be successful. You'll need to commit to taking your medication and seeing me regularly. I'll monitor your symptoms and tweak your prescriptions as needed. You'll undoubtedly experience ups and downs by virtue of the mood swings that are inherent to manic-depression, but together we'll deal with them."

I felt very reassured by what Dr. Bell said. Here was someone who understood my condition and was confident he could, with my cooperation, manage it effectively. He also was a straight shooter. He told me what I have and did not try to sugar-coat my diagnosis. I long had suspected I have bipolar disorder in light of the permanent lithium prescription. Now I had confirmation of my belief. I liked Dr. Bell's view that labels do not matter and his confidence that I could make it as a law professor despite my disease.

Over the upcoming years, lithium continued to keep me from exhibiting any manic symptoms. Hence, my disease was evidenced by a constant state of greater or lesser depression. Dr. Bell frequently changed anti-depressants, and less often sleeping medications, to keep me on as even a keel as possible.

Dr. Bell, of course, worked for the same University where

I teach, albeit on a different campus. As noted, I was very concerned lest my colleagues learn about my condition. Dr. Bell and I went to great lengths to keep things secret. Would the law faculty make someone who has severe bipolar disorder a long-term addition? I cannot say for certain they would have rejected me had they known my history. I also cannot state for sure they would not have done so. Fortunately, Dr. Bell, his successors, and I were able to preserve my secret until it was safe to disclose it. Thus, I will never know the answer to this question.

One last thing happened prior to the start of classes. The Law School Dean contacted me over the summer and suggested I attend a conference of legal writing teachers. I was thrilled to meet with more experienced colleagues. They shared their collective wisdom concerning how to select writing problems, grade papers, confer with students, and generally teach what I had sampled doing in Chicago. I soaked up all the knowledge I could and readied to apply it in my new position.

Unfortunately, one thing I at least thought I heard at the gathering served me poorly. During a general discussion session, several people observed that the schedule legal writing teachers follow fits the needs of those who want a child-friendly timetable in their lives. When at a meeting with the Dean and a few others the question of whom the Law School should hire to teach legal writing came up, I enthusiastically yet naively parroted this comment. The Dean, who was one of the pioneering women in legal education, interpreted what I said as stating I thought women were only fit to teach legal writing. She, not surprisingly, concluded I was some sort of sexist Neanderthal and exploded.

"You mean you don't think women can teach Torts or Contracts or federal income tax?"

"Wha ...?"

"I'll have you know that we have a number of women on our faculty, including me, who teach the same classes as men, and we do so just as well."

"But ..."

"Women have fought for years to be treated equally, and shouldn't be ghettoized teaching legal writing."

"But that's not what I meant ..."

"I can't believe that you feel that way in this day and age."

"But I don't. If you'll let me explain ..."

"You'll see what women can do as you observe your colleagues here. Many of them are far better professors than you'll probably ever be. But enough on this subject. Just be clear, mister, that I'm very disappointed over your opinion."

Her interpretation of what I meant and think is far from the truth. I have been married twice, once to a physician and once to an attorney. I certainly believe women can be professionals and have every right to do so. Still, it took years for me to convince the Dean that is the case. For a long time my repeated efforts to change her perception of me were unsuccessful. As a result, I got off on exactly the wrong foot with my supervisor for the critical first few years of my career.

12

Now that things were set with Dr. Bell I could focus on my new duties. During the 1986-87 year I was assigned to instruct the legal writing class, Basic Legal Skills (BLS for short), to roughly one hundred students. I also had about forty pupils in a legal methods course called Introduction to Law. Hence I taught only first year students, which I did for a number of years. This meant all my time was devoted to the most labor intensive group at the Law School. Today legal writing professors, who typically teach only that course and have no more than a total of fifty or sixty students, complain mightily that they are overworked with that number. Thus, I was grossly overstretched between the BLS and Introduction to Law assignments.

A word about the state of BLS at the Law School in the fall of 1986: The course previously had been taught by a long-term faculty member who originally was not on tenure track. After a number of years he decided he wanted to go for tenure, and the Law School changed his classification accordingly. Unfortunately, as he had to teach a huge number of BLS students—perhaps as many as 180 to 200—he produced no published scholarship. Consequently he was denied tenure. He had lost his job, but under the tenure system was entitled to work one more, "terminal" year. He did so, but with a lack of enthusiasm. The year went very badly, with BLS students flooding the Dean with complaints about their instruction. That meant I inherited a mess. It would take me some time to see

BLS where it should, and in the future would, be.

I did not only have a large number of BLS students. I also was burdened with a faculty member who taught Intro to Law and thought she was responsible for telling me how to teach both that class and BLS. As I had already taught legal writing for a year and had my own ideas about how to do so, there were inevitable clashes. Although I never told the professor this—and to maintain secrecy could not do so—she generated a great deal of stress for me. It, in turn, did not help my medical situation at all. Imagine starting a new academic job and having a senior faculty member trying to dictate everything you do!

I did a good job teaching my mob of BLS students. This was especially true when one considers the conditions under which I had to work. Still, when student evaluations of my teaching came out they were disappointing, although not atypical for a BLS teacher. This could be attributed to several factors. First, as noted, legal writing is undoubtedly the most unpopular course in the entire law school curriculum. Students are not very generous in their comments about a course they generally hate. This is a nation-wide phenomenon, and helps explain why most academics want to avoid the subject like the plague. Since part of the law school compensation model is based on teaching performance, who wishes to teach a class that can lead to low ratings and therefore paltry raises? Add this to possible problems in the promotion and tenure system attributable to "poor teaching" and legal writing clearly is not what most young professors desire to teach. I was told those appraising my performance would factor the unpopularity of the course into their assessment of the students' evaluations. Still, I wondered whether they really did this or whether my future job security and/or salary took a hit every year because of one of the principal courses I taught.

A second reason for substandard student assessments was that like legal writing teachers everywhere I gave multiple grades throughout the year whereas most other courses only had one score, the final exam. As a result, the first grade a student got in law school was on my first assignment. Most law students have strong undergraduate records and are used to getting good grades. Many previously have written papers. They think they know *how* to write.

Unfortunately, the vast majority of undergraduates actually neither are taught to write well nor generally do so. Moreover, legal writing is different from the writing with which students are familiar. Thus, not infrequently a BLS student will earn a C or D on an assignment for the first time in his or her life. This leads to predictable outrage. Students do not appreciate learning that their work is not of the caliber expected of an attorney. To them, writing is writing.

By the time the first semester is over and evaluations are taken, you have students who do not like you as you have treated them worse, grade-wise, than anyone in memory. They rate you accordingly. You then look bad when your evaluations are compared with those of other professors who teach more popular classes *and* have not awarded any grades until after they already have been assessed by their students.

Another issue was the lament of legal writing students everywhere that "I did exactly what [the teacher, i.e., me] told me to do when I met with him and he looked at my draft paper and told me how to make it better. Then, when I got my final version back he criticized what I'd done. He told me to do it a certain way and then marked me down when I did so. He's unfair and inconsistent when he grades papers." Of course, the problem is that the student did not really do as I advised, but *thinks* he or she did so.

Added to all this was the students' perception of me. Again, as at Chicago and as Dr. Hartman had predicted, some perceived me as arrogant, aloof, and weighed down by a superiority

127

complex. They so indicated in their evaluations and marked me down accordingly. I certainly was not trying to be either arrogant or aloof, and frankly was at a loss how to overcome this problem. There was some truth to the superiority issue, as I did (and still do) think both Virginia and Duke are excellent schools and that my academic credentials are very strong. Still, I needed to find a way not to telegraph my feelings to others who would be antagonized by them.

In sum, the BLS class was a real challenge for me. Ironically, I, the perennial outcast with a severe mental illness, had been assigned to teach the least popular course in the curriculum. I had to deal with my mental health issues in that context. It all generated considerable stress for me. I would have had a severe relapse but for Dr. Bell, my medications, and my own stubborn refusal to let it happen. My mood swings were a problem, with the depression becoming severe at times, but I managed to hold on through the year. I would get terribly upset when I got the results of the evaluations, some of which were quite hurtful, but tried not to show my wounded feelings. Instead, I acted as if I thought they were attributable to dislike of the subject matter and not, despite my deep inferiority complex, of the messenger who delivered it. My mood dipped further into depression each time I absorbed more punishment. The long-term effects of this situation were unknown, but worrisome to contemplate.

Despite the problems incident to the BLS class, I actually enjoyed teaching it for several reasons. First of all, I thought I did a good job of imparting a crucial ability to my students. If they listened to what I said, both in class and in my comments on their papers, I knew they would have one of the essential skills they needed to be successful attorneys. I, of course, had no control over how they wrote when they left my course, but I at least had pointed them in the right direction. If it was my job to teach an unpopular, labor-intensive, low-status, yet incredibly important subject I not only would do it, but do it extremely well at that.

I also liked BLS as it put me in close contact with the students. BLS is, by far, the most "personal" course in the first year curriculum. The professors in large-sectioned doctrinal courses like torts or contracts rarely interact with individual students. I, on the other hand, had frequent individual conferences with each BLS student. Accordingly, I actually got to know my pupils. They would confide in me their worries, personal problems, hopes, and dreams. Much as my psychiatrists did for me, I provided support for those in need.

At times I would discover students who had real mental or emotional issues. I would refer them to the appropriate dean, or even the counseling center. As this long predated the presence at the Law School of an academic support officer whose job is to help students succeed and provide them a sympathetic ear to which to vent their feelings, I was it. Indeed, I know I had more empathy for students with psychological or psychiatric disorders than most, if not all, of my faculty colleagues by virtue of my own condition. This was of great value for numerous individuals, some of whom have expressed their thanks and support to me since I have gone public with my story. One former student, for example, sent me the following message: "I don't know if you remember me, but I was a student in your basic legal skills class. I was having a difficult time and you gently suggested that perhaps I should take a medical leave of absence and get help. I took your suggestion. I sought psychiatric counseling at the student counseling center. I was diagnosed with major clinical depression. However, with counseling and medication I was able to complete my degree and even pass the bar. The point to all of this is to say, Thank you. Without your gentle prodding I would have never sought help for myself. You are a shining example of what a person with mental illness can accomplish with treatment and support." I derived considerable satisfaction from helping deserving individuals with problems succeed in law school and the world beyond.

I have far less good to say about the Introduction to Law class, which was intended to pass on basic legal principles to the students. The course had been in and out of the Law School curriculum over the years; when I arrived it was an "in" period. I found the class to be boring and of little real value. If I felt that way, imagine how the students regarded their experience. In any event, I was pleased to join the rest of the faculty in abolishing the course during my second year at the Law School. That left me with one less stressor with which to cope, especially as it eliminated most of my interaction with the meddlesome Intro faculty member. That in and of itself did my mental health considerable good.

As I approached the end of the spring 1987 semester, I saw past the mountain of student papers I had to grade and recognized the professional aspects of the year had been a positive experience overall. I had essentially revamped the way legal writing was taught at the Law School and thought the change was much for the better. I had helped various students deal with personal issues, once again in a positive way. I was ready to spend the summer on scholarly work, both in preparing for the next year of BLS and laboring on an article on which Russ Weaver generously was including me as co-author.

While, like most first year teachers, I spent countless hours at home preparing for class and grading papers, my first year in Louisville was not merely a work experience. As time passed I tried to fit into the community of which I now was a part. At the Law School itself I began to form relationships with several of my colleagues. Unlike in New York, Chicago, or even Jacksonville, I found co-workers who enjoyed my company and included me in various social activities. Russ Weaver, who was single and a little over a year older than I, frequently invited me to parties at his home. Other, more senior, faculty were very nice to me both in and outside school. As I look back, I have friends at the Law School I have known for twenty-five years. They have been there for me through good times and bad, both before and after they learned about my disease. My old suspicion that I would fit in far better in academia than law practice was proving to be true. That certainly made it easier for Dr. Bell and me to handle my disorder.

When I was not at school I also worked to integrate myself into my surroundings. My love of classical music continued and I again did more than sit home and listen to my record collection. Instead, I followed my previous pattern and joined the choir at Second Presbyterian Church, which was located near my apartment. Lucky for me, I had happened onto a church much like Riverside Presbyterian. Second Presbyterian had a very strong music program and although its director was not as talented as Andy Clarke he did a fine job staging works like Handel's *Messiah*. I developed no romances in the choir but still had a venue for my modest musical talent as well as a regular schedule of choir practices and Sunday morning performances to occupy a chunk of my limited free time.

Away from music, I found a way to spend my Sunday afternoons during much of the year. One of my colleagues early on had invited me to join him in an activity that brought me out into the beautiful rural areas outside Louisville. This was the sport of "beagling" at which I became quite adept. Beagling consists of following, on foot, a pack of twenty to thirty beagles as they travel about across fields and fences in pursuit of any rabbits upon which they might happen. Once they spot their quarry they put up a loud, joyous bay and chase the rabbit as fast as they can. Rarely do they catch it (if they do, the local bunny population drops by one), but keeping up with them is much fun and excellent exercise as one participates in what is essentially fox hunting on foot rather than horseback after rabbits rather than foxes. Hares and hounds it is! I met some delightful people in the beagling club who had nothing to do with the Law School. I will never forget going to a rural Episcopal church for the priest, who had close beagling connections, to bless the pack. Thus, I found another unusual hobby to pursue, much as in the case of war gaming and the SCA in college and law school. At least this one was genteel in nature.

In addition to the choir and beagling, I renewed my fascination with handguns. I once again amassed a considerable collection. There was a gun range in the general vicinity of the Law School, and I used to go there to shoot. Thanks to my lithium shakes I was a mediocre shot at best, but I still enjoyed the activity. And, as before, I was prepared should I find myself in need of a final solution to my problems. Thanks to my beagling connections I even got to know a night law student who then was a high ranking officer in the local Sheriff's Department and was in charge of the departmental arsenal. Once a year the automatic weapons had to be put through their paces, and he invited me to help him do so. Together we blew apart a wrecked automobile as we poured in rounds on full auto from a fully automatic Uzi, civilian version of an M16, and so on. Quite an adrenalin rush! This event would have ramifications many years later.

I furthered my libertarian interest and became more civic-minded. At Russ Weaver's suggestion I joined the Legal Panel of the Kentucky chapter of the American Civil Liberties Association (ACLU). We met once a month over dinner and went over the docket of pending and proposed ACLU litigation. As a result, I kept up to date on civil liberties law and had a small voice in deciding which cases were pursued how in the Commonwealth. I was particularly interested in challenges to state endorsement of religion, such as placing copies of the Ten

Commandments on or outside public buildings. This, at least in part, reflected my sentiments about organized religion. Overall, an interesting development in the maturation of a conservative who continued to vote Republican in all elections.

All these activities were important as they helped keep my mood stable and consequently ameliorated my depression. They did not completely offset my work difficulties, but having a life away from the Law School was, as Dr. Bell frequently reminded me, a way not to be "a dull [and also very depressed] boy."

A final, very important social thing occurred during the 1986-87 academic year. Once I moved into my apartment I met my upstairs neighbor. He was a physician who was training to be a pulmonary specialist at the University's Medical School. As I got to know him, I learned he had a younger sister who recently had returned to the family home in Clarksville, Indiana, which is just across the Ohio River from Louisville, following her training as an internal medicine doctor. Jane, who was working as a primary care physician at a local HMO, was a Phi Beta Kappa graduate of Indiana University in Bloomington (the main campus of Indiana University) and an Alpha Omega Alpha (the Phi Beta Kappa of medical schools) alumna of I.U.'s Medical School. My neighbor said various uncomplimentary things about his sister, but through them I learned she was shy, quiet, and unmarried. I decided I definitely wanted to meet her. My neighbor arranged a blind date, and Jane and I went out on Halloween of 1986.

Neither of us wore a disguise, and I took Jane for dinner to a restaurant her brother had told me she and her family enjoyed. When I looked at Jane I saw someone far different from the person her brother had described to me. She was rather shy and quiet, but had a delightful personality. She was somewhat short but I thought very attractive with beautiful hair and skin, sparkling eyes, and a lovely smile. She bore a striking resemblance to the picture of a fine-looking Irish colleen that her ancestry qualified her to be. She was one month younger than I. Almost as soon as I saw her I realized I had found someone I wanted to get to know.

Our first date went appropriately. We discussed our respective families, school experiences, equally solid academic records, jobs, work histories, travels (I had been to most of Europe, while she had been around much of Asia including Japan, China, Southeast Asia, and India), etc. I learned that, interestingly enough, she, like I, had lost a year of her life to illness. In her case, while she was an intern she became so sick that she had to drop out of the internship program and return home for intensive medical treatment and recovery. I did not tell her about my 1983-84 breakdown and recovery because I did not know how she would react to the news. Although she was a doctor and as a result knew something about mental illness from her studies in medical school, that did not tell me what she thought about it. My longstanding stigma concerns generated considerable anxiety when my strong attraction to her was coupled with my very real fear. I would wait until I deemed the time was right for the news and meanwhile crossed my fingers and toes.

Over the coming months Jane and I spent considerable time together as our relationship grew closer. It was a somewhat rocky one, as Jane had severe issues with commitment (or, at least, commitment to me). Still, I doggedly pursued the potential romance. When Dragon, her family Siberian husky to which she was devoted, developed a severe spinal problem while her parents were away I drove Jane and Dragon to Purdue University's veterinary emergency clinic in West Lafayette, Indiana, roughly 175 miles north of Louisville.

The eventful evening began when I called Jane around five in the afternoon. Something about her voice immediately drew my attention.

"What's the matter?"

"It's Dragon. There's something wrong with his back. He's in pain and can't move his back legs."

"Did you call the vet?"

"Yeah. He said there's nothing he can do, and that I should let him put Dragon to sleep. When I asked if there's any alternative he said possibly surgery could help, but nobody around here does that sort of work as it's very delicate and specialized. Vet schools are pretty much the only place it's performed."

"Where's the nearest vet school?"

"Purdue. I'm getting ready to head up there."

"In your car?"

"Yes."

I froze. Jane drove an aging yellow Chevrolet Vega that was hardly big enough to hold her and Dragon. Plus, the car was barely drivable around town, much less on a long trip on the interstate late into the night. Was it safe for her to make such a journey by herself given the condition of her vehicle? And, how would one woman both drive and keep a seriously ill dog under control? I, on the other hand, had a six year old full-sized vehicle in good condition that would be safe for the proposed mercy mission. So long as Jane was with me she could focus on keeping Dragon secured.

"Wait. I'll drive you and Dragon in my car. Dragon can lie across the back seat and you can sit with him and keep him quiet so he doesn't hurt himself. We can drop him off at Purdue and drive back in time for you to go to work in the morning."

"Are you sure? It's a lot of trouble for you."

"My pleasure. You'll just have to stay awake and keep talking to me so I don't go to sleep and wreck all of us."

"Deal."

With that, I loaded up my car, got gas, and drove across the river to Indiana. When I got to Jane's parents' house we carefully transferred Dragon into my car and laid him on a blanket. Jane climbed in beside him and off we went.

We talked quietly as we headed up Interstate 65. It was dark well before we reached Indianapolis but we pressed ever-northward. Dragon would stir occasionally but was apparently in sufficient distress that he lay still so long as Jane petted him, which she did constantly.

We reached Lafayette a little after midnight, where we faced our next challenge: finding the clinic at Purdue in West Lafayette. We turned the wrong way on a one way street and a local policeman pulled us over. When he looked inside the car and heard what we were doing he merely gave us directions and sent us on our way after he wished us luck. By 12:30 AM we reached our destination. Veterinary hospital workers carefully took Dragon inside. They conferred with Jane for a time, and then she rejoined me.

"They say for us to head back to Clarksville and Louisville, they'll handle things from here. They'll probably operate on Dragon in the morning, and then keep him here for several weeks before he can return home. It will be touch and go, but they think we got him here in time."

That was all I needed to hear. We returned to my car and headed south after a stop at an all-night waffle restaurant for some long overdue dinner. Jane was as good as her word and talked to me all the way down I-65. I dropped her off around dawn and then went home and collapsed.

Later in the day, Jane called and reported she had spoken with the hospital and learned the surgery went well. She and her parents regularly telephoned Purdue, and finally brought Dragon back to Clarksville, seemingly as good as new. Indeed, Dragon lived on for a number of happy years until he died of old age. Meanwhile, I had earned many "points" with Jane and her parents for my good deed. This time a dog brought me closer to, rather than away from, a girlfriend.

Around this time I decided our relationship had progressed to the point where I finally should confide in Jane about my disorder. I was in a quandary; I thought I knew her well enough to predict she would react positively to the news. Still, this was a potential deal-breaker for our romance and I was afraid things might fall apart once I told her what I deemed my deep, dark secret. Nervously, I waited until what I deemed the most intimate moment possible. When we completed making love after dinner one night I finally addressed the issue:

"I need to tell you something about me."

"What's the problem?"

"As a doctor I know you're familiar with mental illness, and even treat patients with it. I have a severe mental illness and have been under psychiatric treatment for years. In 1983 I had a major breakdown and spent six months in the hospital. I've fought myself back to even better shape than I was in before 1983."

"What's your diagnosis?"

"Bipolar disorder. I'm chronically depressed because of it and the lithium I take to control it."

"That explains your moodiness and the way your hand shakes."

"Yes. Does this bother you?"

"Not really. Do you have a good doctor?"

"Oh yes, he's one of the top psychiatrists at U. of L. I see him every other week."

"Which drugs are you taking?"

"Lithium, an anti-depressant, and some sleeping prescriptions. Here are the bottles of all that I'm on."

"Do you have a family history? There can be a genetic aspect to mental illness."

"Not that I'm aware of. I don't think there's much of a risk for my children, if that's what you mean."

"Do the people at the Law School know about your disease?"

"No, no one in Louisville knows other than the doctor, his

137

secretary, and now you. Please keep this secret. I'm afraid how my superiors would react if they heard. You know about stigma and mental illness."

"Yes. I'll do so. Thanks for trusting me enough to tell me about it."

And that was that. The status of our romance was not yet clearly defined, but it definitely was a work in progress by the late spring of 1987. Certainly, with Jane I was no outcast. Apparently, she enjoyed my company despite my psychiatric diagnosis. Maybe we had a future together—only time would tell.

13

With the onset of summer came prime writing season. Written scholarship is, of course, an essential part of the career of any academic who works at the college or professional level. It truly is, as my immediate predecessor learned to his sorrow, "publish or perish." My psychiatric condition and the medications I take to control it have always made publication a special concern for me.

Many with bipolar disorder say the disease both helps them be extremely creative and write huge amounts in short periods of time. They point proudly to famous and productive literary geniuses who today are deemed to have suffered from manic-depressive illness like Lord Byron, Ralph Waldo Emerson, F. Scott Fitzgerald, William Faulkner, John Keats, Edgar Allen Poe, and Virginia Woolf. Manic-depression often was a blessing for their work. This behavior, however, was the product of manic phases of their condition. Unfortunately, those in a state of depression have a very different experience.

Bipolar depression markedly slows the mind and the thought process, making it difficult to think or concentrate. In my own case, it takes me an inordinate amount of time to write when I am so afflicted. Beyond that, for many people, including me, lithium, which I took until far into my career, stunts creativity and cognitive function.

I was unwilling to disclose my disease to my superiors at the Law School. In any event, I doubt it would have mattered had I done so. I simply had to buckle down and produce as much as well as I possibly could. I would make up in craft and determination what I lacked in pure imagination and alacrity as I coped with my disease. Like the proverbial tortoise, I would doggedly work to complete my task—"slow and steady wins the race."

As noted, I planned to work on an article with Russ Weaver. First, however, I was burdened with a vestige of what turned out to be the last offering of the Intro to Law course. The focus of both it and the fall half of BLS was having the students do a major project wherein they researched and wrote an extensive memorandum on a complex issue. That paper was graded by both the BLS teacher and the Intro to Law one for each student. I learned I was required to write a "sample" memo the Intro to Law teachers could use in marking the papers. Like the proposed student memoranda, it was to delve into all aspects of the problem. As this predated widespread availability of legal research via computer, the students had to use regular hardbound case reporters in the course of their research. Since there would be inadequate books if all the students were writing about the law in the same jurisdiction—the library only had two sets of state case reporters—the memoranda were set in six different states. Each writing class addressed one or another of them. The bottom line was that I had to research and draft six sample memos. While there were many similarities between them since the same basic fact pattern was used for each, there also were differences. I could refer to those from previous years as a starting point, since the same states were used each year. Still, by the time I finished all six of them, doing my usual quality job, I burned up a chunk of my summer. As I was rather severely depressed at the time, I lost even more key writing time.

Finally, I was able to work on my project with Russ. We were writing about an obscure rule, or "privilege," that lets government keep certain secrets from being disclosed during litigation. It was Russ' field of expertise, and the plan was for him to focus on the operation of the rule. Knowing my background in history, Russ asked me to address the roots of the privilege. While we agreed my contribution would not encompass a large percentage of the total pages in the article, the obscure works I would have to consult would make it intricate. I spent countless hours digging through the basement of the law library where the old English cases and other items were stored. I cited a number of eighteenth and nineteenth century English materials in the course of my encyclopedic footnotes. Even when I turned to United States authorities, I found a wealth of information in nineteenth century sources. The breadth of my treatment broadened as I reached the twentieth century. My total contribution to the article spanned eight pages in print, but that number was deceptive since most of my work was in the footnotes. Had it all appeared in the text, whose type and spacing are larger, it undoubtedly would have been thrice as long.

In addition to my own writing, I also assisted Russ in the overall form of the article. We were very proud of the piece, which was published in a good journal. Others have cited extensively to it since 1988, and it is accepted as the seminal work on the privilege even today.

Considering my health issues and the time I had to devote to the BLS/Intro to Law memos, I had a productive summer. I really enjoyed researching and writing the historical portion of the privilege article. Doing so let me at least pretend I was the historian I always wanted to be rather than the attorney I actually became. Imagine my shocked reaction when the Dean later lambasted me for my "inadequate" contribution to the article. She apparently thought I was supposed to write more than I had completed, whereas in fact I had fully finished the portion Russ Weaver assigned to me. Her previously discussed antipathy towards me made her view more understandable, albeit unjustified. All this explains why, with one exception, I have refrained from any other co-authored scholarship, as when you write it all yourself no one can question later who wrote what or was responsible to do how much.

In any event, the summer was over and I readied to teach my second year at the Law School. I finally was assigned to teach a part of the core doctrinal curriculum, Torts II, in the spring 1988 semester. I would have the entire fall to work towards that goal. I was taking over the new class from a professor who was retiring. By my third year on the faculty I would be teaching Torts I and II along with BLS as my standard teaching load.

Although my fall teaching went well, that was not the most important aspect of that period. Personal considerations instead came to the forefront. I continued socializing with colleagues, beagling once cooler weather descended, and singing on Sunday mornings at Second Pres. The most momentous events surrounded my increasingly serious connection with Jane.

Gradually, I began to shed my lifelong fear of commitment and to focus on establishing a permanent relationship with Jane. I broached the subject of marriage with her. Several hurdles had to be overcome. First of all, Jane needed to know more about the status of my mental health. To deal with that, I arranged for her to attend a session with both Dr. Bell and me so he could answer all her questions. Second, Jane was deathly afraid of guns, and insisted that I rid myself of my collection. I agreed that if we married I would do so forthwith. Third, while I cared little about having children (indeed, by virtue of the events of my youth I affirmatively disliked children) Jane badly wanted to do so. I agreed we would fairly soon after our marriage since we were already in our mid-thirties and time was of the essence.

At this point, Jane was the one with doubts and concerns about commitment. I kept raising the marriage issue, but could not pin Jane down on the point as she vacillated over what to do.

142

I finally issued a sort of ultimatum:

"As you know, I've set aside some money to pay for a nice diamond engagement ring. As you also know, my car's approaching replacement time. This is especially true since I'm driving to Mississippi to spend Thanksgiving with Ramsay's family and I don't want car trouble along the way. If you're willing to commit to getting married I'll buy the ring. If not, I'm buying a new car with the money. You pick."

Jane was unwilling, or unable, to answer affirmatively. Accordingly, I purchased a 1988 Toyota Camry that I broke in on the trip to Mississippi. Inwardly, I was devastated that I was not getting something I desperately wanted. Indeed, the more Jane dug in her heels the harder I pursued her. The last thing I had wanted as badly was to be admitted to law school at Virginia. When I looked at Jane, I saw the perfect partner. She was an extremely attractive, sweet, and caring person. She was a very intelligent peer with a good job. We had much in common. Perhaps most significantly, she was completely non-threatening. In sum, she was the sort of spouse of whom I always had dreamed, and I was not going to give up on her without a fight.

Had I been thinking straight I would have wondered if marriage to someone as hesitant as Jane would be a good idea. Maybe there was something about her of which I was unaware that explained her phobia against commitment. However, I was not thinking straight—love can make you blind. Indeed, the uncertainty worsened my usual state of depression. I had difficulty sleeping, and was increasingly irritable at work. As usual, I depended on Dr. Bell to help me weather the situation.

Despite Jane's obvious reluctance I continued stubbornly to pursue marriage. As I readied to drive to Jacksonville for Christmas I asked Jane to reconsider my proposal and invited her to meet me in Asheville a few days after the holiday.

"Look. Part of what you're worried about is putting on a big wedding. Gatlinburg, Tennessee is the Mecca for easy weddings. Why don't you look into what is available? We can go check it out, and if it looks right take it from there."

"Not a bad plan, but how do we work it?"

"You fly to Asheville and I'll meet you," I said. "From there Gatlinburg is a short drive."

"OK," Jane replied. "I'll book us a room at a nice place there for several days. I'll also look into spots to get married."

In her research Jane came across the Gatlinburg Wedding Chapel. It offered a full package wedding with a Baptist minister presiding. If you got the whole deal you had music, flowers, photographs, a wedding video, and anything else you might want for under $1,000. All you needed was a Tennessee marriage license and you were ready to go. Since Tennessee required no blood test or residency period it could all be done very simply.

We drove over to the Chapel. It was quite rustic and charming. We met the pastor, and immediately liked him very much. He told us to think it over and call if we wanted to go through with it. We could have a time on January 2, and needed to get the license in the county seat in Sevierville on the next day, December 31.

Once we left the Chapel we talked it over.

"What do you think?," I asked.

"It's a very nice place."

"It'll be very easy. Besides, think what those at our jobs will think when they ask what we did for New Years and we say we got married! Ultimately, it's up to you, as I'll marry you anywhere, anytime, anyhow."

I knew this was the crucial moment toward which I had worked for so long. I waited with bated breath as Jane decided whether we would join our lives together.

Jane grew quiet and pensive. Finally, she said "We'll do it."

"Are you sure? If so, we need to call our families so they have time to get here."

144

"Let's call them."

At that, I telephoned my mother and Rick and Ramsay and asked them to come. I further asked Rick to be my best man. When I spoke with Andy Baker and invited him and his wife Susan to be there he not only agreed but also volunteered to help my mother. As it turned out, Andy, Susan, and my mother flew to Knoxville where Andy rented a car and drove them to Gatlinburg. Rick and Ramsay completed my component of the wedding party, as unfortunately Aunt Bet was unable to attend. The next morning I called my landlady and asked her to let Jane's parents into my apartment to get my tuxedo and accoutrements, which she did. Thus, I would be properly dressed for the occasion.

The night before the wedding I was in a (possibly manic?) state of dazed euphoria. I could not go to sleep despite taking my usual sleeping medication. Every time I had the opportunity I started to sing, or hum, or whistle the song "Get Me to The Church on Time" ("I'm getting married in the morning") from *My Fair Lady*.

The wedding itself was lovely and went off without a hitch, as did a post-nuptial group dinner at a Gatlinburg steak restaurant. Jane and I headed back to our new home—Jane's apartment in New Albany, Indiana, also just across the Ohio River from Louisville—as a couple. I truly was in heaven, as I had attained that for which I had strived for so long. I was married, to the woman I loved.

We later were feted by various faculty friends to whom we showed our wedding photographs and video. It was a glorious time to be alive.

14

Spring 1988 was the happiest semester of my teaching career. I was ecstatic the entire time due to my marriage. As promised, I sold my gun collection at a considerable loss as handguns depreciate in value even faster than automobiles. Our honeymoon period went predictably well. I focused all my available attention on Jane, and as a result discontinued most of my outside activities such as attending ACLU meetings or singing at Second Presbyterian. I did continue beagling for a time, although that also eventually went by the wayside.

The biggest problem we faced was the nights Jane was on call, as she would get hundreds of telephone messages when patients throughout the HMO system called in with problems they thought could not wait until morning. This mildly inconvenienced her, as after years as a physician she could go back to sleep immediately after she fielded a complaint. I, on the other hand, always have trouble sleeping and would be a wreck the next day after the constant interruptions. We dealt with this problem by having Jane sleep in the guest bedroom when she was on call. That way I got to sleep undisturbed.

At school, I really enjoyed teaching Torts II. It was a very interesting course, and I prepared thoroughly for it. My hard work was rewarded. I got the excellent student evaluations I consistently have earned over the years for both my Torts I and II classes. Several colleagues later observed that this helped convince them that my usual low BLS marks were more attributable to student dislike for the course than to my instructional abilities. This, in turn, helped me in my quest for promotions and the award of tenure. Even my BLS ratings were high for the spring 1988 semester; one student commented on his or her form that I should get married every semester as it did wonders for my disposition. Dr. Bell and I had little trouble managing my depression as my general state of euphoria overcame it.

As I became a regular Torts teacher I developed a close relationship with Ron Eades, the senior Torts professor on the faculty. Ron is Rick's age (five years older than I), although he always kidded me that we are the same age. Ron mentored me over the years, and was always available to help answer questions about the course. He was an excellent source of information, as he is probably the foremost authority on Kentucky tort law in the Commonwealth. He also stuck up for me with the rest of the faculty. As he was highly respected by our colleagues, he proved to be an invaluable supporter. We frequently worked together, doing things like comparing class grade distributions to insure they were roughly comparable and proof reading each other's examinations. Since I still had stigma fears I did not confide in even him about having a mental illness until years later.

Outside the Law School, now that I was married Jane and I were welcomed into a group of congenial faculty couples who frequently socialized together. These included Ron and Lillian Eades, Ed and Joyce Render, and Bob and Mary Ann Stenger. I was the only untenured faculty member among those in the crowd, which was a good thing as it provided me with even more allies ready to go to bat for me when I was up for promotion and/or tenure.

Summer 1988 brought another period for scholarship. I started my first solo article based on a case on which I had worked while with Judge Snyder. It again let me exercise my love of English legal history, on which it was based. As my depression was still under good control, I had a far easier time researching and writing than the year before. By August I had made good progress on the piece.

Shortly before school resumed Jane and I made a major addition to our family. After reading a story about dachshunds in the newspaper I suddenly felt the urge to renew my relationship with the breed. I raised the issue with Jane.

"I'd really like to get a dachshund. I'll take care of it, so it won't be a bother for you."

"I thought we wanted to have children."

"I know. Dachshunds are good with kids, and don't create allergy problems like some dogs. It'll give me practice at parenthood. Also, remember that pets are good for those with mental illnesses."

"OK. Keep a lookout for an ad in the paper."

I knew I wanted a female miniature dachshund because of my experience with Sue-Sue and Brünnhilde. I decided to go for a red one this time.

In due course I saw the notice for which I was looking, and we went out to look over the litter in question. I immediately saw an adorable female puppy trying to chase a mule in its corral. I knew this was the dog for me, and I named her Brigitte Nutmeg Jones, or Nutmeg for short, in tribute to her distinctive reddish brown color. Now I truly was in heaven, as I had a tiny dachshund with which to play.

I called my mother and said "Guess what?"

"You're pregnant."

"No! We got a dachshund puppy."

"Why would you want to do something like that?"

I quickly changed the subject, as this conversation was not headed anywhere worthwhile.

About a month later Jane began feeling a bit under the weather. She saw one of her colleagues, who ran some tests and discovered the problem. That evening she said "You know how I saw the doctor?"

"Yes. Is everything alright?"

"Well, you tell me. We're pregnant."

"We are? When are we due?"

"Sometime next May. Are you happy?"

"Are you?"

"Of course, I'm overjoyed! You know how much I've always wanted to have children."

"If you're overjoyed, I'm overjoyed."

I called my mother again. "Guess what?"

"Something happened to the puppy?"

"No, she's fine. Jane's pregnant! You're going to be a grandmother again (Rick had three daughters)."

"That's great news. Now you better look for a house for all of you."

She made a good point. Our apartment was already getting crowded, and a baby would occupy considerable space. The news did not create any psychiatric problems for me, and things rocked along at work. Indeed, I grew increasingly proud as I never lost a day there despite periodic dips into the trough of bipolar depression.

Jane looked especially beautiful when pregnant. In due course we started house-hunting, and by late fall located a large modern residence in a tasteful subdivision in New Albany. I finally was able to get all my possessions out of storage, as there was ample room for all both of us owned in our new home. We closed on the house and moved in soon enough to celebrate our first Christmas as a married couple together there.

Spring 1989 saw my courses continue to go well, and I finished my first solo article. I was very excited when a major law review accepted it for publication. Meanwhile, on the domestic front Jane, Nutmeg and I settled into our new home and Jane and I readied for the new addition to our little family. Around the first of the year Jane underwent amniocentesis (*I* had insisted on that as we were both thirty-five at the time of the pregnancy), and the results were that all was OK. Jane's parents spent a great deal of time at our house, where her father was especially helpful as he could fix pretty much anything as well as being a whiz at hanging pictures, performing maintenance on cars, and so forth. We lined up day care for the baby, as Jane planned to return to work about two months after giving birth. I continued to work with Dr. Bell to manage my depression and we generally succeeded at doing so.

After the semester ended I pursued some possible new avenues for scholarship, but Jane and I mainly focused on the impending delivery. Finally, on the evening of May 18 we rented a movie and watched it after dinner. We went to bed, and then early in the morning Jane awoke me and said "It's time."

My initial reaction was underwhelming, as I went back to sleep. Jane awoke me again, and this time made sure I packed the car and headed for the hospital in Louisville after, at my insistence, dropping off the movie at the rental store. We arrived at the hospital and prepared for what was to come. Things seemed to be going fine until an alarm suddenly went off. A delivery nurse came in, looked at some readings, and told Jane something was wrong.

"The baby's heart rate keeps dropping. I'm calling the doctor to get here at once. Meanwhile, we're heading into the operating room in case an emergency c-section is needed."

The expert nurses wheeled Jane's delivery bed into the OR. Someone threw a set of surgical scrubs at me and told me to put them on. When I looked puzzled, the nurse said "Hurry up, you have to sit with your wife. Just don't pass out, as we can't waste time catching you."

About then the doctor arrived. He, the nurses, and Jane all conferred and agreed the c-section was needed. I clearly was the odd man out of this conversation. The operation began, with the surgical staff erecting a barrier of material so Jane and I couldn't see what was going on. Jane was not in any pain at this point, and we had a fairly normal conversation under the circumstances. At one point I peered over the barrier and watched in fascination as the procedure unfolded. I was not really worried, as all seemed to be under control despite the emergency nature of things.

"So that's what fat looks like from the inside."

"What?," Jane asked.

"Oh, never mind."

The doctor called back "The cord was wrapped around the baby's neck, and that's why the heart rate was dropping off. We got in just in time."

Then, the blessed words "It's a beautiful little girl!"

At that, Jane and I kissed one another and the doctor handed Miss Jennifer Lee Jones to Jane. It was midmorning of May 19, 1989.

About the time for Jane and Jennifer to be discharged someone noticed a problem with one of Jennifer's tiny eyes, or tear ducts, to be more precise. An infection developed, and she was rushed into the neonatal intensive care unit. A pediatric ophthalmologist was called onto the case, and Jennifer had to undergo a general anesthesia while he unblocked her tear duct to eliminate the infection. Almost as soon as this was done, the other tear duct grew infected and Jennifer had her second general anesthesia and operation. The child was barely a week old and had been through delivery by c-section and two operations! I was a wreck, after spending most of my time in the n.i.c.u. for days on end, and had to call on Dr. Bell for support. Indeed, I got no work done because I both spent my time in the hospital and grew severely depressed. Fortunately, school was out for the summer so I did not have to teach during this crisis period.

Jane was much more of a wreck. Fortunately, the hospital was renovating some rooms and let her stay in one so she would be available to feed Jennifer on a regular basis. Still, she was stuck in the hospital worried to death about her tiny daughter. Here, being a doctor was not such a good thing, as she imagined all sorts of awful things were going to happen to Jennifer. Sleep was a real problem for both of us. Finally, after almost two weeks the eye infections were gone and we got to bring Jennifer home to her well-equipped nursery.

Now that she was home, another sleep-related problem developed. I still had chronic sleep issues, and a newborn, as is well known, does little good for parental sleep patterns. Jane quickly learned I was pretty useless in the middle of the night. So I could sleep, she made permanent the sleeping in different bedrooms pattern we had developed when she was on call.

Indeed, this was merely a symptom of a greater predicament. Jane, I think, had believed I suddenly would grow interested in children once we had a child. I, on the other hand, took the position that she wanted a child/children so she should care for her/them. I would continue handling the cooking, grocery shopping, lawn and tending to Nutmeg, but the rest was Jane's problem. My mother tells me that my father also believed childcare was for the wife alone, and offered her no assistance. With me, you could add my general aversion to children to the mix. I did help walk Jennifer when she was colicky, but that undoubtedly was too little too late. They say the apple never falls far from the tree.

For the rest of the summer of 1989 I focused on recovering from my mental trauma surrounding Jennifer's early days. I probably should have alerted someone at the Law School about my health issues, but as usual was afraid to do so. Instead, I decided to try to coast into the new academic year. Indeed, I was sufficiently clueless to request a promotion from Assistant to Associate Professor of Law effective the summer of 1990. As

I was satisfied with the quality and quantity of scholarship I had produced in light of all with which I had had to cope, I assumed the senior faculty who decided on promotions would be also. I was sadly mistaken.

15

Workwise the teaching aspect of the 1989-90 academic year went along routinely. As usual, I taught Torts I and II and BLS. On the scholarship front I was having problems since my depression interfered with my choosing a topic for my next article. It is essential, of course, to pick a good subject on which to write. It must be one about which there are no other similar pieces by other academics. By virtue of my teaching assignment I wanted to write a torts-related work, but that is a broad topic and I was unsure what to pursue. The lithium was not helping me creatively do what I needed. Then, Russ Weaver saw an article in the newspaper about domestic violence and suggested that might give rise to a worthwhile article, or even series of articles. I was grateful for his idea. Over the next decade it ultimately led me to write seven articles and speak both locally and nationally—as well as in one foreign country—on the subject. Thus, I became a nationally known expert on this important social issue.

At home all was far from desirable. Jane's mother Shirley was utterly delightful and as a consequence much loved by all. We were devastated when she was stricken with ovarian cancer. At first we thought it was cured surgically, but then it returned and metastasized. The handwriting was now on the wall. Her doctor put her on various forms of drastic chemotherapy but it did nothing aside from make her life miserable in view of the horrendous side effects of the treatment. The one real pleasure in her life seemed to be having us bring Jennifer over so she could play with her only grandchild. For me, this was a nightmare redux as I spent much time visiting Shirley in the hospital or at home. In the process, of course, I watched yet another loved one suffer and gradually but inexorably die from cancer. I was incredibly fond of Shirley, and her condition affected me deeply and depressed me intensely. I had to call on Dr. Bell to help me cope with that over which I had no control. Predictably, my situation adversely affected my work.

My problem was not limited to my reaction to Shirley's decline. Jane was utterly distraught over the situation. Again, being a physician was a bad thing, as she thoroughly understood Shirley's bleak prognosis. Jane would sit at home and weep inconsolably seemingly for hours at a time. Caring for Jennifer would divert her briefly, but as soon as Jennifer went to sleep again Jane was despondent once more. I tried to help her as best I could, but there was really little I could say other than that I felt her pain and was there for her. I arranged for her to see Dr. Bell, who prescribed medications to assist her in dealing with the situation and the depression she developed. These helped her, but she was still miserable much of the time. The only way she could go to sleep at night was for me to sit by her bed and talk quietly to her in a comforting voice until she dozed off. She later said she always appreciated what I had tried to do, but I certainly wished I could offer more than moral support. I knew how much she loved Shirley, and certainly understood the helpless feeling she was experiencing.

As if this were not enough, Jennifer had a greater problem than her bad case of colic. Like many children in day care, she was constantly catching whatever diseases were going around the nursery where she stayed. The pediatrician who worked at the HMO with Jane spent considerable time treating Jennifer's numerous respiratory infections. Finally, by January she was back in the hospital, this time with a severe case of pneumonia. She was very ill, and this time her doctor laid it on the line:

"You *have* to get Jennifer out of day care *right away!* She can't keep on staying sick like she's been doing. She'll just keep getting pneumonia if you don't do something."

At that Jane and I conferred about some alternative. Almost miraculously a solution presented itself: A neighbor of Jane's parents told us about an older lady who would keep one or two children from one family. She lived with her daughter and her family in Clarksville, and as she did not drive you had to take your child or children to her. When we called her we learned the child for whom she had been caring had recently moved to Virginia with his family, and therefore she was available. We went over to meet her and were overjoyed with what we found. She was wonderful with Jennifer and looked exactly like the mother, grandmother, and great grandmother she was. She then was aged about seventy, and said just to call her Nanny.

We immediately retained Nanny for the indefinite future, which turned out to be roughly the next fifteen years. Jennifer recovered from her pneumonia and then thrived since she now had the equivalent to a stay at home mother. My mood rallied a bit as a result.

Nanny became the surrogate grandmother for my family and would go to school with Jennifer, and later her younger sister, on grandparent's day. Every birthday or holiday would be celebrated at Nanny's house as well as ours, and I remembered her on each birthday, Christmas, and Mother's Day with the identical present I gave my mother.

Eventually the senior faculty considered my promotion request. I was shocked out of the relative lethargy into which I had fallen when they denied it. No one questioned the quality of my work, but the faculty said the quantity just was not there. I was granted a one year extension to my contract to teach, and write, at the Law School. My health issues provided a ready answer to the faculty complaint but, as usual, I was afraid to voice it. Instead, I recognized I had to move ahead quickly if I wanted to survive as an academic. I immediately started work on the topic Russ Weaver had suggested to me. Over the next two years I wrote two major articles about the use of tort law to encourage the police to enforce domestic violence laws. They, as it turned out, were enough to insure my survival as a member of the Law School faculty.

In January 1991 the faculty agreed I merited promotion to Associate Professor of Law, and the Law School's new Dean shepherded it through final approval by the University. Meanwhile, at about the same time Jane and I learned we were going to grace Jennifer with a little sister (the amniocentesis told us the gender of her new sibling). Jane and I discussed the name for our new child. We wanted to name her Shirley, but before her death Jane's mother asked Jane to promise not to do so. We decided to honor this promise in the breach, and midmorning on November 13, 1991 welcomed our healthy daughter Anne Shirley Jones (much as the Anne Shirley heroine of the *Anne of Green Gables* series of novels), called Shirley by all, into the world.

At this point, I thought life had finally fallen into place for me. Within a year I reached nirvana when I was voted tenure. This meant I finally had arrived and almost certainly had earned a teaching position at the Law School for the remainder of my professional life. Thus, I had an excellent job, a nice home, a wife I adored, and two beautiful daughters. Jane had the two children she always had wanted and a good job. By now, she had grown tired of working for the HMO and taken a position at the Louisville Veteran's Administration hospital. Slowly, but gradually, she recovered from the loss of her mother. At least there still was a Shirley in her life. Both of us were blessed with Nanny, whose excellent and loving care of our two non-day care, non-virus ridden daughters made so much else possible. What more did I need or have any right to expect? Thanks to Dr. Bell, Jane, and my own hard work I kept my disease well-controlled despite suffering from periodic bouts of bipolar depression. Jane bought me a stainless steel and gold Rolex watch as a tenure present inscribed "Jim Congratulations Much Love Jane 5-21-92" (the day the University's Board of Trustees voted to grant it to me). I still wear it much of the time as it reminds me of the halcyon days of our marriage.

Life puttered along from here. I started work on a new article and was awarded a research grant over the summer of 1993 to cover the time it took me to complete it. By now I was helping more with childcare, getting sick to death of Disney's animated classic *The Little Mermaid* and the PBS television program *Barney and Friends* in the process. Jennifer would watch each on VHS over and over *ad nauseum*.

Soon after the end of the spring 1993 semester, as I recall, we had put the children to bed. Jane approached me.

"Can we talk?"

"Sure. What's up?"

"I've decided I don't want to be married any more. I've rented an apartment in Louisville and am moving there with Jennifer and Shirley. You stay in the house and take care of Nutmeg."

"Whaa??!!" I doubled over as I felt as though I had been punched really hard in the pit of my stomach. "I don't understand. Do you want a divorce?"

"Not necessarily. I just don't want to live in the house with you."

Thunderstruck, I said "What did I do? How do I keep you from leaving?" As I asked that, I thought about all my actions over the years that might have upset Jane. They started with my child rearing philosophy. They notably included the general difficulty of living with someone with bipolar disorder and specifically the times I would grow manic and bellow angrily at anyone around, which of course usually equaled Jane.

"You don't. It has little to do with you."

"But I need you and the girls. How am I going to get along without you?"

"That's not my problem. While I hope I'm wrong, I'm afraid you'll either end up dead or in a psychiatric hospital."

With that, Jane turned, went into her bedroom, and shut the door in my face.

I was dumbfounded. I did not know how to react as I saw my whole world fall apart around me. It reminded me of 1983 and the events that led to my breakdown and stay in Highland. I liked neither of Jane's predictions, but could see why they might be accurate. What was I to do?

I called Dr. Bell and tearfully recounted what had just happened (this was really the first time since the emotional maelstrom of Highland I had responded in that way). He told me he was sorry and for me to try to hold together until he could see me in his office, which he would do forthwith. I then tried to think who else to call. Since I had few friends, I was at a loss. I considered calling my mother, but quickly concluded doing so would not be helpful. I finally telephoned Aunt Bet. She heard me out, said how sorry she was, and asked me if I would like to come over to Henderson and stay with her while I tried to figure out how to proceed. I thanked her for her offer, and said I would get back to her. I then tried going to bed, but sleep would not come. I would not sleep well again for a long time.

16

The next morning things looked just as bleak as the night before. Jane's father came over, helped her pack up a load of things both in her car and in his, and left me staring vacantly at them as they pulled away. I was so distraught over the situation that I literally could not imagine what to do next. After meeting with Dr. Bell, who could only counsel me to take things "one day at a time" and to advise me to call him immediately should I start to become suicidal, I called Aunt Bet.

"I'm totally devastated. I guess that's why mostly I sit around and cry. Even though I've seen my doctor, I'm afraid I'm going to have another breakdown like in '83."

"As I said, don't you think it will help you to come over here so you aren't alone?"

"Well, maybe. But what will I do?"

"You can be with me. We'll tell the rest of the family you just came over for a visit and you don't have to discuss Jane unless you want to. We can go on walks every evening and see everyone you love in Henderson. You can even get a temporary membership at the YMCA and go there every day for some exercise. Didn't you tell me one time that exercise helps you when you're depressed?"

"It does. OK. I'll call when I'm ready to head over."

In addition to all my other problems, when I found myself crying uncontrollably I felt even worse. What sort of man cries, I thought? As a result, my depression only spiraled down even further.

At this point, I contacted the Dean and advised him I wanted to surrender my research grant as certain "family issues" required my attention. I took Nutmeg to the vet to board and fled Indiana as fast as I could.

When I reached Aunt Bet, she was as loving and caring as I could hope. I moved into her guest bedroom and she nursed me to try to maintain my mental health. I purchased a one month membership at the Y and took full advantage of all it had to offer. We visited with family and old friends, all of whom were glad to see me. Things seemed to brighten a little.

Fortunately, I still had Nutmeg. When I returned to Indiana she would be waiting eagerly for me. At this point, little did I know how important Nutmeg would be for me. Over the coming years she would drive home what I had learned years before with Sue-Sue—pets really are important to those with mental illness by virtue of their companionship and unquestioned love.

Nutmeg was truly a unique animal. If Susie was smart, Nutty was even smarter. She understood a large vocabulary, often amazing me when she responded appropriately to what I said to her. She also knew what I was thinking or feeling before I knew myself. She was totally attached to me, and also was very fond of Jennifer and Shirley, who reciprocated her feelings (which she manifested with much jumping, tail wagging, and licking). Thus, when they came to see me they would get to see their old friend as well. That would help insure a positive visitation experience. I loved Nutty's beautiful red coat, as well as the flecks of grey that were beginning to appear on her muzzle. She was thin, weighing about twelve pounds, and bore the aristocratic bearing of a pedigreed member of her breed. Her knowing, liquid, and soulful eyes made her wisdom and devotion apparent, and totally endeared her to me. She was so smart that I could trust her outside without a leash, as she would obey my commands instantaneously even when she faced the temptation of a squirrel or rabbit across the street.

Nutty was an Oscar-winner when it was time to beg for a tasty morsel from me or someone we encountered, as she had the lean and hungry quiver, with one paw pitifully raised up, down pat even when she had just been fed. She was utterly fearless, as she had demonstrated when, as noted, she chased a mule a thousand times larger than she; Nutty thought she could take on any dog or other animal, regardless of its size or disposition. Still, she was extremely friendly with everyone; she never met a stranger, and as a result was popular with all we met.

One of my favorite memories of my time with Jane was the night we were enjoying a fried chicken dinner when for some reason we were called to the front door. When we returned to the kitchen table I was flabbergasted, and tremendously amused, to see Nutty, quite the athlete, standing on one of the kitchen chairs with her front legs on the table and tossing a piece of chicken off to the side of the table to another dog, who was streaking past her. It reminded me of some sort of football lateral play. Maybe Nutty had been paying attention to the games I watched on television! One never forgets a delightful moment like that, or the perpetrator of it. Were there any lingering doubt, this incident proved once and for all that Nutty was no dummy, and ingenious to boot!

I knew having Nutmeg would help me weather the storms that lay ahead of me in the world I now faced. For much of my free time, I would be alone other than with her for the foreseeable future. She was always overjoyed to see me when I came home for the day, and would eagerly curl up in my lap as I watched television or talked with my few friends over the telephone. I loved to go on long walks with her that got me the exercise I desperately needed given my depressed mental state. Every night, she slept under the covers of my bed snuggled next to me such that I did not feel quite so lonesome. Indeed, she seemed to care for me far more than Jane ever did during all our years together; she certainly had no commitment issues. I could expect no more of Nutmeg, and could not ask for a better friend.

While I tried to recuperate enough to return to New Albany from Henderson I spoke with Dr. Bell regularly and tried to follow his advice. Also, fortuitously for me, I had a friend on the faculty who had gone through a divorce some years before. She still remembered the experience well and was willing to commiserate with me and offer me support and the knowledge that eventually things would get better. I called her daily and poured out my heart to her.

Although I did not realize it at the time, my friend was functioning like the support groups that have proved so important to me in the years since mid-1993. I must have been an extremely boring conversationalist, as I tended to cry and say the same things over and over—again, my inability to curb my emotion did not further my self-esteem. My listener patiently emphasized and reemphasized that I could live through the end of a marriage, and that many before me had done so. These talks, my time at the Y, and Aunt Bet's endless encouragement held me together, averting a very severe depression and the resulting trip to the hospital Jane had predicted.

After a few weeks, I decided it was time to return to Indiana and at least go through the motions of resuming my life. I rescued Nutmeg from the vet and moved back with her into a four bedroom house all for the two of us. Jane continued to pay part of the mortgage and utility bills, but there was a greater financial burden on me than when we were together. More frequent visits to Dr. Bell added to the drain on my resources. Money, however, was not the main problem. *Loneliness* was the big issue. I was, by now, used to life with others, and it was very traumatic to be living alone. As I tried to prepare for a new academic year I realized I needed to take steps to resolve matters with Jane. I clung to the hope we would reconcile, but it simply was not happening. Each time I saw her I read her actions to see if she had altered her feelings. Unfortunately, while she was civil towards me she never seemed to miss me or want to get back together.

I spoke with Nanny, who of course knew Jane very well, about the collapse of my family.

"What do you think about what's happened?"

"I don't understand Jane at all. She needs to stop acting as she is and focus on having a good life with you and Jennifer and Shirley from now on."

I appreciated Nanny's sentiments. Over the coming years she often tut-tutted to me over many of Jane's actions and choices. Still, I of course understood that she could not take sides between Jane and me. Her role was to take good care of Jennifer and Shirley, and she fulfilled it exceptionally well for years. The relationship between Jane and me was not in her purview.

By now I would see the children on a weeknight and on weekends. Eventually this solidified into me cooking them dinner. As Jane did not know how to cook, these would be their only home cooked evening meals of the week.

A local shopping mall contained an amusement park, and Jennifer, Shirley, and I spent countless hours there riding the same rides and often eating at the same fast food court restaurants (thus cutting back on the number of home cooked dinners during those weeks) over and over. When the girls were small I would have to take them into the men's room and fit the three of us in a stall while Jennifer used the facilities and I changed Shirley's diapers (this long predated changing tables in men's restrooms).

I tried to put on a brave face for the girls, and they seemed to enjoy their time with me. I imagine from their perspective they actually liked things better than when Jane and I were together as now I focused total attention on them rather than pretty much ignoring them. Still, I found seeing them very upsetting and depressing as they reminded me of their mother whom I so desperately still loved.

Eventually I recognized our marriage probably was over. I took the, to me, epic step of taking off my wedding ring. More importantly, I set the legal machinery of divorce into motion.

As noted, Jane said she did not necessarily want a divorce, she just did not want to live with me, her husband. However, I knew that an invisible clock was ticking. Once she lived in Kentucky for six months she could file for divorce there and whatever advantages Indiana law provided to me would be lost. Accordingly, I telephoned a relatively recent graduate of the Law School I knew socially (I never had her in class) named Jean who I knew practiced in the largest firm in New Albany. After the initial pleasantries, I cut to the chase:

"You have a license in both Kentucky and Indiana, correct?"

"That's right. Why?"

"My wife recently left me and I may need to file for divorce. Do you know anyone who does Indiana divorces?"

"I do Indiana divorces. I have considerable experience in the field."

"My wife Jane has moved to an apartment in Louisville with our two daughters. She says she doesn't want to file for divorce. I'm afraid she just may be hoping I'll hold off long enough for her to file in Kentucky."

"Well, on the one hand it's always cheaper to have the other spouse pay to file, as it's more work to file than merely to respond to your spouse's petition. Also, it may be emotionally more satisfying for you to make her take the initiative. Finally, you'd rather be viewed as the victim than the aggressor in the suit, and the aggressor is usually the one who files. Here, however, all this will be offset by the disparity between Indiana and Kentucky divorce law. As you say, you need to act before she files in Kentucky."

"What should I do?"

"Can you meet me for lunch tomorrow at Kunz's restaurant in downtown Louisville?"

"Kunz's is where Jane and I went for our first date in 1987."

"Can you meet me for lunch tomorrow at Kunz's?"

I could see that Jean was no sentimentalist. "Yes."

"See you at noon."

Jean was very businesslike. She explained what I should expect, including a range of what things would cost. Whenever I tried to talk about my emotional issues, including my despair and my having bipolar disorder, she coolly directed me back to the task at hand.

"Your disease may prove relevant as the case proceeds. For now, talk to your psychiatrist about it, not me. I'm a lawyer, not a therapist. Never confuse the two."

By the end of lunch I hired Jean to represent me. She told me what information she needed me to gather for her and bade me farewell. As I would come to learn, I had a pit bull in my corner. I sent her the information she wanted and sat back to see what would happen next.

Around this time I recognized I could no longer keep the situation from my mother, and I told her and her then-new second husband about things. I was surprised when she was sympathetic with my plight and even invited me to come visit them in their home on Long Island. I did so and had a very pleasant time, which included trips into New York City for Broadway shows and even lunch at the famous Sardi's. At least temporarily, I could depend on my mother as well as Aunt Bet for familial help.

I continued to see Dr. Bell regularly, and he tinkered with my medications to try to keep me going. He suggested that I get into a therapy group. When I said I was willing to do so he arranged for me to join one run by a local Ph.D. in psychology.

The group consisted of roughly ten participants, many of whom had been divorced, plus the leader. When I got the opportunity to speak at my first meeting I talked loudly and emotionally about my situation. The leader had difficulty reining me in, and I kept interrupting others as I strove to tell my tale of woe. After the meeting the leader indicated I should listen to others more and sound off less myself.

At the next meeting I continued where I had left off. It was as if I did not really want feedback from others, I just wanted a pulpit from which to speak. If the truth be known, I was exhibiting the racing thoughts and rapid speech that cannot be interrupted that are characteristic of the floridly manic.

After the meeting the leader again indicated he was not pleased with the nature of my participation with the group. When a third meeting saw the same pattern, he kicked me out. Imagine what *that* rejection did to me! Dr. Bell tried to make light of the situation and said we would shelve the group idea for the time being. Later, I derived great benefit from another kind of support group.

Despite Jean's admonition to the contrary, I was so desperate for any sort of help I could muster that I frequently called her to discuss this or that issue. Really, I just wanted to bend a friendly ear, and I did view her as some other type of therapist to supplement what Dr. Bell provided to me. Jean figured out how to cure me of this behavior—after a month or so she sent me a large bill for the time she had spent talking with me. I *never* called her thereafter unless the matter at hand truly required her attention!

Around this time the fall 1993 semester began. I spoke as part of the orientation program for the entering first year students. I was quite preoccupied, and depressed, when I took my turn. I thought little about my performance afterwards other than to be vaguely dissatisfied with my effort. As it later turned out, I had made quite an impression on at least one of the students who heard me. This would turn out to be very important within the next few years.

Somewhere around this time I got the bright idea I should try target shooting again. Consequently, I bought an expensive handgun at a local gun store. Because of my severe depression, I had other things at least indirectly in mind. When I mentioned my purchase to Jean, she immediately insisted I sell it back to the gun dealer. She said she would no longer represent me unless I did so. Meekly, I followed her instructions. This was as close as I came to suicide during these days, so that part of Jane's prediction did not come true.

Dr. Bell suggested that Jane and I go through "closure" counseling. When I asked what that was, Dr. Bell explained it was a way to end a relationship as positively as possible. While he did not say so, it was also a means to convince one like me that things indeed were hopeless and the marriage was irretrievably broken.

Jane agreed to participate, and Dr. Bell referred us to John E. Turner, L.C.S.W., probably the premier marriage and family counselor in Louisville. We had several sessions with him, and eventually Turner carefully explained to me that all really was lost and that I had to go on with my life without Jane. We would still have dealings attributable to having children together, but that interaction would be it. Jane effectively was lost to me forever.

Despite my poor mental status I knew enough to be extremely impressed with Turner, and at my request he agreed to meet with me a few times alone. The upshot of these sessions was that it was not anyone's fault that the marriage had ended and that I did need some sort of assistance to help me through the trials yet to come. He recommended that I attend the Crescent Hill Baptist Church Divorce Recovery Support Group, an organization that met every Sunday evening and even had a nursery for the children of group members. I followed his advice, and as a result had my Sunday evenings occupied for the next four years. Meanwhile, I found in Turner someone upon whom I thought I might call at an appropriate time in the future. Eventually, he proved to be even more important to me than the support group at Crescent Hill.

In the meantime, the divorce was getting increasingly nasty. Jean did not like Jane's attorney at all, and the feeling was mutual. Moreover, Jane's lawyer had a reputation as a legal street fighter and brawler. On one occasion, he moved to transfer the case to a different county in Southern Indiana. His stated reason for doing so was that I had been a gun collector in the past and was known (by Jane) to have a mental illness. This led, according to him, to the conclusion that the matter should only be adjudicated in a courthouse with a metal detector at the doors, and the courthouse where the action was pending was not so equipped. While I really did not care by this point what happened so long as the divorce was over soon, Jean said I could not have the public record reflect the motion being granted and thus me being branded as some sort of homicidal maniac. I saw her point and told her to fight it out. We prevailed and the case stayed where it was, but the battle cost me considerable emotional energy and money. Indeed, I rather suspected part of Jane's lawyer's strategy was to wear me down with legal expenses in the hope of getting what her side wanted because I no longer could afford to contest things.

The motion in question, and the battle over it, proved to be utterly unnecessary. I never went to court while the divorce was pending.

The winter of 1993-94 saw my life at a nadir. In January Louisville suffered its worst winter storm on record, with nearly two feet of snow and a temperature of around twenty-five degrees below zero. The area shut down, and while Southern Indiana dug itself out, Louisville was buried for some time. The University shut down for a week. I was pretty well cooped up with Nutmeg as my only company. I could not even see Jennifer and Shirley, as they were locked in by the snow in Louisville with Jane. I held on as best I could, but felt my mental health grow worse and worse. It became harder and harder to teach class and perform my other obligations.

It was time to get rid of the house, which by now was an albatross around Jane's and my necks. We put it on the market in spring 1994, and after a few months had a buyer. As closing day approached I went apartment hunting back in Louisville as I no longer had the need to live in Indiana. Eventually I found a nice place with two bedrooms very near where I lived when I first reached Louisville. By virtue of my poor mental status, I lacked the energy to look elsewhere. The guest bedroom was the perfect size to accommodate Jennifer and Shirley, and I bought them a set of twin beds to go with the toys, VHS tapes, and other items I would keep for them when I moved. I packed my things into boxes and put many of them in a ministorage unit near my new apartment.

On moving day I felt incredibly sad and depressed when I saw all my possessions removed from the house where I had been so happy and unpacked in my new "bachelor pad." I drove around our street in New Albany one last time and then headed across the river. At this moment I truly realized that an important phase of my life had come to an end. Over the next few years my only trips to Indiana were to pick up Jennifer and Shirley from Nanny's house or to attend preschool and kindergarten events at the New Albany Lutheran church where Jane had enrolled them. Meanwhile, Nutmeg had the run of my new apartment and spent most of her days asleep in the sun on my bed (I had a stool set up to make it easy for her to jump there). As I always said, she had a fourteen hour bladder, and thus was a perfect roommate.

Early in my marriage I had pretty much, at least temporarily, abandoned my interest in listening to classical music. As a result, my huge record collection rested in numerous boxes in

171

the basement of our house. It was almost as if I now had a life with a wife and family so I no longer needed to hide in the world where I earlier had spent so much time. When I left the house I probably needed music as much as ever, but instead I donated the entire compilation to the New Albany Public Library and got a nice charitable income tax deduction for doing so. Therefore, I was without ready access to recorded music for the first time in many years. Eventually I rediscovered my special world, this time in the form of the new technology of cds, and retreated into it once again.

17

ow that I was back in Louisville I had to try to cope with my new life. As most know, divorce itself, especially for the one who does not want it, is a very upsetting and profoundly depressing event. In my case, my psychiatric condition probably made it worse than for almost everyone who has to face it. I dragged around the Law School as I attempted to fulfill my duties but was aware my poor mental health hurt my teaching and general ability to do my job. My condition must have been pretty obvious, as one day Ron Eades commented that I seemed depressed. When he said this I knew he thought I needed some form of medical intervention. I indicated I appreciated his concern, but I never said I was in regular therapy and on numerous medications.

The depth of my despair was as great as I ever could recall. I had all the symptoms of a classic bipolar depression: I had serious problems sleeping despite the numerous sleep medications I took, was constantly hopeless and irritable, lacked energy, had difficulty concentrating or deciding what to do with my life, and was chronically suicidal such that Dr. Bell always asked during each appointment about the severity level of my suicidal thoughts rather than merely whether I had any. The lithium and other medications continued to control the worst symptoms so that I could continue to work. Still, the peaks and valleys were there, with horrible valleys the predominant condition. At least through all this period I stayed alive and out of the hospital, thus defying both parts of Jane's prediction.

I did what I could to improve my functioning. I returned to the choir at Second Presbyterian, which put music back into my life, gave me something to do on Thursday evenings and Sunday mornings, and provided some level of sympathy from the choir members who knew about the pending divorce that brought me back into their midst. When I could I went to the Y and got the exercise I needed. I resumed my role as a member of the ACLU legal panel. I practically lived with Dr. Bell, who constantly tinkered with my medications to give me the benefit of the latest in pharmacological knowledge. Indeed, he frequently consulted his Medical School faculty colleague Dr. Manoochehr Manishadi, who was known for his talent in that aspect of psychiatry, and applied his insights to me.

Over the summer of 1994 I fled to Long Island again to be nurtured by my mother and stepfather. In the process I abandoned all hope of producing scholarship during that period. My stepfather also owned a large ancestral home in Henderson (he had been my mother's high school sweetheart prior to the upheaval of World War II) and I took Jennifer and Shirley over for an extended visit that also exposed them to Aunt Bet at an age when they were old enough to appreciate her.

I actually enjoyed my time in Henderson, finding my mother truly rallied to my assistance. Indeed, she grew quite angry at the woman who had so hurt her child.

Without a doubt, the single most important contributor to my recovery from the trauma of my divorce was the support group at Crescent Hill. It was run by its own alumni, so all there knew first-hand the pain of divorce. Moreover, they were what I often referred to as "dumpees," or those who had been cast aside by their spouses for new lovers, mid-life crises, financial woes, or any of a thousand other reasons. "Dumpers" never seemed to attend a support group, whether as they were happy to be free of their former spouses and accordingly needed no assistance, afraid of meeting their former spouse at the group, or merely aware they would not find a very receptive audience from the "dumpees" there.

Crescent Hill Divorce Recovery Support Group had been founded in 1981 by one of the true heroes I have met during my life, Jerry Smith. Jerry worked in the counseling field, and when he himself got divorced saw the need for a group like Crescent Hill and founded it. Years later it, and he, were there for me during my hour of need. Indeed, it is still going strong over thirty years later with Jerry still at the helm. I never told anyone at Crescent Hill about my illness. I never really needed to do so as most there were depressed. They thus exhibited symptoms similar in kind, if not degree, to mine.

The standard Crescent Hill Sunday night gathering would start around five. I would arrive a little before then and if Jennifer and Shirley were with me would take them to the nursery where children their age spent group time. They really enjoyed it, so for them it was a fun occasion. At the meeting, Jerry would make some opening remarks and ask anyone attending his or her first meeting to see him so he could assign the person to a small group. On occasion he would remind everyone of a basic tenet of the organization: what was said there stayed there. He also would pass the hat so those who could afford to contribute towards the cost of childcare during the meeting could do so if they wished. I always gave whether or not Jennifer and Shirley were with me as I had the money to do so when many others did not and I knew it was essential to have free childcare available to all who wished to attend meetings. Then, all would scatter to their small section of eight to ten members and a facilitator. There generally were from six to eight sections operating depending on the number attending the group. Every few months the sections would fold and the overall group would be reshuffled such that you would get a new facilitator and a new set of "supportees." Consequently, a varied Crescent Hill experience was assured.

In the section meeting each person would have time to describe what he or she was facing. Most of us found someone else who had experienced the same thing and could offer helpful insight into the issue. All at the session could offer advice or reassurance. Not infrequently, when a member faced an important, and stressful, court date someone from the section would accompany him or her for moral support. Most were angry with, or even hated, their spouses.

When I first came to group I was a basket case and little help to anyone else. As I gradually got enough support from others to be something close to my own self again I became the resident legal expert. In the process, I learned more than I ever wanted to know about the details of Kentucky divorce law about which I frequently was asked to expound. I always prefaced any response by noting I was not a licensed Kentucky attorney and inquiries should be directed to the questioner's attorney, not someone unfamiliar with all the legal and factual details of the case at issue.

I was one of the few males in attendance, as apparently "dumpers" usually tend to be husbands. This could lead to occasions of severe "man bashing," but before it went too far I always reminded everyone that we were all in the same boat and I was not the enemy, just another victim of an inhuman process.

By about 6:30 all would have had the chance to speak and get advice and comfort from the others in attendance and we would break for the week. But that was not the end of the Sunday event. Most of the group, including me as well as Jennifer and Shirley when they were with me, adjourned to a local restaurant for a communal meal and informal social gathering. There we really got to know one another, as well as get pleasure from some good food.

Everyone there enjoyed the occasion, which was the social

high point of the week for many group members. I cannot even guess how many burgers with bacon, mushrooms, and blue cheese I consumed during my four years at Crescent Hill! You can only imagine how valuable it is to be able to look forward each week to leaving your empty apartment and get support from, and enjoy a meal with, others who are in your situation and hence your friends and allies. Each week my participation with the group briefly would raise the veil of depression and despair that had enveloped me ever since Jane's departure.

I could always count on Crescent Hill because we never missed a Sunday. On holidays special gatherings were held, usually at a group member's home, which could be quite festive. Each attendee would bring food or drink so there would be plenty for all. Indeed, Crescent Hill met on every holiday during the year, including Christmas and Thanksgiving, so no one ever had to face those events alone or even only with children. I remember attending and enjoying parties for events I never really celebrated when married such as Memorial Day, Labor Day, and Independence Day. Thus, the group tried to show its members it cared about them and consequently arranged for them not to be alone at what once were "family" occasions.

For those who felt ready to go beyond the safe confines of Crescent Hill and plunge their toes back into the waters of the outside world, other social venues were available. Most Fridays a group would gather at a local watering hole where drinks and dancing were the order of the day—there I learned the intricacies of the line dance the "Electric Slide." We would go as a group and stay as one, so the women did not have to associate with strange men and yet could dance pretty much as often as they wanted. The men found themselves worn out from dancing with our female group compatriots. Times like this reminded me of Saturday evenings at Highland where I would dance and cut up with my friends and colleagues. It helps explain why I consider all support groups pretty much the same whether they are based upon marital or mental, inpatient or outpatient status.

What was I to do when I was not involved with Crescent Hill? For both work and entertainment purposes I bought a home computer (the Law School bought all faculty work computers in the late 1980s) on which I spent countless hours playing various games and surfing the Internet.

At some point after the collapse of one's marriage it becomes time to re-enter the dating scene. Considering the vulnerable emotional state of many at Crescent Hill, romance inside the group was not encouraged. Still, all involved were adults, and nothing was forbidden other than a relationship between a facilitator and a member of his or her section. I met a veterinarian my age and we dated for several months before our relationship ended like most immediately post-divorce ones, badly. Similarly, I struck up some Internet connections, but none of them went anywhere either. I would need a bit more time before I really went on with my life, romantically-speaking.

There were occasional good moments, in retrospect, over these days. When one is in the sort of crisis where I found myself, you remember the small favors others do for you. I will never forget the action of Bob and Mary Ann Stenger in November 1993. At that point, all knew about my marital collapse and ongoing divorce proceeding. They thus were aware that I was alone and far from family. Bob and Mary Ann reflected upon what sort of Thanksgiving I probably would have under these circumstances and invited me into their home to celebrate the holiday with them, their two sons, and a few others. Rather than having to endure time at the practically empty house in New Albany or a relatively joyless Crescent Hill gathering, they gave me a few hours of happiness and festivity that stuck with me for some time. They probably will never know what this meant to me.

Despite all these concerns, the central focus of my life continued to be my job. Depression may have limited what I could do, but I had to carry on as best I could. In 1994-95 I was on sabbatical in the spring semester during which I was going to write another major domestic violence article and teach as a visitor on the law faculty at the University of Leeds in Leeds, England. While in England I also planned to spend a long weekend in London and surrounding areas and take a two week tour of Scotland, Wales, and Ireland (the "Celtic fringe").

First, however, came the fall of 1994 when I finally was scheduled to use my knowledge from law school and Davis Polk & Wardwell and teach Decedents' Estates to a day and an evening section of the class, roughly 150 students in all. Had I been thinking clearly I would have been worried. It is difficult to teach Decedents' at the best of times, let alone when severely depressed, sometimes suicidal. As it was, I just thought I would muddle through what should have been one of the highlights of my academic career, the fulfillment of my dream of the last twenty years.

In August came an omen in the form of a letter from Jean advising me that my divorce from Jane was final. Whether this was a good or a bad one remained to be seen. It certainly inexorably ended an important period of my life and left me despondent just as my career required maximum effort.

I spent countless hours preparing for the Decedents' classes, barely staying ahead of the students in the process. Still, I was not really up to presenting the information in the best possible way. Indeed, I was so far gone that I have almost no memory of the semester. Students later complained that I "read from the book" in class. This was true in a way, but only because I had inscribed my encyclopedic notes there. Being new to the course, I tried to cover far too much in the semester, ultimately teaching 1,200 pages out of the casebook. I was not familiar with the nuances of particular material until after I was done covering it, and by then we had moved on to the next day's work. I therefore did a poor job of telling the two classes the matters upon which they really needed to focus. Today, by comparison, I cover less than 900 pages during a Decedents' course and regularly indicate what students are likely to encounter in practice. My reward is a much happier class, and the good teaching evaluations that accompany it.

The 1994 classes were veritable cattle calls. As I was covering the same material in both my day and evening sections I let students attend whichever they pleased on any particular day. I never knew how many students I would have in a specific period until it actually began. On Thursday nights I often would face over one hundred students, who would hit the local bars after class to celebrate the end of another week of classroom drudgery.

By the end of the semester many of the students in my two classes hated both my class and me. They absolutely excoriated me in their teaching evaluations, complaining about all I had done or tried to do. It is not uncommon for a professor to receive less than stellar reviews when he or she teaches for the first time a complex course many students wish they did not need to take in the first place. This is even truer when the professor (gasp!) violates the unwritten rule law students should never be expected to do mathematics, which is an important component of the Decedents' class. Still, my evaluations were truly awful as a consequence of the way I taught the class and an additional factor: unjustified gossip that spread about me and an alleged relationship with a student in the class. It left me devastated and in shock that only grew worse when I actually read the totally horrible things students had written about me.

The Dean made a point of insuring I knew how bad the reviews were, and promised they would weigh against me for both salary and promotion purposes over the next three years, after which they would be too old to be considered. This would have been a perfect time for me to explain the medical issues that would have mitigated matters. Given my post-divorce mental status I probably should not have been working at all, much less teaching Decedents' Estates for the first time to nearly 150 students. As always, however, I was unwilling to share this information with anyone at the Law School.

I cannot fault the Dean for his reaction to the situation, nor myself for not daring to go public even with him about my mental illness. The result was yet another example of the unfortunate impact of stigma. I burned up many hours of Dr. Bell's time trying to keep things in perspective and not spiral out of control into the intensity of a depression that would have required inpatient treatment and probable disclosure of my disease to the Dean and others at the Law School.

So what was the story behind the alleged relationship between me, age forty and newly divorced in the fall of 1994, and Kathleen Ann Murphy, then a never-married second year law student enrolled in my Decedents' class at age thirty-four? All hearkened back to my talk during orientation for the 1993 Law School entering class. I was speaking about case briefing, an important skill for new law students. Unbeknownst to me, Ms. Murphy, an incoming first year student, was checking me out, and in particular looking for a wedding ring. Since by then Jane and I had been separated for several months, as noted I recently had garnered the strength to remove my ring. As a result, she could see I apparently was unattached.

Ms. Murphy was an evening student. My Decedents' Estates class was the late class in the evening, so it ran from 7:25 until 9:05 PM. Many nights she would come to me with a question or just to chat after class. I am tall and thin and very much the WASP; Ms. Murphy is short, a little round, and Irish to the core (what would you expect of someone with a name like hers?). Hence, we were an unlikely looking pair. Gradually, I started to unload my problems on her. The more we talked, the more I got used to interacting with her. She was an excellent listener, so I felt very comfortable with her.

Other students noticed me spending time with her, and started the rumor that we were dating. This was not true, but there was nothing I could do about the situation. I was not going to let idle student gossip stop my conversations with Ms. Murphy, which I found extremely helpful. Neither would I make some sort of public declaration that there was no relationship between us. What would that have accomplished other than merely making matters worse by calling further attention to the issue? I would just let the Law School gossip mill grind away and appear to ignore it.

Often on Thursdays after class a group of students would go a bar located near the Law School for some "power drinking." They encouraged me to come along, and on occasion I accepted their invitation. I would always sit with Ms. Murphy and several of her best friends. This socializing helped boost my spirits, as well as cement the growing bond between me and the group in general and Ms. Murphy in particular. So far as I was concerned we all were social equals, as most in the group were not that much younger than I, and one was older by three or four years.

One Saturday when I had visitation with Jennifer, age six, and Shirley, age four, I took them to the large shopping mall where the Louisville Disney store is located. While we were there we ran into Ms. Murphy and her best friend from school. We chatted, and I introduced them to Jennifer and Shirley. They especially liked Ms. Murphy, something I noticed.

As the semester wound down, Ms. Murphy and I parted ways. I assumed the separation would be permanent, since I taught no other classes she could take. I wished her well, and thanked her for being such a receptive listener. Later, after I turned in my anonymously scored course grades I learned she had earned a

C+ in my class. While that was not a bad grade, I could not help thinking that it would surprise her classmates if they learned of it. Had she really had the sort of relationship with me rumored by the class gossips they undoubtedly would have expected me to have awarded her much better than that!

18

Considering the tumultuous ending to the fall semester and the impending doom of the return of the Decedents' evaluations in January, my sabbatical did not start particularly auspiciously. Still, the ability to research and write from home without having to teach or attend committee or faculty meetings at the Law School was intoxicating.

When I got the bad results, I ruminated over them for a few days of severe depression. I discussed them with Dr. Bell, endured a few sleepless nights, and then made the conscious effort to move beyond what could not be changed and instead focus on the main events of the semester and summer: writing my article and going to the British Isles to teach, travel, and rejuvenate. I did both exceedingly well. The article was among my best researched and written, as well as most important, scholarly pieces. The trip to Yorkshire; London and environs; and Scotland, Wales, and Ireland both thrilled and relaxed me. What could be better for an English history buff like me than to be in London on the fiftieth anniversary of VE Day where Queen Elizabeth the Queen Mother helped lead the ceremony? By August 1995 I was rested, reasonably happy, and ready to resume work in earnest. Indeed, I had big plans for the coming year. They started at Crescent Hill.

By now I regularly had been attending Crescent Hill sessions for two years, and had improved greatly from my mid-1993 condition of depression and devastation. In fact, in the eyes of Jerry Smith

I had progressed enough to become a facilitator and minister to the needs of the next generation of Crescent Hill attendees. I was extremely honored and flattered when Jerry approached me about the position, and of course immediately accepted his invitation. I underwent some training in how to be a good facilitator and then readied to join the ranks around the beginning of October. I would spend most of the next two years fulfilling my obligation, always trying to live up to the outstanding examples of those who had worked with me from 1993-95.

I had an even larger goal for work: I applied for promotion to the rank of full professor of law. Typically, a professor at the Law School goes up for promotion the year after tenure. I, of course, had not done so considering the more pressing matter of the separation and divorce and its impact on my delicate psyche. By mid-1995 I had written two post-tenure articles. I had partially written one prior to the vesting of tenure in July 1993. I completed most of it, however, after the initial shock of the divorce. This was the article for whose writing I gave up the summer research grant in 1993 because I knew I could not do it justice. I thought it was now appropriate to go for the promotion.

The fall semester should have gone uneventfully, or even very well, for me on account of the psychological boost of the sabbatical. This was true even though, at the request of the Dean, I then was teaching a one class overload to help meet the curricular needs of the Law School. It was short one-half of a faculty member and thus needed me to teach a third, still labor intensive first year course. Unfortunately, my health once again failed me, dragging me down in the process. This posed a particular problem attributable to my already being somewhat over-stretched by virtue of the teaching overload.

Unlike my usual pattern, on this occasion I fell prey mainly to multiple physical ailments rather than to a psychiatric one. In addition to my usual gastrointestinal problems, I unfortunately developed, simultaneously, two totally unrelated, but serious, medical problems. Each required surgical correction. One was a painful neurological condition in my left foot that was severe enough that it continues to bother me to this day. The other was an excruciating inguinal hernia in my left groin. Note that both involved my left leg between the groin and the foot.

Finally, in truth, the sheer weight of all with which I had to deal hindered my mental health as well.

I wanted to avoid interrupting my teaching schedule during an extended recovery period. To do so would greatly have inconvenienced the Law School administration, which would have had to find someone to cover for me for an unknowable amount of time in three different classes. Hence, I delayed the surgeries until the end of the semester. I did so even though I really needed immediate pain relief.

This was particularly true since I was hurting in two different places in the same leg at the same time. The discomfort had a cumulative effect that made matters much worse than they otherwise might have been. Indeed, neither surgeon could really tell me what to expect after the repairs because of the wild-card soreness multiplier I faced. And, of course, the worse the pain got the more serious the depression and resulting inability adequately to teach my classes became.

Lest I be less than candid, I also delayed the cures as I wanted to be visible around the Law School during the semester at the end of which would come my promotion vote. In any event, I scheduled both operations so I would only require one general anesthesia immediately after the promotion vote.

I was surprised and extremely disappointed when the Dean advised me that I essentially had been denied the promotion on the ground that I had insufficient publications since tenure. I had "only" written two articles since 1992, and this troubled the faculty promotion committee. It denied me when it knew I had gone through a psychologically devastating divorce during this period. It understood I only applied once I finished the major domestic violence article and thereby, in my mind at least, demonstrated a renewed focus on scholarship.

Unbeknownst to the faculty, any discrepancy—and I do not believe there was one—was due in large part to the post-divorce bipolar depression and medication side effects I had not disclosed. To complete yet another perfect storm scenario, all this happened at the same time that Jane, for whom I still carried a torch, advised me that she had gotten, or was getting ready to get (I forget which), married again. Imagine my mental status at this time! Fortunately I had Dr. Bell to monitor my illness and guard against the ever present risk of an act of suicide.

Needless to say, I was quite upset over what I considered to be unwarranted and ungrateful treatment by the Law School. If you view the situation dispassionately, the faculty was unaware of my disorder and its impact on the quantity—if not quality—of my scholarship. It did, however, know the divorce had left me seriously depressed for several years. It also knew both that I was teaching a significant overload at the request of the Dean for the convenience of the Law School (being a "team player"), and had postponed much-needed surgery to alleviate chronic severe pain in large part so as not to inconvenience the Law School ("taken one for the team," to use another colloquialism).

By virtue of the quality of my post-tenure writings and the background that underlay them, I still believe the faculty acted unjustly with its vote. I recognize that it did what it thought was right, but I viewed it as, perhaps unintentionally, kicking a loyal colleague when he was already down. And, I was down there, at least in significant part, in order to assist the Law School in a time of need. The event reminded me of the major rejections of my life such as in childhood, by the fraternity in college, by the University of Virginia Law School, and by the many law firms that declined to hire me despite my outstanding credentials. For the first time in many years I felt like an outsider, an outcast, and my old inferiority complex resurfaced. It again was me against the world, and the world was winning.

Over the years after I finally became a full professor, it somehow helped when I saw others denied promotions on several occasions. This was the case, first of all, as while I usually both disagreed with the denials and voted against them, at least I saw the same thing happen to others as occurred to me. Second, when they took place I saw colleagues on the promotion committee struggle with deciding how to vote such that it clearly was not a matter taken lightly. Like most severe, but non-fatal wounds, mine eventually healed, but it took many years to do so.

In the fall of 1995, three things left me in a horrendous state of mind when I underwent the double surgeries. These included being aware how the faculty treated my promotion request under all the circumstances that were known to it, Jane's marital news, and the mental health matters stigma prevented me from disclosing but nevertheless colored my thinking. Indeed, I was depressed, devastated, and extremely angry at the faculty, the Law School, and the world at large all at the same time. My bipolar tendency to ruminate over problems went into overdrive! This was one of the rare occasions in my life when I have wondered both whether there really is, in fact, some higher being above us all and if I somehow had offended or angered that entity such that it had dumped travails akin to those of Job upon me.

One additional problem, one of my own making, had hindered me in the fall semester. I had hired a second year student to act as my student research assistant and help me with the various duties I had to perform. This semester she was to aid me with the extra things I had to do as a consequence of the teaching overload. In addition, she was to work with me in finalizing the publication details for the domestic violence article I had written during my sabbatical and the summer thereafter. Unfortunately, she proved to be more of a hindrance than a help for me. She always had some reason why she could not do what I asked when I requested it. This was, most notably, her obligations as a member of the law review.

Although I never told the student I was frustrated and unhappy over her behavior, I ruminated over it at some low level whenever I saw or thought about her. As chance would have it, she wandered by immediately after I learned about the denial of my promotion. She had yet another excuse why she had not done what I had asked of her. I exploded and told her I would not need her services any further. She would later remark that she could not understand why I appeared to be so angry with her. That could be attributed both to my already enraged state of mind and her behavior, which long had justified dismissal.

At this point I realized that when I returned to school after my surgery I would have no one to help me try to teach, in my severely impaired condition, the two classes I still had left to me. As I reflected upon my options, I remembered the very capable Ms. Murphy. I knew based on our conversations the previous year that she was always in dire financial straits. I also felt she both would be interested in working with me and would be the kind of research assistant I needed—someone who would go above and beyond the call of duty to assist me in any way she could. Thus, I contacted her during the brief time before my surgery and offered her the position, effective January 1. She immediately accepted, and therefore I at least knew that after the operations I would have someone on my team upon whom I could rely without hesitation.

The surgery was extremely painful and debilitating. I was fortunate that Rick had volunteered to stay with me until I could function alone. There was, however, a bigger problem to face than the pain and temporary disability. I had had several previous surgeries in the years since I went on lithium, and somehow got the idea recovery would come easier were I not on psychiatric medication. Accordingly, prior to the surgery I foolishly, and on my own, stopped taking my lithium and anti-depressants. I developed a bipolar psychosis from the anesthesia for the surgery itself and the Demerol thereafter for pain, and then I lapsed into a severe depression.

I had great difficulty grading my Torts I examinations after this, and called the Dean about it:

"Yes?"

"This is Jim Jones. I have a severe problem."

"What's that?"

"I can't finish grading my Torts exams."

"Why not"

"I can evaluate each individual paper, and have raw scores for all of them."

"Good. So what's wrong?"

"I can't decide what score deserves what grade."

"Haven't you been plotting grade curves for nearly ten years?"

"Yes," I answered, suddenly sobbing loudly, "but I just can't do it now. It's the surgery, I can't make hard choices anymore, or not now anyway."

This clearly was not what the Dean wanted to hear, an apparent collapse by a faculty member in the middle of the key grading time.

"Would it help if you had more time to finish grading?"

"I don't think so," crying even harder. "I just can't pull myself together."

"I know you just had multiple operations. Have you talked with your doctors about this?"

"No, I don't see how they could help."

"Shall I come over and work with you as you set your curve?"

"No, I'll come up with something. I'll do my best to be fair.

That's the most I can do for the time being."

With that I managed to come up with a proper grade distribution. I of course never told the Dean the real reason for my problem, the runaway bipolar depression—recall that one suffering from it has difficulty thinking, concentrating, or making decisions such as how to proceed with the grade distribution process. I am not sure what the Dean, who I doubt viewed a weeping male subordinate favorably, made of this episode, but based on later events I suspect he construed things far from the way they actually were. At least I could understand that my health crises might have left me at the mercy of my emotions. Maybe crying was a symptom of bipolar disorder and hence not something over which I need feel embarrassed?

At this point, rather than restart my medications I just felt sorry for myself and stayed depressed for some time until I finally resumed my lithium and anti-depressants and they kicked in during the winter of 1996. As noted, a large number of people who have bipolar disorder frequently suffer severe consequences when they stop taking their medicine. They do so for various reasons such as they do not like the medication's side effects, feel better and foolishly think they no longer need the drugs that maintain their sanity, cannot come up with the money for the very expensive psychiatric remedies, etc. This, however, marked the only time in over twenty-five years that I failed to take my prescribed medications. That fact answers part of the question of how I have been successful over the years despite having a severe mental illness: I can afford the drugs and I take them religiously, compliant with my doctors' orders. I only go to doctors I consider to be first rate, and I then follow their advice.

When it was time for Rick to return home, he fully stocked my larder before he left. I called Ms. Murphy and asked if she could drop Nutmeg off at the vet to board until I was able to hobble outside with her when she needed to go. Ms. Murphy was happy to do so, and it was quite simple to engineer since we shared the same vet, one of her classmates and close friends who today is one of the few attorney/veterinarians in the nation. I gave her directions to my apartment and Rick met her at the door. Together they escorted Nutmeg to her car and the two headed off for the vet. Rick commented on how nice Ms. Murphy appeared to be and how lucky I was to have her working for me. I agreed wholeheartedly. He then accepted my very sincere gratitude for all his help and headed off to the airport. I truly could not have gotten through the surgical ordeal without him.

I holed up in my apartment for some time. Eventually I concluded although I could not drive yet I now could get around the apartment complex and would love to have Nutmeg's company again. Thus, I called Ms. Murphy and asked her if she could retrieve my darling for me. She immediately did so. When she knocked on the front door, I was overjoyed. Nutmeg ran into my apartment and jumped into my waiting arms. "Thank you so much," I said to her while petting and kissing Nutmeg, who was furiously licking me in return. "You don't know what it means to me to have Nutty with me again." We chatted for a few minutes about my health and other routine matters. Then, she prepared to leave. "Do you have to go?," I asked. As I said this, I opened my arms wide. She rushed forward into my embrace.

Kathi stayed for a long time that day, and returned on a regular basis. We quickly became a monogamous couple, and I came to love her very much. I gradually for all intents and purposes forgot about Jane and shifted my attention to Kathi, who seemed to have great concern for my well-being. She would fix dinner for Jennifer and Shirley when they came for weekend visitation. Later, she helped them hand carve a pumpkin on Halloween. She also taught them to make cookies, an item they thought could only be bought in the store already prepared. Not surprisingly, they became extremely fond of her. I noted this fact.

193

I felt vaguely uncertain about the propriety of our highly
secret relationship. My concern was that someone might think
it possibly violated some unwritten University or professional
standard of conduct. I consoled myself with first, she was no
longer my student and there was no romance between us until
a year after she was in my class; second, she was over thirty-five
and as a result I was no cradle-robber; third, we never went out
in public together so we would hardly embarrass the Law School
through some indiscretion; and last, what did I care what the
people who had denied me promotion thought?

About this time, Dr. Bell retired at age eighty and I went
to his colleague Dr. Manishadi. He handled my medical needs
until he left private practice in 2000. It was a real blow to lose
an excellent psychiatrist twice within four years, but I coped as
best I could. I started seeking therapy from John Turner at the
same time I went with Dr. Manishadi, and remain under his
wonderful care today, over fifteen years later. Most who suffer
from bipolar disorder will tell you they need a good psychiatrist
to handle pharmaceutical treatment and a good therapist for
other attention. I have been blessed with both since Dr. Bell
stopped filling those capacities for me in 1996.

So now things would go better. I gradually would recover my
physical and mental health, teach BLS, finish the publications I
had in progress, and perform my other duties until the semester
came to an unsatisfying, but final, conclusion. I then could focus
on writing a new article and a planned visit on a teaching exchange
at the University of Natal-Pietermaritzburg in the Republic of
South Africa. WRONG! A series of misunderstandings and
misperceptions by the Dean turned the rest of the spring 1996
semester into a total nightmare.

After a delay attributable to my continued health problems
I resumed teaching BLS in late January 1996. I was, however,
really in no shape to do so. All that spring I was depressed and

irritable by virtue of the severe postoperative pain I endured and the gap in medication concern. The problem was exacerbated by having a disorder that produces depression and irritability when one is stressed by things like physical infirmity. I do not think either the foot or hernia repair surgeon really had focused on the difficulty of managing the exponentially magnified pain from simultaneously operating at both ends of the same leg. For example, I could not sleep on my left side as doing so irritated the main nerve in my left leg and caused severe shooting pains in it. This problem persists to this day.

I believe that at some level the Dean recognized I had legitimate pain issues, but he discounted them because he basically misperceived me. He was convinced my principal problem was that I was angry over the promotion denial. He then concluded as a consequence I was being difficult by pouting and generally being as uncooperative as possible. In fact, things were far more complicated than that. I do not deny that I was angry over the promotion denial. Despite that, my actions were driven by my poor physical and mental condition rather than a juvenile reaction to a negative career event. Had I felt I could confide in the Dean about my psychiatric disorder things might have gone differently, but I did not.

Once I turned in my Torts I grades, the first major problem involved the scoring of BLS papers. As I was handling two BLS sections that year, the overload the Dean had asked me to teach, I faced a mountain of BLS memoranda from the fall semester to grade. The task, quite frankly, overwhelmed me. That might have been the case for anyone who was struggling with the pain that was devastating me, but was even truer for one who was deeply depressed from bipolar disorder.

It did not help matters when, as is their wont, the students developed a feeding frenzy and barraged the Dean with complaints over the slow return of their fall papers. Rather than just telling my pupils that things do not always go as planned for an infinite variety of reasons and they would have to wait until their ill teacher could grade their memoranda, he chose to side with the students. When he put additional pressure on me it only made me more upset and depressed and consequently further slowed my grading.

Eventually I finished grading the papers, but by then the Dean's views apparently were set in cement. Things were so bad that when I had briefly to set the BLS papers aside in order to meet a publication deadline on the journal article I had written during my sabbatical, the Dean joined the students in saying I should not have been working on anything other than the BLS papers. He had the same reaction when I spent a few hours writing a short piece for the Louisville *Courier-Journal* newspaper about a pending domestic violence issue. When your boss castigates you for spending a brief period timely editing or writing important scholarship that is significant for both your reputation and that of the Law School you truly are in a no win situation.

Another alleged problem was my "lack of collegiality." This sprang from my membership of many years on the faculty committee that supervises students on academic probation and hears petitions for readmission from students who have been academically dismissed from school, the Reinstatement and Probation Committee. In 1996 each committee member was supposed to serve as academic advisor to a certain number of the probation students (today all are advised by the committee chair). When it was time to divide up the probation students among the committee members I said I was too sick to serve as an advisor and others would have to cover for me. True to my illness, I did this in a rather abrupt fashion. Some on the committee complained to the Dean. He may well have concluded continued anger over the promotion denial caused me to be difficult, although he never said as much.

All came to a head in May when the Dean issued his annual evaluation of my performance and announced my raise for the year. He rated me in the second of four categories, that for one whose performance overall was satisfactory but needed improvement. In so doing he criticized my Decedents' teaching in the fall of 1994, my 1995-96 BLS performance, and my "abrupt" withdrawal from the advising of probation students in spring 1996. I immediately requested he reconsider his decision on several grounds. These included both that he did not adequately consider the impact of my health concerns and that part of my problem was teaching the extra BLS section pursuant to *his* request the year before. When he finally responded over a month later, a period during which I ruminated myself into a terrible state, he declined to reconsider his decision. He discounted the lack of collegiality problem, but only after effectively condemning me for it. He stuck to his guns on the teaching issue. He found a pattern between the poor Decedents' evaluations of the fall of 1994 and the BLS ones for the year just concluded. Since I did badly with the Decedents' course when I had said nothing about any well-being issues, he reasoned BLS must have been a problem for more than health concerns.

It was a masterful handling of my complaint. It left no real basis for appeal, as my surgery was not an issue in 1994. In fact, there was a clear nexus between the two years. Both featured bipolar depression run amok, once primarily from a divorce and once from the effects of multiple surgeries. Unfortunately, I felt I could not discuss this connection with anyone at the Law School. Instead, I dropped the matter.

I could talk about this in broad terms with one person whom I trusted above all others—Kathi. When the BLS teaching evaluations were ready, I handed them to her.

"Do I want to read these?"

Kathi shuffled through them.

197

"No. Nothing good will come from that. Just file them away for future reference purposes."

"OK." I did so. I do not believe I ever looked at them, as I was already horribly depressed and had no need to exacerbate the situation.

Why do I talk so much about the merits of my teaching two BLS classes in 1995-96? I do so because the issue greatly affected me for an extended period of time. It generated great angst and significant depression that hurt me badly. Even more than that, I pursue it due to what it says about stigma. Had I not been afraid to disclose my mental illness I readily would have explained to the Dean its impact on me at both the time of the Decedents' and the BLS classes. He, usually a reasonable man, then may well have seen my problems in the two courses were connected and health-related and viewed me quite differently. Instead, I kept quiet as I was afraid of stigma and was found wanting as a result of my silence. How often do those with severe mental illnesses suffer mentally and/or financially as a result of such considerations? It is hard to say, but probably more often than one might like to think.

I left for my teaching exchange almost immediately after the rehearing denial. Although I would be gone for six weeks, Nutmeg was not inconvenienced at all as she did not have to stay with the vet. Instead, I hired Kathi to reside in my apartment and care for her. She moved in as I left for Africa. By the time I returned in August Nutmeg adored Kathi. I noticed that as well.

My own mood greatly perked up after my journey to the Republic of South Africa, Swaziland, and Zimbabwe in July-August 1996. I taught domestic violence law at the University of Natal-Pietermaritzburg in South Africa for three weeks. During that time I was entertained royally by the faculty there. I kept up with Kathi through multiple e-mail messages each day.

While in Pietermaritzburg I was particularly valuable when I helped prepare a submission to the South African government. It concerned ways to reduce domestic violence in that nation, where it long had been a problem of epidemic proportions. The piece, based on my knowledge of what is done in the United States, later was cited roughly fifteen times by the South African Law Commission in its report concerning how best to reform South Africa's Prevention of Family Violence Act of 1993. This reform was instituted, based in large part on the report, in South Africa's Domestic Violence Act of 1998.

I later wrote one article and co-authored another, both of which eventually were published in South Africa's leading law review, comparing South African law on domestic violence with that in the United States.

My legal/public policy work followed a three week tour of southern Africa, including of Cape Town and the Cape of Good Hope; Victoria Falls; the great South African game reserves; Voortrekker historic locations such as that of the 1838 Battle of Blood River; the place of the famous armored train incident of Sir Winston Churchill during the Boer War; and most of all the best known battle sites from the Zulu War of 1879, Isandlwana, Rorke's Drift, and Ulundi. The visit to the latter three places thrilled me to the core. I had been fascinated by them ever since the film *Zulu* appeared in 1964 and I then read all about them over thirty years before I actually witnessed them. The entire trip was truly the experience of a lifetime. When else was I likely to be up close and personal in the bush amidst lions, leopards, Cape buffaloes, elephants, rhinoceroses, hippopotamuses, crocodiles, giraffes, zebras, antelopes, black and green mambas, and vultures? It greatly improved my view of the world. It is hard to be depressed when in a place like that! In fact, I almost reached a manic state, spending excessive amounts on gold jewelry and African souvenirs for Jennifer, Shirley, Kathi, and most of all myself. Still, I regret nothing about that trip, and it did wonders for my mental health after the travails of the previous year. I remember it as if it were yesterday, the greatest journey of my life.

19

Upon my return from South Africa I took several days to catch up on my sleep after my twenty-plus hour trip home from Pietermaritzburg. Then, I showered my three girls with gifts. It was like Christmas in August! In particular, I bought Kathi several nice jewelry items, although none was the diamond ring she probably hoped for most of all.

There was a reason for the latter discrepancy. Much like Jane nine years before, I was having serious commitment issues. Unlike Jane, I had a reason for being gun-shy—the total emotional devastation that followed my separation and ultimate divorce from her. I had real concern whether I could survive another such episode. Kathi often reassured me that she had no intention of ever wanting to be with anyone other than me. As she put it: "Murder yes, divorce never!"

Kathi never pressured me at all. Instead, she just spent most of her time with me; was wonderful to Jennifer, Shirley, Nutmeg, and me; and waited patiently to see what, if anything, would happen. I could not have asked for anything more than that. Still, I had "doubts."

Since people with mental illness have difficulties maintaining long-term relationships (those with schizophrenia rarely marry at all), my concern was not without some justification. John Turner, Dr. Manishadi, and I went around and around this issue. Turner once told me that "the average second marriage lasts six or seven years. As a result, if you get that, all after it is gravy." I thought this was an interesting way of looking at things. I hoped if I did marry Kathi our relationship would endure until the ladle days. I ruminated over the matter seemingly for days on end. I remember thinking that if John Turner, the foremost marriage counselor in the region, "thinks marriage to Kathi is a good idea, who am I to disagree?"

Kathi and I took several overnight trips safely away from Louisville so we could be a couple out of hiding. I thoroughly enjoyed the freedom we had doing so. When I discussed the marriage issue at divorce group I got the lukewarm reaction I should have expected. Most there never expected to marry again and wondered why I would consider doing so. Still, Jerry Smith married another facilitator after being divorced for over twenty years and both seemed very happy. It was not an impossible prospect. You just needed the right partner and the right mutual feelings to give it a shot.

Kathi either really loved me or was a great actress who pretended to do so, and I had feelings for her that seemed like love. It was different than the emotion I had when I was courting Jane. This time I had a willing, caring, and nurturing target. With Jane, there had been a tracking and shooting of the prize stag aspect to my pursuit of her. I now was in a healthy adult relationship. I often said I did not know what love felt like but I was fairly certain this was it.

Now that I was reassessing my feelings for Kathi, I had to address the same issue that so bothered me with Jane: when to tell her what about my mental illness. As with Jane, I feared that Kathi might head for the hills if she learned about my psychiatric history. However, it seemed doubtful that Kathi, who very much seemed to want to be with me, would abandon me over a treatable illness. Besides, I was not convinced marriage was the right idea. Maybe an acid test for marriage to Kathi would be her reaction to my disclosure. In any event, I told Kathi about my medical history at dinner one evening in the fall of 2006. She hardly blinked, and assured me that it would give her great pleasure to spend many years helping me care for myself.

"You seem to cope with things very well. How else could you have kept this secret for so long? If you have problems, we'll deal with them. After all, I'll be with you in sickness and in health."

Following my pattern with Jane, I arranged a session with John Turner where he explained to Kathi what she could expect from me and my disorder. I wanted her to enter marriage with her eyes wide open after full disclosure. What he said did not appear to bother her at all. Meanwhile, I began talking with my attorney Jean about a prenuptial agreement, but as the fall of 1996 proceeded all remained an open issue.

On the academic front, I taught my BLS and Torts classes. Despite being cursed with the fear of public speaking that bothers so many with bipolar disorder I also spoke three times on domestic violence, including once at the Sixth Annual National Conference on Domestic Violence of the National College of District Attorneys in Atlanta. All three talks were well-received. At around this time I additionally spoke to the members of the University's Department of Psychiatry. I was very proud to appear before Drs. Bell and Manishadi as a legal expert rather in my usual role as their patient. In the scholarship arena I was working on one of my South African articles.

Even before I knew all these things were going to happen, I demonstrated the stubborn obstinacy I have exhibited on occasion and applied once again for promotion to full professor of law. I figured I would play a new game: I would apply for promotion each year, and the faculty committee members could do whatever they chose, damn them! We would see who blinked first.

As it turned out, it was a short contest. For whatever reason the committee approved my promotion, which took effect on July 1, 1997. I, a person who suffers from one of the most serious mental illnesses known, had reached the pinnacle of my profession. That is a height that is sufficiently lofty that few reach it, healthy or not.

Again exhibiting some political confusion, I rejoined the ACLU Legal Panel and was a proud, card-carrying member of the ACLU. How someone could be a confirmed Republican and ACLU member was a little difficult to reconcile, but it again showed my libertarian tendencies. As I grew older and saw more of the world I became more tolerant of those who were different. Perhaps coping with your own secret makes you empathize with others with issues of their own. In any event, a political transformation was slowly, but inexorably, occurring.

Back to my personal life, I realized that I could not stay on the fence regarding Kathi forever. She was graduating in May 1997 and undoubtedly would not wait indefinitely for me to commit to her. As I thought about it, I came up with the following: (1) I loved Kathi. (2) Jennifer and Shirley loved Kathi. (3) Nutmeg adored Kathi. (4) Kathi appeared to love Jennifer, Shirley, Nutmeg, and me. (5) John Turner thought marriage was a good idea. (6) Jean thought it was OK so long as we had a good pre-nup. With all that, it seemed to be a no-brainer. To sum it up, when I asked Jennifer and Shirley how they would feel about me marrying Kathi they replied, practically in unison, "Cool!" So, cool it was.

In November 1996 I suggested that we go to Indianapolis for a weekend where we could go out in public together. Kathi immediately agreed. I booked us a room in one of the finest hotels there and made a dinner reservation at the best restaurant in town. I was trying to keep my intentions secret, but I probably gave them away when Kathi initially suggested we go on December 13 and I instantaneously said "No! I never do anything important on the thirteenth!" I guess I am not very good at keeping on my poker face.

When we arrived in Indianapolis we checked into the lovely and romantic hotel and did some sightseeing. Then, it was time for dinner. We dressed up for the occasion and walked a few blocks over to the restaurant. The food was delicious, as everyone said it would be. At the end of the main course the waitress brought us each a glass of sparkling wine as I secretly had arranged for her to do. I then started to talk.

"Kathi, you've come to mean a lot to me. Indeed, I realize that I love you very much. You've become an incredibly important part of my life, as well as the lives of Jennifer and Shirley. I'd like to make our relationship a permanent one."

At this point, I dropped to one knee and retrieved from my coat pocket the small jewelry box I had secreted there.

"Kathi," I said tenderly and emotionally, "Will you marry me?"

As I did this I handed her the three-quarter carat diamond engagement ring that was in the jewelry box.

Kathi glowed as she said immediately "Yes, I'd love to marry you."

And that was that. We embraced, kissed, and enjoyed our wine and an outstanding dessert (I can arrange things well when I really try to do so). As Kathi later noted, several elderly women sat at a nearby table. As I acted, they said "Oh look, I think he's gonna." Then, when I dropped to one knee they said "He's gonna!" When I pulled out the ring, they said "There he goes!" Glad to provide entertainment to the others in the restaurant.

After dessert we headed back to the hotel to call our friends and relatives with the happy news.

As we walked, Kathi recognized the voice of one of my colleagues on the Law School faculty: "Isn't that David Leibson?"

I listened and said: "Dammit, it is!"

We then scurried down a side street to avoid being seen. It turned out that U. of L. was playing Indiana University's basketball team in the Indianapolis domed stadium that evening.

"We drive two and a half hours to be able to be out in public and this happens!," I complained.

Kathi said, hopefully, "No harm, no foul."

I have never known whether or not Leibson saw us.

Once in the room, we took turns calling people. My mother actually sounded happy for me. Sadly, my stepfather, who would have thought the world of Kathi, had died a few months before so she never got to meet him. In view of the relative sizes of the Jones and Murphy clans, Kathi was on the phone much longer than I was.

When I looked back on this event, I realized all that had happened since 1993. Then, I was depressed, devastated, and even suicidal over the end of my marriage to Jane. Now, I was overjoyed as I looked forward to my life with Kathi. Amazing the change a few years can bring! Fourteen years later, I am as happy with Kathi as one could ever wish to be. She is my friend, lover, confidante, and partner in all things for life. I have every hope I will be married to her until I die. From her perspective, I am fine mentally almost all the time. When I get grumpy she just ignores me unless I take matters too far. Then, she squelches me quite effectively. And, as she says, "You're my 401(Jim) plan—if I die first I don't need a retirement plan, and if you go first everything goes to me." She has a good sense of humor (and of reality)!

Thank goodness she decided to go to law school at U. of L.! The fates knew what they were doing when they saw me get a job in Louisville.

Mother, of course, wanted to meet Kathi. We promised to visit her during spring vacation. I told Mother Kathi was a paralegal so we could fly under the radar as much as possible. That was true, as she had a degree as one and worked in that capacity. I did "forget" to mention that she was also a law student who would graduate shortly. I told Rick about the pending nuptials and asked him to be my best man again. He agreed to do so and asked no other questions although he knew perfectly well who Kathi was.

Despite my usual "silence is golden" policy, we decided to let a few of my colleagues in on the news, most notably the Stengers, Eades, and Renders. None seemed bothered in the least and all kept our secret.

Somewhere about this time I learned something interesting: back in 1993 when I spoke at orientation, Kathi called her best friend that evening and said "I've just seen the man I'm going to marry." In other words, I had been in the cross-hairs all this time and never knew it. How Kathi could conclude that based on my talk escapes me. Anyway, they say the man is always the last to know! Also, I later discovered Kathi had picked out her wedding dress long before I proposed to her. I guess confidence is a good thing, but I wish I were a little less transparent (it is unsettling when your wife knows your every thought faster than you do yourself).

Needless to say, my mental status was good for most of the fall of 1996 and spring of 1997. After all, I had had a wonderful trip to Africa, been promoted at long last, and was getting married soon. I still occasionally grew depressed, but easily could overcome the disease considering all the good things that were happening.

There was one big manic incident in the spring. I was, as then was usual, the faculty advisor for the BLS class mock appellate oral argument session in which all BLS students in the Law School participate. For many of them, it is their only law school experience at speaking in court. I always found that event to be stressful, as it involves 150 or so first year students, forty or fifty attorneys who volunteer to act as "judges," and the Law School Moot Court Board that handles most of the details.

In 1997 I was working with a student Moot Court Board officer who was not interested in the insight I could offer. Instead, that student decided to reinvent the wheel. Some of that student's ideas did not work out well. One, in particular, proved highly problematic. Rather than sending copies of the briefs the students had written to all the attorneys who were hearing their arguments (in other words, send copies of student A's brief to each of the three attorneys who would judge A's argument), as usually was done, the student sent out only some of the briefs. I learned this when some of the attorney "judges" complained that they were hearing arguments of students whose briefs they had not been sent, and thus they felt unprepared to hear the arguments.

I searched out the moot court officer. "Hey, some of the judges say they didn't get copies of all the briefs for the arguments they're hearing. What happened?"

"Oh, I decided only to send out a sampling of the briefs since I figured the attorney judges wouldn't have time to read all of them."

"You only sent out some of the briefs."

"That's right, I already said that."

"You decided, on your own, that you'd change the way things have always been done and mail out only some of the briefs."

"Yes. Again, I already said that."

As I pondered this answer, the situation bothered me greatly for several reasons. First, I had angry volunteer judges who always made a point assiduously to read the briefs for all the arguments they were going to judge. Second, and more importantly, like the other BLS teachers who depended on me to insure the Moot Court Board handled things properly I had required the students to provide enough copies of their bound briefs so that each judge would get a copy. I now faced the prospect of having students who had paid some of their scarce funds to have bound briefs provided to all their judges possibly discover that some of those judges would never see the briefs because of the unilateral action of the "creative" moot court officer. As a result, I was, perhaps predictably, not particularly happy with the moot court officer.

208

Faced with this situation I could have reacted calmly, mollified the judges and students, and muddled through as best I could. I was, after all, an advisor rather than the one "officially" in command of the event. However, I grew uncontrollably, and manically, angry. I started to shout at, and jab my finger in the direction of, the moot court officer.

"You did *WHAT*??!! What possessed you? How could you do something like that without consulting me first? Just who do you think you are to pull a stunt like this?"

A junior colleague with whom I had worked for several years and who was also teaching BLS tried to intervene and calm me down: "Now don't yell at her over this."

"I'll yell at her if I want to yell at her. She deserves to be yelled at. And besides, what business is it of yours? I'm in charge of this fiasco, and you're just along to watch the show. So mind your own business and get out of my face!"

I was so outraged and out of control that in the heat of the moment I could not even remember the name of this colleague, with whom I was not on very good terms at the outset. Instead, after some sputtering I referred to her with a generic female title ("lady" or "madam" or "Ms." or the like—I was so enraged and irrational that I really cannot recall what I said). The faculty member later complained to the Dean that I had acted in a sexist way by not using her name. It may have appeared that way to her, although at that point I would have reacted the same to anyone, male or female, who tried to intervene in an effort to blunt my tirade.

Eventually I apologized to the judges who did not get the briefs, making up some bogus excuse about a mix-up in the mailing process, and promised them it would not happen next year. I also prayed the first year students never learned what had happened and demanded the money they spent on the unused copies back. I hoped all was over at that point. No such luck.

The junior colleague complained to the Dean. First, she said that I had yelled excessively at the moot court officer. Second, and undoubtedly more significantly to her, she claimed I had been rude and used sexist language against her.

I do not think the Dean was totally unsympathetic with my predicament. Still, he could not just ignore the situation after the colleague complained. The Dean insisted that I apologize for my actions in writing to both the junior colleague and the moot court officer. I of course did not explain to the Dean why I had reacted in this fashion to this stressful situation. Yet again, even though I now was a tenured full professor I was afraid of being stigmatized by students and faculty alike if my secret came out. Hence, I just wrote the letters and moved on, raging inwardly the whole time.

I did derive some ultimate benefit from the moot court problem. First, I immediately asked the Dean to relieve me from supervising the BLS oral arguments since it was clear the Moot Court Board was not interested in working with me. He granted my request. Much better, I pointed out to the Dean that I had been teaching legal writing to first year students since 1985 when I was a Bigelow. I then respectfully requested to be allowed to teach other things in the curriculum. The Dean agreed to that as well. As a result, I started teaching Decedents' Estates, Torts I and II, and a written advocacy seminar (an advanced, upper-class version of BLS) as my regular course load. Since 1997, I have only taught BLS once when a colleague was on sabbatical. I am no longer considered part of the BLS faculty.

After the oral arguments were completed I graded my BLS briefs, finished Torts II, and prepared for Kathi's graduation. All her relatives were very proud of her as she was the first member of her immediate family to finish college, much less professional school. I may have been even prouder, as I knew from personal experience what she had accomplished. Indeed, I had done it at age twenty-four rather than thirty-seven and had a father who paid for it all rather than having to make it on student loans and meager salaries from various jobs.

Kathi's father rented a suite at a local hotel for a party to celebrate the event. Prior to the actual ceremony we got some pictures of Kathi and me together in our respective academic gowns and hoods—quite the memorable shots! I do not remember who spoke at the ceremony but recall being incredibly proud when Kathi walked across the stage and held up her diploma in triumph to the cheers of her family and friends. She had done it after four long years of working forty hours and going to school four nights a week. The party was lovely and several of my colleagues, including Ed Render, made an appearance. At this point, depression was the furthest thing from my mind!

After graduation, I told Kathi to vacate her apartment and move in with me. There was no sense in wasting money on rent for two different places. I also advised her to give up her paralegal/law clerk job until mid-August. She was going on my payroll so she could concentrate on studying for the bar exam while spending her spare time planning a wedding. I was still working as a facilitator at Crescent Hill but gave my notice effective early August; I did not feel it appropriate for me to counsel the sad individuals who were in the process of a divorce when I was a happy newlywed.

I worked on various wedding details while Kathi studied. I chose music, addressed invitations, wrote our vows, and selected the place for the ceremony. Since neither Kathi nor I had any strong religious connections (I had quit the choir at Second Presbyterian for the last time several years before) we decided the proper forum was Crescent Hill Baptist Church, the home of the support group that had so helped me over the prior four years. One of Kathi's classmates was a non-practicing Baptist minister and he agreed to perform the service, so all was set in that regard. Ironic that I, who was raised in the Presbyterian Church and educated in a school run by the Episcopal Church, have been married twice in the Baptist Church.

Jennifer and Shirley were the flower girls. Both Mother and Aunt Bet were able to attend. I was especially glad Aunt Bet could be there, and she became very fond of Kathi in the coming years. Mother planned an elegant rehearsal dinner at a local country club that had a reciprocal arrangement with one of hers in Jacksonville. Everything was far different than when I married Jane. It was planned well in advance and there was no question that all wanted the marriage to happen. I did insist on a pre-nup (I was not going to be burned twice) that Jean prepared and Kathi signed after being advised by a lawyer and friend who worked with her boss.

Finally the end of July rolled around. Kathi headed off for the two day bar exam endurance test while I waited nervously. When Kathi returned I took her out for a celebratory dinner and heard her express her certainty that she had failed the exam. I told her time would tell and to get ready for the wedding. I am proud to report that in July 1997, when Kentucky saw its worst bar passage rate in memory, Kathi was, as she later put it, one of "the few and the grateful" who passed the first time she took the test.

The wedding was beautiful, and the next day we flew off to the cool place (I hate hot weather) upon which we had agreed for our honeymoon, Anchorage, Alaska. We embarked there on an unforgettable one week cruise to Vancouver, Canada. Following the pattern I had set in South Africa, we bought jewelry items at practically every stop and generally had a fantastic time. At the end of the cruise we flew back to Louisville. Kathi resumed her job pending the bar results and I started my twelfth year at the Law School. We decided to stay in my apartment for the time being.

Interestingly enough, now I assumed the role of Jane and

started having doubts whether the marriage was a good idea. Kathi was at least initially unaware that I was ruminating over the matter with John Turner and requiring extra medication from Dr. Manishadi to help deal with my distress. Eventually I grew louder over my concerns, making something of a fool of myself in the process. Turner repeatedly counseled restraint, and gradually I came around to giving the marriage a chance to succeed. At this point, I am very glad that I did so.

From her side, I am proud to report that Kathi has never expressed any regret at having married me. This is true despite the notoriously poor marital success rate of those who suffer from my disease. We have stayed together despite the travails of the coming years.

20

Kathi and I bought a house in Clarksville in 1999 near where Nanny lived. It was good to get all our things out of storage and be in a place with plenty of room for the two of us. My health held up reasonably well despite some early issues ranging from double cataract surgery to a few bipolar flare-ups.

At around the time we moved to Indiana Kathi and I discovered a history-linked activity we pursued fervently for five years and occasionally thereafter. One of the attorneys with whom Kathi practiced was the captain in command of a Civil War re-enacting unit. He invited me along to an event at a Union fort just south of Louisville and I was immediately captivated by the hobby. I spent considerable funds purchasing uniforms, leather goods, and firearms I used as either a Union or Confederate soldier. My attire depended on the need of the particular event and the unit with which I was serving. At one point I belonged to three regiments, two Union and one Confederate. As I portrayed both officers and enlisted men I had a full complement of handguns, swords, bayonets, and one rifled Enfield musket. I even had an original 1866 sterling silver key wind pocket watch that still keeps perfect time and Civil War-era pairs of binoculars and spectacles. Kathi had appropriate garb also and we traveled all over Kentucky, Indiana, Ohio, and Tennessee attending events. We even got outfits for Jennifer and Shirley and took them to engagements. These included the period balls that were held on Saturday nights to the strains of Civil War music played by authentic musicians.

215

Eventually we took matters to a higher level when we realized I am a near double for Confederate General Braxton Bragg, commander of most Confederate troops west of the Appalachians from mid-1862 until late 1863. I grew an appropriate beard and had a uniform exactly like that worn by Bragg hand-tailored. I then developed a talk as General Bragg that I gave throughout the region. Some of my programs were before large groups of Civil War enthusiasts who accorded me extremely warm receptions, including lots of loud applause. Bragg had led the unsuccessful 1862 Confederate invasion of Kentucky, and I became the unofficial Bragg for the Commonwealth. I spoke every year at the reenactment of the climactic Battle of Perryville. I collected various Bragg memorabilia, including an authentic Bragg autograph, that I maintained in a Bragg mini-museum that traveled with me. This was another illustration how far I had come from my early fear of public speaking. Now I was appearing before large groups and performing in first person much like actor Hal Holbrook does as Mark Twain. Most significantly, I was even one of the main characters in a film about the 1863 Battle of Chickamauga. Even though it was a direct to VHS effort, I had acted in a real movie!

As noted, in 2000 Dr. Manishadi left the University. Fortunately, he handed me over to the elegant and extremely well-qualified hands of his colleague Dr. Lounette Humphrey. Dr. Humphrey took excellent care of me until late 2002. Then, as noted, the psychiatrist wife of one of my junior colleagues on the Law School faculty joined the University's psychiatric group. Exhibiting the paranoia of many with my condition, I was concerned lest somehow word about my illness might reach the Law School. Accordingly, I asked Dr. Humphrey to refer me to another psychiatrist after sixteen and one-half years with the same group. I expressed some irritation to Dr. Humphrey over what had occurred.

"Why didn't you warn me?"

"Warn you what?"

"Warn me that Dr. Janet Wood has come to work here. I think I spotted her before she saw me. I've been hiding behind a magazine in the waiting room praying she didn't see me before you fetched me. That's why I sprinted into your office and closed the door behind you."

"What's wrong with Dr. Wood?"

"She's married to one of the assistant professors at the Law School, remember? I told you a long time ago I never wanted to be exposed to her."

"Now I recall. I'm sorry. Frankly, the whole thing slipped my mind. I'm sure she'd never say anything to her husband, as that would be a gross breach of psychiatrist-patient confidentiality."

"You may be sure, but you aren't the one who's kept his mental status a secret from those at the Law School for over sixteen years. I don't like running risks. One little slip will do it."

"Well, let's go ahead with our session today. Later I'll speak with her without giving anything away and see if she saw you. You think how you want to handle things from here on."

"OK, fine. Meanwhile, when we're done today, please run interference to make sure she doesn't see me on the way out."

Later that day Dr. Humphrey called me.

"I spoke with Dr. Wood. She saw nothing, and frankly seemed hurt that I thought she'd have said anything if she had."

"You didn't, I did."

"What do you want to do?"

"I don't know. I have to think about it. For now, keep me on the book for my next appointment with you."

"Fine."

I went home, pondered the matter, and discussed it with Kathi. Then, I wrote Dr. Humphrey a letter: "Upon reflection, I have concluded that the present situation makes it impossible

217

for us to continue working together. I cannot feel uncomfortable every time I visit my psychiatrist because of the near certainty I will encounter Dr. Wood. Therefore, I would appreciate your immediately sending me referrals to doctors who have offices elsewhere and otherwise are not affiliated with University Psychiatric Services and Dr. Janet Wood. I need the referrals quickly so I can make an appointment with my new doctor, considering the inherent delay in getting new appointments, so there is no interruption in care. I will hold University Psychiatric Services responsible for any present or future breach of my right to privacy. Needless to say, I am not happy over this overall course of developments. I have been a faithful patient of your group for sixteen and one-half years, and feel that I have been driven away by circumstances completely beyond my control. However, they are also effectively beyond your control, so at this point we need to move forward and work together to insure continuity of my care and the confidentiality of my situation."

A few days later I received a handwritten letter from Dr. Humphrey: "I am very sorry that you will no longer be my patient because I always enjoyed seeing you. However, I recognize that being anxious every time you come to the office is not in your best interest. My recommendations for referrals are [the following]. I will prescribe for you until your new psychiatrist takes over. Again, my regrets that you had to leave my practice."

Dr. Humphrey referred me to, among others, Dr. Deborah Quinton, an excellent and extraordinarily dedicated psychiatrist in private practice in New Albany whom I chose to consult and who remains my doctor today. As I quickly established, I finally am older (by a few years) than my psychiatrist!

Nutmeg continued to be extraordinarily dear to me even after my marriage to Kathi. Indeed, I viewed her as at least equal to Sue-Sue, if not an even better friend. As I saw it, Nutmeg pretty much "single-pawedly" got me through at least two years of sheer hell during and after the divorce process before I found Kathi. Moreover, she was there for me even after that time, a constant friend and companion. As she grayed and developed back problems as she grew older (she was nearly ten) I nursed her desperately, paying whatever it took to keep her alive and well. Indeed, her vet, only half-jokingly, once said he was afraid if anything happened to Nutmeg he would not graduate from the Law School. The faculty has to vote to approve each graduate and he purportedly feared I would blackball him in retaliation for her death. Nutmeg shared my bed even when I was recovering from the 1995 surgery and it probably was not sterile to have her there. After Kathi and I were married Nutty slept with us, and when Kathi's loud snoring and early work hours led us to have her sleep in a separate bedroom Nutmeg stayed with me. I talked incessantly about Nutmeg when teaching class, using her as an example whenever an issue about a pet arose. Gradually she became quite famous around the Law School. Like Sue-Sue, she occasionally bore the burden of my manic rages, but generally she got total love and devotion. I would say she was spoiled and pampered, but she deserved all the good things she got.

Once I became Dr. Quinton's patient all rocked along reasonably well until 2003. At that point, disaster struck twice during the same year. I recovered reasonably successfully from the first occurrence, but the second threw me for a real loop.

The first issue was one of the normal, but temporarily overwhelming, events of life. The previous summer Aunt Bet learned she had tongue cancer. She needed major surgery, removal of most of her tongue, to resolve the problem. Since it was such a major operation she was having it at Duke Hospital, about sixty miles from Henderson. As I knew she needed help getting through this ordeal I told her I would come over for the surgery. I would stay in her house in Henderson and drive over to Duke in Durham every day. She herself had arranged to stay in a nursing home in Henderson for a time after the surgery until she was able to be on her own again.

It was really awful to see what Aunt Bet went through. The surgery was incredibly hard on her, and she was still in the hospital when I had to head home two weeks later. Gradually she regained her ability to speak, and I called regularly to keep track of her health. She did very well in the nursing home. Indeed, she grew to like having others take care of her, as she had been on her own for much of her life. One weekend Kathi and I surprised her by driving over to Henderson to visit her. It was a thrill to see her cry for joy when she saw us.

While we were there we took her home for a few hours. She really enjoyed seeing all her things again. She planned to move back into her house once she was well enough to do so. Unfortunately, that was not to be.

For most of my adult life I had spoken by telephone with Aunt Bet several times each month, if not weekly. It was harder to call her when she was in the nursing home, but we still spoke regularly. Then, early in 2003 I got the dreaded message that she was very ill and in the hospital. She had developed a urinary tract infection, and then sepsis set in. A cousin on the scene advised me that the doctor said she would not last long and that she kept repeating my name as if she were trying to hold on for me to arrive.

"Tell her she's always done everything for everyone else, and now to do what's best for her. Kathi and I are with her, we love her, and she doesn't have to wait for us."

Thirty minutes later the cousin called back and said Aunt Bet, a devout Baptist for all her eighty-nine years, had gone home.

Kathi and I drove to Henderson immediately. The relatives there had had Aunt Bet cremated, and her remains were in a lovely brass-colored container shaped like a box with dogwood flowers all around it. As Aunt Bet was a great gardener and adored flowers, I thought it a particularly appropriate selection. After the memorial service, we went out to the cemetery plot and saw her interred near her parents and my father.

Rick was unable to attend the funeral as he had been suffering from lung cancer for over a year. We should have been co-executors of Aunt Bet's estate, but his poor health led me, the Decedents' Estates professor, to agree to be sole executor. I waived the executor's fee to which I was entitled out of the estate assets in gratitude to Rick for nursing me after my 1995 surgery. This whole situation was very hard for me. Some of what I encountered was a normal grieving process, but I also saw my level of depression, and thus my overall mental status, worsen significantly. When all was over, I somehow pulled myself back together. Aunt Bet, whom I always had loved so much, had left me enough money to purchase the Toyota Camry I still drive today—I gave Kathi the 2001 Camry I then was using—and to pay off the mortgage on our house. Pictures of Aunt Bet are scattered throughout our home; it is a living memorial to someone I dearly loved and never will forget.

The second problem of 2003 was even more of a crisis than Aunt Bet's unwanted, but not really untimely, demise. In the fall a routine blood test showed that over the last few years I had experienced a gradual increase in the calcium level in my body. After a series of tests my primary care physician and I learned I suffered from hypercalcemia, an excessive amount of calcium in my blood. That can, among other things, lead to osteoporosis, severe digestive tract disorders (it exacerbated my already compromised digestive system), kidney stones, irritability, depression, inability to concentrate, and even death. Hardly what someone who already dealt with the symptoms of bipolar disorder needed! It was created by hyperparathyroidism, an excess of hormone from one or more of my four parathyroid glands, which are part of the body's endocrine system. The parathyroids have nothing to do with the thyroid gland other than being scattered around the neck near it; they secrete the parathyroid hormone that governs the calcium levels in the body. In order to repair the difficulty one must undergo a parathyroidectomy, a fairly involved type of neck surgery, to remove the malfunctioning gland or glands. Usually the source is a growth on one gland, but on occasion one can have multiple defective ones.

I now decided to retire as General Bragg. I did not need to be out in the heat in a wool uniform under the circumstances. I shaved my beard and became merely a law professor rather than a commanding general once again.

As soon as Dr. Quinton heard about the problem she, who is as much of a medication expert as Dr. Manishadi, noted that multiple parathyroid failure is a rare side effect of long-term lithium ingestion. Neither the endocrinologist nor the head and neck surgeon on my case were really familiar with this fact, and each was skeptical that it was the source of my problem. In any event, as 2003 came to a close I faced the prospect of delicate surgery in the area around my vocal cords early in 2004. If it cost me my voice, a potential complication, it would leave me at a real career disadvantage since it would be hard to teach law classes if I could not talk.

Before 2003 ended, however, I faced a different type of challenge. Earlier in the year Kathi and I, who enjoy going on cruises, thought it might be fun to take Jennifer and Shirley on a December one to the Caribbean. Unfortunately, their school schedule only allowed them to go during Christmas week. As we knew they never would agree to leave their mother alone at that time the idea seemed to be dead in the water. Then, Jane suggested that she accompany us on the trip and even volunteered to pay for Jennifer and Shirley to go. This created the unusual prospect of taking a vacation with both my current and ex-wife.

Kathi and I discussed the matter with both each other and

Dr. Quinton and John Turner. We reflected on the generally positive relationship the three of us have with one another. For example, when Jane's second husband died I sat with her in the church at the funeral and consoled her such that the minister thought I was a brother or other close relative. Moreover, when her father died I attended the visitation at the funeral home as well as the funeral and held an umbrella over her at the cemetery to keep her dry while she headed under cover during a torrential rainstorm. We all decided it would be desirable for Jennifer and Shirley to see the three of us on good terms with one another close up. In addition, I did not mind saving several thousand dollars of trip expenses. Hence, Jennifer, Shirley, and Jane shared one cabin while Kathi and I were ensconced a safe distance (two decks above them) away. We all five did some activities together, while at other times the girls would go off with either Jane or Kathi and me. Overall, they got to swim with dolphins, scuba dive, helmet dive, snorkel, and generally have a great time. Thank goodness a thunderstorm canceled the parasailing!

Every night the five of us had dinner together in the main dining room, where the waiter and assistant waiter treated the girls like queens. Indeed, Jennifer did not like being treated like this as she thought it was wrong for people to wait on her. Our budding egalitarian maintained this opinion even after we explained the wait-staff made their money from tips, and thus wanted to make you happy with their service.

On the last night of the cruise, the waiter, who was from an eastern European nation, pointed at the five of us and said:

"What is relationship?"

Jane answered "First wife, second wife, children with first wife."

That pretty much said it all. The waiter looked both a bit surprised and perplexed.

Soon after our return home I learned the surgery would be necessary. When it was performed in January 2004 it disclosed that the disorder was in fact caused by long-term ingestion of lithium that had destroyed three of my four parathyroid glands. Accordingly, I could no longer take the old "gold standard" friend that had handled my disease since 1983 lest I risk losing my remaining parathyroid gland and having a system whose calcium level would run amok. Because of this illness I had to resign from a university committee on which I had served for about seventeen years, chairing it for most of that time. The surgeon wanted me to take large doses of calcium orally to replenish that which the hyperparathyroidism had leached from my bones, but it severely upset my stomach. Instead, I had to have intravenous infusions of calcium until everything was where it should be.

One incidental, but significant, side effect of the surgery was that it permanently narrowed my esophagus. As a result, objects I once could swallow like large pills, pieces of prime rib or steak, and so on periodically get stuck in my throat. Then, I have the frightening experience of having to move the obstruction past the partially blocked area so I can swallow safely once again. This can be very embarrassing when it occurs in public.

Once again, I wanted my medical problems to affect my students as little as possible. Consequently, I only took ten days off for the surgery. As things turned out, I might have been wise to have spent more time recovering.

Dr. Quinton was optimistic that she could manage my bipolar condition without lithium. Her hope proved ill-founded.

After the surgery Dr. Quinton immediately started to wean me off lithium and onto an anti-seizure drug also used for bipolar disorder when lithium is not available as a mood stabilizer. Unfortunately, it is very common for one rapidly taken off lithium to suffer very severe adverse effects. Before I could build up to a therapeutic dose of the new medication I had a full-blown manic episode three days before Law School graduation in early May that was attributable to severe stress and sleeplessness. I imagined, among other things, that a bus on the interstate as I was driving home and a tree in our back yard as I was attempting to mow the grass both tried to attack me. Things got so bad that I started screaming at Kathi and throwing things around the room until she stepped outside. Never a smart thing for a husband to do! At some level I recognized that things were badly wrong, and I called John Turner at home for his guidance.

"Mr. Turner, I think I'm really manic or something."

"Why do you say that?"

"Well, I think a bus and a tree attempted to hit me. Then, I got really upset at Kathi. I screamed at her and starting hurling stuff in the kitchen. She went outside to get away from me."

"When did all this happen?"

"She just went out in the yard a few minutes ago. I thought I should call you."

"Good idea. I want you to take the cordless phone outside right now and ask Kathi to come and talk with me. Then, I want you to leave the phone for her and go take a nice long hot shower. Someone will call you back shortly."

"Alright."

I did what he said, and saw Kathi coming to the phone as I headed back inside. Then, I showered, singing Mozart opera arias in their original Italian at the top of my voice as I did so— once again, in a time of crisis I turned to music. After a while I finished and dried off. Just then the telephone rang and when I answered (or Kathi got me, I cannot recall which), Dr. Quinton was on the line.

"Hello James [Dr. Quinton was very formal when addressing me], this is Dr. Quinton." She spoke extremely calmly and soothingly, but authoritatively and firmly.

"Hello Dr. Quinton, how're you?," I said somewhat giddily, slightly slurring my words.

"I'm fine, how're you?"

"Oh, I've been better. I really don't feel very well." Just then I started to cry.

"You sound like you're having a hard time. John Turner called me and said it's been a rough day for you."

"Yes," I got out between sobs, "a tree and a bus attacked me and I yelled at Kathi and flung things all about."

"That doesn't sound very good."

"No, I don't think so." Suddenly everything seemed funny, and I started to giggle. "I've been singing Mozart in the shower!"

"Really?"

"Yes, you wanna hear?"

"No, that won't be necessary."

"But I sing really well."

At this point I clearly was ultradian rapid cycling. That is a condition where the mood of a person with bipolar disorder swings from mania to depression and back very quickly, making the affect vacillate wildly in the process.

"I'm sure you do. Do you think you're safe to stay at home with Kathi tonight?"

"You mean will I try to hurt myself or Kathi?"

"That's right."

"No, I don't think so."

"Do you promise?"

"Yeah, I guess so."

"OK, I trust you. I'm going to call in a prescription for some medicine I think will make you feel better. I'll have Kathi pick it up for you to take."

"What kind of medicine?"

"Don't worry about that right now, just promise me that you'll swallow it. It'll probably make you go to sleep."

"Good, I need some sleep as I'm very tired. Can I go with Kathi to Walgreens?"

"Sure, if you'd like and she agrees. Then, tomorrow morning

I want you to call my office when you get up and let me know how you're doing."

"OK, I'll do that."

"Good. Now, let me talk to Kathi."

I sat patiently while Dr. Quinton conferred with Kathi. Then, we had dinner while the prescription for something called Risperdal was filled. After dinner we picked it up, I took the proper dose, and almost immediately passed out dead asleep.

The next morning I took the Risperdal, which I later learned is classified as an atypical antipsychotic medication used for schizophrenia and acute mania. I then called Dr. Quinton's office. When I was connected with her I complained "I don't like Risperdal. It makes me feel really spacey, and it's hard for me to stand up."

"Will you try taking it today and see how you do? If you can't, you may have to go into the hospital for a while."

"The hospital? I can't go into the hospital, I have to go to graduation Saturday and teach summer school starting on Monday."

"Well, we'll have to see whether you're well enough to do those things. Right now, promise to take your Risperdal and have Kathi call me in the morning, or sooner if you run into problems."

It is hard to describe how it feels to take an antipsychotic for the first time. You are extremely sedated, and often somewhat dizzy. You move very slowly, often shuffling your feet. You try to work your brain, but thoughts move very slowly and erratically. It is probably a cross between how a large animal like a rhinoceros feels when shot with a tranquillizer dart and how a person reacts to being pole axed. Or, it is like being a mindless zombie in a movie like *Night of the Living Dead* except that you do not eat human flesh.

By the next day I was almost incoherent and grew extremely upset. Kathi called Dr. Quinton: "I'm really worried about Jim.

He says he won't take the Risperdal because it makes him feel strange and he has to be ready for graduation. Then he mumbles about hurting, or killing, himself."

"Put him on."

Kathi brought me the telephone.

"James, Kathi says she's concerned that you might try to harm yourself. Are you thinking about doing that?"

"Maybe."

"Well, I think Kathi should take you to a very nice psychiatric hospital near your house called Wellstone Hospital. Let the people there talk with you for a while. They may think you need to stay for a time, but it will be nothing like as long as when you stayed at Highland in Asheville."

"Where is it?"

"It's in Jeffersonville [the town next to Clarksville]."

"You say it's a good place? Is it private and discreet? I don't want people at the Law School to know I'm there."

"Very much so. Since it's in Indiana, I doubt you'll see anyone who'll know you or tell anyone in Louisville."

"Will Kathi be able to visit me?"

"There is regular visitation, yes."

"Will you be my doctor while I'm there?"

"No, the hospital has its own doctors, but they're excellent. You'll like them."

"Will they talk with you?"

"They'll call me whenever they think they need to."

"Do I really need to go there?"

"When I consider how you've been feeling and since you don't want to take the Risperdal, I think it's a good idea, yes."

"Can I take a shower and eat lunch before I go?"

"Yes, you can do that. Just don't wait too long."

"OK, I'll pack a bag and we'll go as soon as I finish lunch."

"Good, now let me talk with Kathi again while you get your shower."

228

"OK Dr. Quinton, whatever you say."

After lunch Kathi and I got some things together and we prepared to drive to Wellstone. I had been listening to the soundtrack from the movie *Oh Brother, Where Art Thou?*, and put "Keep on the Sunny Side" on in the car and sang it really hard all the way to the hospital.

"There's a dark and a troubled side of life. There's a bright, there's a sunny side, too. Tho' we meet with the darkness and strife, The sunny side we also may view. Keep on the sunny side, always on the sunny side, Keep on the sunny side of life. It will help us ev'ry day, it will brighten all the way, If we'll keep on the sunny side of life."

I had printed out the words to the song from the Internet, and they seemed to fit perfectly with where I was emotionally. I knew I was in a very dark and stormy place, but hoped to see the sun again in due course. I kept hitting the replay button on the car stereo and sang the tune over and over, doubtless driving Kathi crazy as I did so. Somehow, this little mantra helped me, and I felt better as I sang. Yet again, the calming effect of music worked for me when I was in a truly desperate spot.

Once we arrived at Wellstone we went into the admission area. An admissions specialist talked with me for a time, asking a number of questions. In particular, he wanted to know whether I might hurt myself. Unbeknownst to me, I was already in a locked area so I could not leave unless someone let me out. At the close of my interview the specialist told me that I needed to be admitted for an unknown period of time.

It was very hot in the admission area.

"I don't want to stay here, it's hot and I hate hot places," I said.

"It's nice and cool back in the actual hospital," the admissions person said.

"Show me."

At that, we walked back to the ward and it was quite cool. As we walked back to admissions, I said "Fine. Is there smoking here [I remembered Highland]?"

"Not inside the building, no. There is a little courtyard where smoking is allowed, and you can go there periodically during the day if you want to smoke or just to be outside for a few minutes."

"That's good. I can just stay inside and be away from the smoking. I'm willing to stay here."

"Good. Let's see about getting you a room"

While we waited for this to happen I talked with Kathi. She clearly, had I really focused on her, was stressed to the max. Her husband, the breadwinner of the family, was about to be admitted to a psychiatric hospital for an indefinite period of time and with a questionable prognosis. Still, she put on a brave front and worked to seem normal and cheer me up, as I was now in a severely depressed mood as I contemplated what was happening to me.

The hospital person returned and said "There's just one minor problem. The psychiatric unit is all full. However, we're in luck, as there's an empty room in the c.d. [chemical dependency] ward next door. You can stay there until a bed opens up in psych."

"Absolutely not!," I practically shouted. "I'm not a substance abuser, have never been a substance abuser, don't trust substance abusers, and won't be housed in a substance abuse unit!"

"But that's all we have available, and it'll only be for a little while."

"No, never! Send me to another hospital!"

The man turned and looked quizzically at Kathi.

"You've touched on a nerve. Rightly or wrongly, Jim thinks there's a difference between those, like him, with a mental illness like depression, schizophrenia, or bipolar disorder and those with a substance abuse problem. He feels that way because of his experiences in other hospitals, especially the one in North Carolina where he was a patient for six months. He doesn't think chemical dependency is really a mental illness."

"OK, many people feel that way. I'll see what I can do."

I had become very agitated at this point, and Kathi focused on calming me down. "I'm no druggie or alchi and won't live with those who are," I mumbled a tad incoherently.

The man returned. "The nearest psych bed is in Seymour. Do you want it?"

"But that's fifty miles north of here!," Kathi exclaimed. "I can't be driving back and forth from there!"

"OK, I've changed my mind about staying in the hospital. We'll just go home again."

Kathi looked very uncomfortable with this prospect. "Let's call Dr. Quinton."

"OK."

Kathi made a call, and spoke for several minutes before handing me the telephone.

"Hello James."

"Hi Dr. Quinton."

"I've talked with Kathi. You need to stay there at Wellstone."

"No. I won't be in a substance abuse unit."

"But it's only for a short time."

"I don't care. I refuse to do it. I want to go home."

"That isn't going to happen. First, Kathi doesn't feel that would be safe for either of you. Second, based on what you told the hospital worker if you try to leave Wellstone will put a seventy-two hour hold on you while you are evaluated. That might end up with you being committed, and you know how you've told me you never want that to happen to you."

"I feel trapped. What should I do?"

"Have you thought about talking with John Turner? I know you trust him."

"Good idea. I'll have Kathi call him."

"Tell Kathi to let me know what you decide."

231

Now, poor Kathi had to track down John Turner. Always resourceful, she was able to do so and put him on the phone with me.

"Jim Jones, what's going on?"

"They want to hospitalize me, which is alright, but they want to put me with substance abusers, which isn't."

"Well, that's a dilemma. Let's talk it over. What do you think you should do?"

"I don't know," as I started to cry. "I just want somewhere cool to be able to rest. I'm very tired."

"Why don't you talk with the folks at Wellstone and see the best arrangement you can work out?"

"Well . . . ."

"Let me talk with the Wellstone person for a minute."

Another muffled conversation, and the phone was handed back to me. "Wellstone is ready to agree to the following: You only stay in the c.d. unit until a bed opens up in the psychiatric unit, which should be within a day or so. You get your own room in the substance unit, with no roommate, and no one enters your room besides hospital personnel and you. You can go and visit the psych unit whenever you want for however long you want. Basically, you'll be like all the other psych patients other than where you sleep. Jim, you really need to agree to this, as it's the best thing for you. More significantly, it's very important for Kathi. She's at the end of her wits, and you have to cooperate here."

"What does Dr. Quinton think about this?"

"Why don't I call, explain it to her, and have her call you back with her advice."

"Alright."

Kathi and I talked for a few more minutes. It was, by now, nearly Friday evening and we'd been at Wellstone for over three hours. Then, I was called to the phone again.

"Hello James. I just finished talking with John Turner. He

explained what he's worked out for you, and I think you should take it. It's the best we can do. You just can't make Kathi commute to Seymour for you. You'll see less of her, and it'll be harder to call her as it'll be long distance. Finally, Wellstone's much nicer than the hospital there. What do you think?"

"Oh, OK. I'll do whatever you say."

"Give the phone to the Wellstone employee who's there with you."

After a brief conversation with Dr. Quinton, the deal was struck. I told Kathi goodbye, and that I would call her later. I then was ushered back to my room, where I unloaded my things.

It was a very comfortable room, and the temperature was perfect. And, the people at Wellstone were as good as their word. One of the psychiatric workers came over from the psych unit to interview me and inventory my things. I disrobed so he could inspect me for scars, self-inflicted wounds, etc. I exchanged my shoelaces and belt for harmless cable ties and gave him my razor and other "sharps" for me to check out when needed. I discussed my dietary needs, and those were attended to promptly. As soon as this was done I asked to go over to the psych unit day room and was immediately allowed to do so.

Once there, I sat down by the television and met some of my fellow patients. They seemed very pleasant, much as those at Highland. Since it was Friday, dinner was on the unit, and I got something to eat. I called Kathi and told her all was well and that I looked forward to seeing her during visiting hours Sunday afternoon. I then settled into what was to become a routine for over three weeks.

Within forty-eight hours, I was transferred into a room with a very agreeable roommate in the psych unit. We had our own bathroom with shower, and each had a desk unit with some drawers and hanging space for clothes and other personal items. I now was reasonably happy, and ready to work on getting better.

In the process, when I reflected on all the tears I had shed over the last few days I was no longer at all ashamed at having done so. I realized crying was just part of my disease, that I had gotten through it in the past, and that I would once again. A major weight off my shoulders.

21

Shortly after I was admitted I met my psychiatrist, Dr. Paul Phillips. Dr. Phillips looked very kind and approachable, and he proved to be both. He had an affinity for tasseled loafers, which I also loved to wear prior to my 1995 foot surgery. Infinitely more important, he had a long-haired dachshund he brought with him when he made weekend, and maybe even some weekday (I cannot remember for certain), rounds. Thus, when he saw me I got to play with his dachshund. That, of course, made me extremely happy.

During our first meeting Dr. Phillips and I discussed my diagnosis and care.

"You've suffered an acute manic episode, undoubtedly the worst of your life. It'll take a while for us to get you back to where you can function again. You're pretty sick right now because of the lithium withdrawal. Let us take good care of you."

"Did I do something wrong?"

"Not at all. No one did. Dr. Quinton always knew there was a distinct risk this would happen as you went off lithium, but she had no choice. Sometimes bad things happen due to no one's fault and you just have to make the best of the situation."

"When life gives you lemons, make lemonade."

"Right. We'll make lots of lemonade in the coming days."

"How long will I have to be here?"

"Let's hold off on that until we see how you do, OK?"

"But what about graduation and summer school?"

"Graduation is out of the question. Summer school isn't for a few days, so we'll talk about it then."

"OK," I muttered, "but I hate to miss graduation."

I quickly discovered that the Wellstone nurses and other psychiatric workers were outstanding. It was not a long-term care facility like Highland. Few, if any, like Highland are left in the managed care world of the twenty-first century. Still, Wellstone was excellent nonetheless. A great hospital has a wonderful staff, and Wellstone was no exception. All were very attentive, and as at Highland always ready to provide a friendly ear when you needed help with a problem. One nurse, in particular, reminded me very much of my beloved Nell. I picked her as my personal confidante and mother confessor. Like Nell, she worked the evening shift, and would always make time to talk with me.

Also like at Highland, I made a number of friends. Once again, I found that some of the kindest, most understanding, and most giving people with whom I ever get to be acquainted are fellow psychiatric patients. They comprehend what you are going through as they are in the boat with you, and you all row together. We shared the dayroom with one another and had psychotherapy, arts and crafts sessions, exercise in the gym, and meals as a group. Consequently, we got to know one another quite well, and helped each other as the need arose.

The immediate problem was graduation. Ordinarily I would not have minded missing it and just would have let Kathi return my cap and gown to the Law School. This year, however, one of my all-time favorite students was getting her degree. She had started in the evening division and had me for Torts I and II. I had taken some steps to protect the rights of evening students when they were being threatened. As a result she had bought a special book, had her classmates sign it, tied a ribbon with a nice bow around it, and presented it to me. It remains on my desk at work, one of my most prized possessions.

As graduation time approached on Saturday afternoon I got increasingly uncomfortable. Finally, I started to cry. When another patient asked me what was wrong I told her I was very upset.

"Why?"

"Because I'm letting one of my favorite students down by missing her graduation."

"Oh," she responded, and wandered away.

A few moments later, one of the hospital workers came to console me.

"Right now the only place for you is here in the hospital. It's sad that you have to miss something that's important to you, but you can just do the best you can. I'm sure the student will be so excited to graduate that she won't be offended that you aren't there."

"Do you really think that will satisfy her?"

"You can always tell her later that you missed the ceremony after your parathyroid surgery suddenly made you very sick. Meanwhile, focus on getting better so you can return to your usual life."

Years later, when I told this story to the alumna in question she was speechless.

"Why Jim, I don't know what to say. I noted you weren't at graduation, but just assumed you were taking a well-deserved break from school."

"I would never have skipped your graduation unless I was locked up or sick. Both were true here. I grew extremely sad and wept profusely when the hour for the ceremony arrived and I wasn't there."

"I'm so sorry. Again, I never would have suspected this in a million years."

"You probably never knew how much some very special students like you mean to their professors."

My next significant issue involved the movie that never should have been shown in a psychiatric hospital—*A Beautiful Mind.*

The psych unit had a DVD player and a small library of movies to view on it. One of them was *A Beautiful Mind*. It, of course, is the multiple Academy Award-winning version of the story of 1994 Nobel laureate in economics John Forbes Nash Jr. Early in his career Nash, a brilliant mathematician, made groundbreaking discoveries that are still important today. Soon thereafter, he developed paranoid schizophrenia, which debilitated him for many years. Finally he recovered to a considerable degree, but essentially lost years of his life to severe mental illness. Thus, to cut to the chase, the film was the story of an academic's descent into despair and a madness that robbed him of much of his career. For obvious reasons, I found it profoundly disturbing. Even today, I can barely stand to watch it.

I worried for some time in Wellstone whether my fate would parallel Nash's, only without the ultimate recovery and Nobel prize-like recognition. I was desperately afraid I would lose my job and end up destitute and homeless as a result of my illness. As by this time I was a tenured full professor at the Law School this was highly unlikely to occur, but I ruminated on it constantly nonetheless. It took considerable effort by Dr. Phillips, the hospital nurses and other mental health workers, and my fellow patients to pull me out of the tailspin into which I fell after watching *A Beautiful Mind*.

As Dr. Phillips said: "You aren't John Nash, and your prognosis is very different. You have bipolar disorder, not schizophrenia, and you already proved in 1983-84 that you can recover from a severe breakdown like you just suffered. While there are no guarantees, you should be able to work again pretty much as well as ever once your brain has time to rest and recover. Just concentrate on getting better a little bit each day, and don't let a movie devastate you like this."

As I thought about Nash and me, each had depended on his mind as the key to success in life. Reflect on the despair you feel when that linchpin suddenly becomes your worst enemy!

In retrospect, I think it was highly irresponsible of Wellstone to have this movie in the collection it showed to patients. Similarly, I do not think *One Flew Over the Cuckoo's Nest*; *Girl, Interrupted*; *Prozac Nation*; *Shine*, or other movies portraying severe mental illness or life in a psychiatric hospital belong in such a place. Patients there have enough problems without potentially upsetting them with stories about madness.

The next, far more significant, concern Kathi and I had to face was summer school. I was scheduled to teach my written advocacy seminar during the summer, with classes starting two days after graduation. I already had the syllabus, assignment, and all other important documents printed out and copied before my breakdown. This bought us some valuable time. Kathi went in my place the first night of class, told the students I was ill, passed out the handouts, and announced the two guest speakers I had already lined up for the second meeting. They appeared and spoke. Consequently, the entire first week of class was covered. That, however, did not take care of the longer-term issue—that I was going to be staying in Wellstone for some time. I would be in no shape to teach summer school, or even during the fall 2004 semester.

Sam Marcosson is one of my best friends on the faculty. Sam happened to be one of the associate deans at the Law School in 2004. With my consent Kathi contacted him and explained my dilemma. As she later related to me, she first told him that no one at the Law School had ever known I have bipolar disorder. Since 1986 both excellent medical care and my own effort had seen me do well enough to perform my Law School duties without anyone ever suspecting the truth. Then, she noted that I could no longer maintain the silence of the previous eighteen years. My recent surgery and the medication change that followed it had combined to create a very serious manic breakdown. It would probably be months before I could teach again at all, and even longer before I would be back to normal.

Kathi then asked Sam what she should do. She noted that I was desperately afraid I was going to lose my job, or at least be wiped out financially. I felt very paranoid and did not believe her when she said she did not think that would occur. Sam offered to talk with me over the telephone. He also told Kathi she would have to meet with the Dean, who happened to be a nationally known expert on disability law, to discuss matters.

Sam called me at Wellstone. "Jim, I'm really sorry to hear what you're going through."

"Yeah, it's pretty awful. The people here are really nice, but I'm terribly worried over what's to become of me long-term."

"Yes, Kathi told me that. I can't predict the future, but I don't think it'll be as bad as you fear. The Law School will work with you on this."

"But if it's like 1983 it'll take me a long time to get back to normal, if I ever do at all!"

"There are things like medical leaves with pay and partial teaching loads available to help you. Kathi can discuss all of them with the Dean. You just need to devote your efforts to getting better and not worry so much about things down the road."

"It's very hard for me to do that. Part of my disease is catastrophising, and I'm doing a great job of it right now."

"Well, as your doctors probably have told you, try to get through one day at a time. You take care of you, and let Kathi and me deal with the Dean."

"What do I do about my summer course? It's already started, but obviously I can't teach it."

"Leave that to the Dean and me. We'll get someone to cover the class."

"Good. That takes a load off my mind. Also, what about my spring exams and papers? I can't go over them with my students

240

so long as I'm in here."

"Don't worry about that. Faculty are gone all the time and that delays exam reviews. I'll take care of it."

After a deep breath and long pause I continued: "I hope everybody at the Law School doesn't find out about this. I've always been afraid of how I'll be treated if word ever gets out. That's why I've always kept it secret."

"You don't have to worry about anyone hearing anything from me or the Dean. We both know we're legally and morally obligated to keep your situation private. If anyone asks me what's wrong, I'll just say you're suffering from the results of your surgery last January. That's true, in a way. No additional detail is needed."

"Great. Thank you very much. You can't know how much I appreciate your help for Kathi and me. I'm locked away in here, and also my mind isn't working very clearly, so you're very important."

"No problem. Just concentrate on your treatment and doing what your doctor says."

Within a few days Kathi made an appointment with the Dean and met with her. The Dean said someone else would handle my summer class, and also that she would not expect me to teach in the fall. She explained to Kathi that the University, in appropriate cases, can grant a faculty member a medical leave with full pay for a six month period, and that she thought I might qualify for one. She asked Kathi to get a letter from Dr. Quinton that explained my situation and said she would take it from there. Dr. Quinton wrote such a letter in which she outlined my condition and concluded my severe mood lability, anxiety, and decreased concentration made a medical leave necessary. The Dean then approved a leave. This, as one might imagine, took a huge load off the minds of both Kathi and me. I would continue to receive my salary and benefits through the end of the year. By then, we would have a better idea what I could do.

Kathi later said having to tell Sam and the Dean about my illness was one of the most terrible things for her about my breakdown. This was because she knew how hard I had struggled, successfully, to keep it hush-hush for so long—eighteen years—even when disclosure might have helped me. Fortunately, Sam and the Dean did as he had said and told no one what was really wrong with me.

It was fortunate that when Kathi and I had our wills drafted a few years earlier we signed mutual powers of attorney. As a result, Kathi had mine and used it a good deal. She wrote checks on my account, thus paying household and other bills at a time when I was in no shape to do so. She filed for benefits under the long-term disability insurance policy that had supported me in 1984 while I was in Asheville. It again paid me the $1,000 per month benefit once Kathi produced the power of attorney that told the insurer it had to deal with her. In general, Kathi handled everything extremely capably such that I had no problems with which to deal. In my debilitated state I depended on her totally, and viewed her as sturdy as the Rock of Gibraltar. She had called both Rick and my mother to tell them where I was and kept them updated on my condition.

Only years later did Kathi tell me how terribly worried she was at this time. She met with John Turner regularly for support. Apparently, she cried a good bit of the time she was with him. She surprised her father, who thought she could handle anything, when she fell apart while meeting with him shortly before I was discharged from Wellstone.

Throughout my time at Wellstone, Kathi had to manage both the varied obligations of a practicing attorney and the many difficult and time-consuming demands I and my illness placed upon her. For example, she had constantly to field telephone calls from me. I was quite imperious, and got very angry if she did not drop everything to talk with me. So far as I was concerned, the most important aspect of her life was dealing with me and my needs.

After I had been in the hospital for a week or so I indicated how much I would like to see John Turner. Although he did not ordinarily make "hospital calls," he agreed to come and visit me. I really appreciated his doing so. I never asked him what he thought when he saw me, but I imagine I looked far different from the competent law professor with whom he was used to working.

What was a day in Wellstone like? All fell into patterns that reminded me of the ones I had followed in Highland twenty-one years before. When I awakened in the morning I would take my meds, of which there were a number, and check out my shaving gear and do my basic morning ablutions.

Before breakfast I might sit in the dayroom and look out the large, undoubtedly shatterproof floor to ceiling windows at the bird feeders and other pleasant outdoorsy things that were located there. Squirrels were always trying to steal food from the birds, and I thought it oddly appropriate to have them near the human "squirrels" in Wellstone. A number of types of birds were there as well. I remember watching doves, goldfinches, and my all-time favorite, cardinals—the mascot of the University of Louisville—in abundance. Small lizards and various insects completed the nature scene. I spent many hours watching the little vista the Wellstone designers had been kind enough to provide for us.

In due course, one of the attendants would lead us to breakfast in the spacious dining room. The food at Wellstone was excellent, with the main cook there moonlighting at Denny's, and there was always plenty of it. Soon after I arrived I met with the dietician to explain my special needs produced by my gastritis and other digestive problems, and the right food was always waiting for me.

After breakfast we would return to the dayroom and wait to meet with our doctors. Unlike Highland, all Dr. Phillips' patients did not meet together for a discussion of everyone's condition (I suspect changing patient privacy laws may have forbidden such a thing), but we each would have an individual session with him. When I met with him we discussed how I was doing and where I stood insofar as eventual release was concerned. As Wellstone doctors believed strongly in Risperdal, I stayed on it. Fortunately, by now I had adjusted to it. Accordingly, it did not produce the distress I suffered when Dr. Quinton first ordered it for me.

However, I knew Risperdal was an antipsychotic, and did not like taking it. "As I understand it, people with psychosis have had a break with reality, are delusional. I'm not delusional. Why am I taking an antipsychotic medication and thus implying that I am?"

"Calm down. Antipsychotics are used for those who are delusional, who you would say have schizophrenia or the like. But you're wrong to think they're the only ones for whom we prescribe antipsychotics. They are the best way to treat severe mania. There's no question you have that."

"In other words, people with bipolar disorder take antipsychotics?"

"All the time. Up until now you were on lithium and it controlled mania for you. Now that you're off it, you're manic. To make you not manic, and keep you that way, you need to be on an antipsychotic."

"But don't antipsychotics have some severe side effects? I remember people on them at Highland for a long time had many problems, including grimacing and moving their mouths and heads around all the time."

"Like all drugs, there are side effects. They can include weight gain, high cholesterol, diabetes, dry mouth, and sedation. Probably their worst problem is causing the movement disorder called tardive dyskinesia you witnessed in some people at Highland."

"Well, what about these?"

"We can control high cholesterol and diabetes through medication if you develop them. Sedation is an issue, but as you've already learned from taking Risperdal, once you get used to a drug it becomes less and less of a concern. Tardive dyskinesia is bad, but the newer, atypical antipsychotics like Risperdal are much less likely to cause it. If it develops it's usually a lot milder than what you saw at Highland. The folks there were on the older form of antipsychotic like Haldol or Thorazine that is much more prone to leading to severe tardive dyskinesia."

"How will being on an antipsychotic affect my ability to do the scholarship part of my job?"

"That's a little hard to predict at this point. It'll affect your ability to concentrate, which I imagine could be a problem for you. Again, however, over time you'll get used to it, so it may turn out, at least eventually, to be a non-issue. This is one of the things you'll just have to wait and see about. Meanwhile, look at the bright side—you'll probably find it a lot easier to sleep now."

"I still don't particularly want to take something called an antipsychotic."

"Stop worrying about how the medicine is classified and just be glad it's available to make you able to function. Otherwise you'll probably never be able to work again rather than recovering fully as I'm certain you eventually will do."

I even now did not really like it, but I had no real argument to counter what Dr. Phillips said.

After we met with our doctors there were events scheduled pretty much every hour. They included various types of group therapy led by staff members, including the excellent social worker who dealt with families, long term placements of those for whom a short-term hospitalization would not suffice, and discharge planning. These sessions were not as valuable as the Highland group Dr. Gawarowski conducted. Since Wellstone was a short-term facility people were constantly coming and going so there was no stability of group membership. As a result I often would forego a group meeting and go back to my room for a nap instead.

Naps were important for me as I was not sleeping well despite being on numerous sleeping meds. I would wake up at three or four in the morning and wander about the unit. There was always food available there, so I would sit at a table in semi-darkness and eat rice crispies to tide me over until breakfast. I also would visit with the night nurses and attendants, getting to be pretty friendly with several of them. The lack of sleep was, of course, not a good thing as it worsened my manic symptoms. I would have to be able to sleep before I could go home.

Scattered throughout the day were "smoke breaks" in the little courtyard in the center of the hospital. I recalled all too well the large number of smokers at Highland, and was glad to be in a smoke-free indoor facility. As a sop to the smokers, they could cluster around a hospital worker with a lighter and have a few cigarettes in the courtyard. They would go there, rain or shine. Non-smokers could go out as well. Since it was the only time one ever actually was outside while at Wellstone I sometimes would do so. I would huddle with other non-smokers as far from the smokers as possible while enjoying some fresh air and sunlight.

After lunch, there would be other types of therapeutic activities, most notably arts and crafts. As always, this was a pleasant time. I made a number of presents for Kathi, which I proudly would present to her when she came for visitation.

Even more fun than arts and crafts was the physical activity period before dinner in the gym, which featured a basketball goal and a volleyball net. We played horse in basketball, but as I am a lousy shot at the best of times it was not my favorite activity.

Volleyball was always enjoyable and I am sure would have been amusing for others to watch. The games generally featured the psychiatric patients on one team and the chemical dependency ones on the other. You had people who were full of antipsychotics against others who were at least temporarily substance free, and therefore essentially normal. My team was as tipsy as if it were drunk—people would hit wild shots in all directions, or even have the ball hit them in the head because they were so sedated that they were very slow to react. Accordingly, there tended to be the foreseeable routs on behalf of the c.d. patients, but it was entertaining nonetheless. At other times the teams would be mixed, and then the c.d. players would try to help their psych teammates play as well as they could. "Come on and concentrate. Just hit the ball toward the net and we'll get it over for you. You're playing like you're high or something!" Even with that encouragement, the team with more c.d. patients generally won. As I explained the problems of the psych patient competitors to the c.d. ones, "you try playing when you're almost comatose." In any event, by dinner time all had an appetite.

After dinner came telephone time. You could sign up for the right to make telephone calls, and wait your turn to do so. Conversations were limited to around ten minutes, and I would religiously talk with Kathi every night. As noted, at times I would wheedle a buzz during the day, but that was not a sure thing like the evening one. I would tell Kathi how I was doing, how much I loved and missed her, and how much I looked forward to seeing her during visitation.

Visitation itself was on Thursday evening and Sunday afternoon. Each session lasted for an hour and was held in the dining room. I got very upset if Kathi was not there exactly on time—to me, work demands or traffic jams were irrelevant. I would sit at a table with Kathi and enjoy the thrill of seeing her. She never looked as beautiful as at those sessions. No matter how elementary my artistic effort may have been, she always acted as if my arts and craft gift for her was a treasure. I tried not to whine too much, but at times I would beg to come home. Kathi always said I had to wait until Dr. Phillips thought I was ready to leave the hospital. As soon as she left, she had to call my mother and Rick to report on my condition. Another onerous task for her!

One Thursday evening was particularly memorable. Dr. Phillips knew how much I loved and missed Nutmeg as I talked about her incessantly, especially when he had his dachshund with him. He decided it would be very therapeutic for me to see her, so he let Kathi bring her to a conference room off the dining room to spend an hour with me. By then Nutmeg was sixteen and somewhat feeble; she was almost totally white in color as she was weighed down by extreme old age yet she still wore her always endearing expression, her eyes bright through her cataracts. I hugged and kissed her as long as I could—she truly was my beloved Nutty, and her visit helped me recover.

Just to show that I still had a bit of a sense of humor, one day I decided to see if I could escape. Perhaps it was the old wargaming spirit evidencing itself once more. I had no particular goal, other than perhaps to walk over to a nearby discount store for a change of scenery. As I had no money or identification on me, I could not have gotten far. I reached outside the locked portion of the hospital but was apprehended before I made it any further. I lost my dining room privileges for the day as a result, which angered me considerably, but I suffered no long-term detriment.

Kathi and I had several meetings with the hospital social worker as she went over my progress. Eventually she suggested a family conference, including Jennifer and Shirley, so she could help us break the news about my condition to them in a controlled situation. Up until then I had never told them that I have a severe mental illness.

Once all were settled in the conference room, we discussed my illness. I was in a very emotional state and sufficiently impaired that I do not really remember most of the details of the conversation. I do recall that when Shirley heard I have bipolar disorder and have had it for her entire life, she, who was twelve at the time, burst into tears. I was devastated by this reaction, but I later learned that when children that age hear news they cannot really handle they cry. Jennifer took the history of my disease more calmly, but I am sure she was distressed over what she learned about me. In any event, the genie was now out of the bottle, and the social worker painstakingly explained my disease and probable recovery to Jennifer and Shirley. Overall it went well, and helped them understand aspects of my personality and behavior that may have perplexed them over the years.

Not too long after this visit Dr. Phillips decided I was ready for less rigorous treatment and thus could be discharged into Kathi's capable hands. I had been in Wellstone for over three weeks, which was an eternity for a twenty-first century private psychiatric patient.

My release was with the understanding I would participate in the hospital's day program—Intensive Outpatient Program, or IOP—every morning during the week. IOP was a sort of therapy group for those who needed care but not enough to be inpatients. It included many recently discharged Wellstone patients like me. I stayed in IOP throughout the summer even though I neither really liked the dynamics of the group nor its leader. It gave structure to my day, as I had it each morning. I then would go home for lunch and spend a chunk of the afternoon at the Y so I was not alone too long before Kathi came home. Also, it gave me ready access to Dr. Phillips, who continued to work with me in concert with Dr. Quinton. Therefore, I was being treated by two outstanding psychiatrists at the same time. I was, not surprisingly, very glad to be home and back with Kathi, Nutmeg, John Turner, and Dr. Quinton.

In 2004 I was "lucky" both to have good health insurance and to have had the parathyroid surgery before my stay in Wellstone so I had already met my insurer's annual individual maximum out-of-pocket expenditure limit of roughly $2,250 (this amount does not include any co-pays) before I got there. Hence, my stay and the IOP charges cost me nothing. Had I been uninsured I do not know how much my Wellstone visit would have been, but I imagine it would greatly have exceeded the $10,000 per month charge at Highland in 1983 (when you factor in inflation, $10,000 in 1983 was roughly $18,875 in 2004). I shudder to think what I would have done if I did not have an excellent job and the good insurance benefits that accompany it.

About a month after my discharge I developed akathisia, severe anxiety and restlessness, as a side effect from the Risperdal. I could not sit still and felt I was about to jump out of my skin. It was so bad that when Kathi took me to a movie to divert me those around us complained to theatre management as I was moving so violently that I was shaking their seats. When I discussed this with my doctors they concluded I needed to be hospitalized to get matters under control. Although I was only in Wellstone for three or four days this time, it was my second psychiatric hospitalization in the same year. Not a goal to which to aspire.

At around this time, Kathi decided to leave the self-employed solo practice of law for the safer realm of government service. She learned that a local state trial, or circuit, judge had an opening for his "staff attorney." The holder of this position is the same thing as a law clerk such as I had been for Judges Tjoflat and Snyder— the personal assistant to the judge who handles whatever legal or other tasks are proffered to him or her. Kathi went to interview with the Honorable Martin F. McDonald, who had been a circuit judge for about six months and a lower-level judge for about ten years, when she learned from his then-staff attorney that she was leaving his service. When Kathi met with Judge McDonald—or

Marty, as he is known to his friends and colleagues—she had a rather unique interview. She went prepared to discuss her background and the nature of the position. Instead, the Judge regaled her with the tale of going machinegun shooting with a certain beagling law professor roughly fifteen years before; yes, this was the former deputy sheriff and night law student with whom I had been friends so many years ago.

As Marty finished the story, as I understand it, he turned to Kathi and said "so do you want the job?"

"Uh, absolutely!"

"When can you start?"

"Uh, two weeks?"

"Fine. Go down to the court administrator and fill out the necessary paperwork. See you soon."

And that was that. I like to think of this as a job won equally in the classroom, private practice, and loading and emptying nine mm automatic Uzi magazines.

What was my overall mental status at this point? Much as in 1983, my brain had short-circuited very severely and as a result I was almost completely dysfunctional. Memory and reading were real problems, and I had incredible anxiety issues. Without the lithium that for years had kept my feelings under strict control I was incredibly emotionally labile, such that tears frequently flowed freely (again, at least I understood they did so because of my disorder and thus I was not ashamed over them). I had so much trouble reading that I had to check out books on tape from the public library and listen to them to try to engage my mind. Ponder the plight of a professor of law who depends on books on tape for mental stimulation! It was some time before I could really focus enough to read the simplest volume. Sleep, or the lack thereof, became a real problem. Like many with my disorder, I was deathly afraid of change, and just leaving the house made me terribly uneasy. The thought of travel away from my little sphere of safety in Clarksville and, to a lesser degree the Louisville area, was unthinkable.

Risperdal could be taken orally every day. It was also available as Risperdal Consta, a shot in the buttocks that only had to be taken every two weeks. Dr. Phillips eventually put me on Risperdal Consta, as was done with a number of Wellstone patients. I later read that Risperdal Consta, when administered to those with affective diseases like bipolar disorder, is more likely than other atypical antipsychotics to trigger tardive dyskinesia. After a while, I started to notice that I had involuntary repetitive movement of my mouth and tongue. This was exhibited by pursing of my lips when my mouth was closed and having my tongue stroke against one of my bottom molars. As it happened, I had a gold crown on that tooth. As I massaged my tongue there over and over the gold grew thinner and thinner until the crown came off. I then had to have my dentist install a porcelain one that he said I could not damage by rubbing. This took care of that issue, but I was still concerned over the mouth movements.

Eventually, I asked Dr. Quinton "Who can tell if I have tardive dyskinesia?"

"I can."

"Oh. Do I have it?"

"You've had a mild form for some time."

"Why didn't you tell me?"

"I didn't want to upset you. Now that you're off Risperdal Consta [which I had been for some time] it's unlikely to get worse. Moreover, atypical antipsychotics tend to mask the symptoms."

"You mean they both set it off and make it less obvious?"

"That's right. Try not to worry about it. You have such a mild case that others won't even notice it unless you call it to their attention."

"You recognized it."

"I'm trained to spot it. Ordinary people aren't. I don't

think you'll ever be like the Highland patients you saw where it was conspicuous."

That may have been the case, but puckering and pursing of my lips and rhythmic circling of my tongue, especially when under stress, continue to bother me even today. Moreover, I eventually developed painful symptoms of TMJ (tempomandibular disorder of the jaw and face muscles) due, at least in part, to stress and the tardive dyskinesia. It also, fortunately now only intermittently, still plagues me, requiring me to wear a bite guard during much of the day—generally excluding when I am engaged in public speaking, such as teaching class—and at night.

I had a far worse problem than either tardive dyskinesia or TMJ: severe suicidal urges set off by the bipolar depression that afflicted me. I did not return to Wellstone for them until November. While there I discovered what it is like to be on suicide watch with, as noted, someone on the hospital staff observing your every move during both the day and night. Still, the compulsions tortured me throughout the summer and fall. For months Kathi worried every day whether when she opened the garage door when she came home from work she would find me dead in my car from carbon monoxide poisoning, or when she entered the house I would be hanging from the ceiling fan in the living room. Imagine the sheer hell through which I put her, although to me, as discussed earlier, she would only be collateral damage if I actually killed myself.

Dr. Quinton was sufficiently concerned I would attempt suicide that she had Kathi lock up all the weapons in the house, including my reenactor's collection of reproduction Civil War swords, bayonets, knives, and functional percussion cap pistols— along with the lead balls, percussion caps, and black powder needed to fire them—in a closet to which I did not, and still do not, have a key. She was wise to do so, as on numerous occasions I was sorely tempted to employ them.

Since my story has become public, many have asked why I did not just get rid of all the dangerous items. The answer ranges from I still went to the occasional Civil War event and needed them there to the same dual reasons I first articulated twenty years before: I wanted to have them around both to show I would not use them and to have them available as the tools to end my life if I chose to do so.

Although the medical leave excused me from working at the Law School during the fall of 2004, I was in desperate need for something to do to wile away the hours each day. I had to give myself a reason to live and to rehabilitate myself as I had done with Scott Jarvis in 1984 in Asheville. Before I left IOP I discussed this with the group, as well as Kathi, John Turner, and Dr. Quinton. I settled on the triumvirate of the Y, volunteer work, and auditing a class at the branch of Indiana University in New Albany.

Exercise at the Y was, as always, very therapeutic for me. My nerve-damaged left foot prevents me from participating in many athletic activities such as jogging, running on a treadmill, or otherwise putting pressure on the foot. Fortunately, the Y has a set of recumbent exercise bicycles I can ride pain-free. Thus, I can travel many miles, and burn off lots of calories, each day. The bike was (and is) an excellent antidote for stress, and also helped me both lose thirty pounds I had gained from my meds and lower my cholesterol, for which by now I also was on a regulatory drug. Thanks to the combination of exercise and medication my cholesterol dropped from a potentially dangerous level to a normal one. It has stayed there despite the proclivity of my antipsychotic for increasing it.

I searched around for an appropriate volunteer job. Once a week the Louisville *Courier-Journal* prints a list of available opportunities. I settled upon doing something at the hospital where I got my Risperdal Consta shots and where Dr. Quinton and my primary care doctor are on the staff. I met with the volunteer coordinator, and although I never disclosed my health situation we settled on something low stress and not mentally demanding. As a result, several days a week I sat at the table outside the outpatient surgery department from which I ushered patients and their friends or family into the pre-op area, transported patients around via wheelchair, and informed family members when they could go see their loved ones in the recovery room. Alternatively, I worked at the main visitors' desk and escorted people back to radiology, the lab, etc. This was truly mindless work, but was about all I felt I was capable of doing. I did get to know some of my fellow volunteers, and learned that I was both practically the only male and the only one under about age seventy in the group. No one ever asked me why I was volunteering rather than working for money, but I am sure my colleagues wondered what an apparently able-bodied man in the prime of life was doing there. At least I was helping others as I labored towards returning to the Law School in 2005.

My most challenging activity was auditing a twentieth century history class. That required me truly to engage my mind, as I was in a university setting. I felt as comfortable as I could under the circumstances, as it was the familiar locale of a history class such as I had attended numerous times at Virginia. I had never studied much of the subject matter, or at least that post-World War II, in any course. However, unlike the rest of the students, and the professor for that matter, I had the advantage of actually having lived through the latter half of the period in question. Consequently, I remembered events like the Cuban Missile Crisis, the two Kennedy and King assassinations, the Vietnam War, the Watergate scandal, and the fall of the Berlin Wall the rest of the class regarded as ancient history about which they knew little. Still, I stressed out about my performance to an incredible degree, and nearly had a mini-breakdown upon the first test in the course. Imagine my surprise and exhilaration when I earned an A+! It did me worlds of good, and I was as proud of it as any of the many achievements during my life. Maybe I could do it, could make my mind work again, could go from the role of student back to that of professor without falling apart or otherwise embarrassing myself and the Law School! I showed off my test to Kathi, Dr. Quinton, and John Turner, and think I even called Sam Marcosson about my "accomplishment."

I continued on in the history class for a good portion of the semester, earning As on various other assignments and tests (the other students in the course probably hated me as a "curve buster") until I had made the point to myself that I really was much closer to normal than I had suspected. Then, I stopped going to class and began to focus on getting myself ready to teach in the spring.

At Dr. Quinton's suggestion, I also enrolled in a meditation course she hoped would help me deal with stress to go along with John Turner's efforts to teach me cognitive behavioral therapy. I attended several classes, but when the teacher went into the details of crystals and chakras I could not take it and actually walked out, never to return. I place no more credence in "New Age" spiritualism than traditional religion.

Unfortunately, not all was well. Despite my work at the Y, the hospital, and the college, I continued to suffer a great deal from my disorder. I slept either not at all or twelve to fourteen hours a day. Indeed, sleep was the one real respite I had from the extreme mental anguish I felt. Unfortunately for poor Kathi, who would have liked to be able to relax after a day in her new job, the evenings were always horrible. I would weep inconsolably from despair and the sheer pain of depression. Kathi would say that "I don't know how to help you" as she watched me sink deeper and deeper into a morass. To make matters worse, one horrible weekend in September I absorbed two tremendous blows that shattered me.

First of all, on Friday we got the call that my brother Rick had died. Because of fear how I would react, Kathi talked with my sister-in-law Ramsay and did not put me on the phone with her. Although Rick had battled cancer for several years, he had been doing well of late so the news was both a huge and unexpected shock. On account of my already fragile emotional state, I was totally numbed by the report that my only sibling was gone. I really had grave difficulty absorbing it. All I could say, over and over, was "poor Rick," and my depression went into freefall. Kathi was really worried if I would weather this storm. I eventually called to offer Ramsay my condolences, although I had a hard time talking. Needless to say, considering my then-paralyzing fear of travel I could not attend the funeral.

The next day saw a complete emotional meltdown. For several days Nutmeg had been having serious problems, and Kathi and I took her to the vet. I had a premonition of a dire diagnosis, and left my glasses in the car. When our old friend and longtime veterinarian examined her, he, who is usually quite the jokester, got very serious.

"Jim, I've never had to tell you this before, but Nutty is in very bad shape. She's in pain, and there's really nothing I can do for her. Her systems are all shutting down, and it's only a matter of a few days. I'm afraid it's time."

I was speechless for a minute or so. Finally, disconsolately, I said: "Go ahead."

"Do you want to stay with her?"

"Yes, I owe her that."

At this point, as the vet went to get the lethal injection, Kathi ran out of the room.

As the vet shaved Nutty's leg to make it easier to give the shot painlessly, I started to cry uncontrollably; it was a good thing I had left my glasses in the car as they would have been a real hindrance. I told Nutty over and over how much I loved her, frantically kissing her, patting her on the head, and rubbing her tired old body while the vet gave her the terminal medication. As I saw the light in her eyes flicker and then vanish shock nearly overcame me. The vet gently led me out of the room, as I was in a daze and could barely walk.

By virtue of my already extremely weakened state the loss of my dear friend through two marriages and one divorce, probably quite predictably, totally overwhelmed me. It took me months to recover from this trauma. I know that the loss of a pet upsets anyone, but my illness and my total devotion to Nutmeg made it hit me like a thermonuclear explosion. In days of despair and severe depression, some of the darkest of my existence, I had focused my affections on her, hung onto life in large part for her sake, and now she was gone. I still do not know how I survived the double whammy of that weekend.

Today, as I look back over my sixteen years plus years with Nutty I am flooded with happy memories. I have had few relationships in my life that have been as close as mine with Nutmeg. To me she had anthropomorphized into a person, and a wonderful one at that who loved me unconditionally through everything. I responded accordingly to her, almost worshipping her in the process. I will always remember Nutmeg with great fondness.

The aftermath of this horrible weekend was interesting. I e-mailed Ron Eades about Rick's death, and also mentioned Nutmeg's demise. Ron, in turn, e-mailed the faculty and staff of the Law School and advised them of what had happened to my family. I got a number of supportive messages and cards regarding both deaths. Specifically, I got several sympathy cards expressly for the death of Nutmeg. Ron later commented to me that he was surprised when he heard from so many people who said that they were particularly sorry to hear about Nutmeg. She had become famous around the Law School from when I discussed her as an important member of my family with roughly fifteen years worth of students.

Now my "secret" was known by Sam, the Dean, and the other associate dean who was in charge of the schedule and thus had had to be told as well. Kathi and I decided that I should share my story with my oldest friends on the faculty, the Eades, Renders, and Stengers. We managed to have dinner alone with each couple and to share my news at that time. All expressed great surprise, but were totally supportive. They offered me any aid I might ever need and agreed to keep my disclosure secret. Ed Render, in particular, was completely flummoxed; he was utterly amazed I had kept my disease a total mystery from everyone at the Law School for nearly eighteen years and only had it come out then when my medications failed me. This was the second real surprise I had kept from everyone, the first being my romance with Kathi. I think the couples all wondered, at this point, what else I might be hiding!

It is said that time heals all wounds. That must be true, as gradually I got past the events of September 17 and 18. Despite my brief November hospitalization, I really was getting better. I was incredibly anxious as January, and the return to the classroom, moved inexorably closer. Still, deep down inside I thought that with the supportive rocks of Kathi, John Turner, and Dr. Quinton by my side I at least *might* be able to make it back, albeit slowly as in 1984. I had tried to follow their collective advice to the letter since my breakdown, putting in my time at the Y for exercise, the hospital for socialization, and the university for mental stimulation. Hence, I had worked to bring both my mind and body into something approaching normal functioning. Only time would tell whether I had succeeded in doing so.

22

January 2005 saw me return to teaching, but only on a part-time basis. The Dean had been kind enough to make things as simple for me as possible. Rather than teaching two courses in the spring semester as I normally would, she let me handle one in the spring and one in the summer. She counted them together to equal the full spring load. In addition, she relieved me of all service and publication duties. As a result, all I really had to do was teach my appellate advocacy class once a week for two hours per session in the spring and twice a week for two hours each time in the summer. It is hard to imagine an easier workload, a more undemanding segue back into my job, than this.

Despite my undemanding situation, I freaked out over it. Anxiety coursed through me in waves as I was convinced I could not handle a course I successfully had taught many times before. Indeed, I always got excellent evaluations in that class. It was really ridiculous, in retrospect, how I would go home the one or two days I taught and wail to Kathi:

"It's so hard, I can't do it!"

"Yes you can. You need to get a grip on yourself and give yourself time to recuperate. You made it back in 1984 and can do it again now."

John Turner and Dr. Quinton delivered essentially the same message. I agreed to try to tough it out and spent much time at the Y to reduce my stress level. I also took frequent tranquillizers chemically to accomplish the same thing. Finally, I bugged Kathi to death with incessant telephone calls at her office seeking reassurance, complaining about non-existent problems, expressing anxiety, etc. etc. I was amazed when I eventually learned my teaching evaluations for the spring class were excellent.

During the summer of 2004 John Turner suggested I join a support group for those with bipolar disorder, and I followed his advice. The first meeting I attended I was so overwhelmed with emotion that I broke down completely, crying for the entire hour-long gathering as I related my story. Just as when I got divorced, I found the support group incredibly helpful. All those in attendance could relate to my problems as they had experienced them as well. They regularly reassured me while I dealt with these concerns. As I often say, "No one knows better the path one with mental illness must tread than others who walk the same road themselves." The group meets every other Sunday evening. It also features a support group for loved ones of those with my disease that Kathi has found to be very valuable for her.

By the fall 2005 semester I again taught a full load, Torts I and appellate advocacy, but did no service or scholarship. I barely held on through the academic year. I continued to suffer intense anxiety, for which Dr. Quinton heavily medicated me. She added a drug commonly used to fend off stage fright. Before each Torts class I, who do not believe in organized religion, had to state my usual mantra plus recite the Lord's Prayer and cross myself repeatedly. I always desperately hoped I would be alone on the elevator all the way down from my office on the second floor to the classroom in the basement as then I could do so without interruption. Although I had taught Torts I over fifteen times, I repeatedly had to read the book to prepare for class. I neither could remember what I had done in the past nor what I had just read and reread. During class I stood frozen at the podium by my book, wracked by the fear I would lose track of where I was unless I had immediate access to it.

Each night I would come home from school, say I could no longer go on, and cry yet again.

Kathi, in response, would declare "Remember you don't do well in the evening. Take your bath, go to bed, and remember, tomorrow's another day." She also regularly reminded me to "take things one day at a time" and "to focus on the positives" and not the negatives, as was my habit. I am sure she grew tired of this daily routine, and the veil of pessimism through which I viewed the world.

My terror of traveling meant I missed the celebration, put on by his former law clerks, honoring Judge Tjoflat, to whom I owe so much, for thirty-five years of service as an active federal judge. True to form, as soon as Judge Tjoflat heard I was not coming because of health concerns he called me to see what was wrong. Somewhat nonplussed, I explained that the previous year I had suffered a breakdown from the medication problem that was as severe as that of 1983 and that I had not yet recovered from it. He wished me a speedy convalescence and said I should come see him the next time I was in Jacksonville to visit my mother. As was clear, Judge Tjoflat keeps up with his former law clerks even after over twenty-five years.

At this point in my recovery, Nanny died. It was like the passing of a dear relative. We were all treated like family before, during, and after the funeral. In particular, Jennifer and Shirley were grouped with all the blood grandchildren at the service. Both were predictably devastated by the loss; Jane, Kathi and I felt it deeply as well. Fortunately, by that time Nanny had raised both my daughters to be well-mannered young women. She could have done nothing more important than that.

Finally, the fall semester was over. I was convinced it was a total disaster and that my students had seen me as the fraud I believed I was. Imagine my astonishment and temporary relief from my crippling anxiety when I got excellent evaluations in Torts I and good ones in appellate advocacy. Indeed, I later spoke with a Torts student who assured me that I seemed no different from any of the other first year professors. In fact, she said I had been one of the best who had taught her class that term. The students had no idea I was terrified of standing in front of, and speaking to, them.

One might think this positive reinforcement would have cured me of my fear, but no such luck. The spring semester picked up right where the fall had left off, anxiety-speaking. Gradually, however, much as in 1984 I improved somewhat as the months passed by. I was devastated in the spring when I got mediocre reviews from the relatively few students who filled out evaluation forms in my appellate advocacy course but survived emotionally since I got very good Torts II ones.

In the summer of 2006 I taught appellate advocacy again and this time got strong evaluations. In addition, I left home for the first time since my 2004 breakdown when Jennifer, Shirley, Kathi, and I went to Tampa for my niece/goddaughter Borda's wedding. Since Rick could not give her away, she asked me to do so. I agreed as I could see no way around it but was petrified at the prospect of the trip itself, much less of walking Borda down the aisle. John Turner discussed this with me for weeks and suggested various cognitive exercises to get around my fear. As it was, Kathi practically had to pry me out of the house and into the car to the Louisville airport. I was sure I could not get the right food, or sleep, away from home. This was not totally surprising. People with bipolar disorder hate change of any sort and travel is, by definition, change. In addition, the trip would expose me to my entire family for the first time in over a decade. That made me very nervous. I was so bad off that I was terrified of the security gate check at the airport even though I ultimately passed through it without a hitch.

When we got to Tampa things went far better than I expected. Everyone was very kind to me who was, after all, a secondary player in the unfolding drama. Borda was incredibly sweet, writing me the loveliest note I have ever received. In it she said that "I never really knew the role of a godfather. Now I see it is to stand in for my father at important events if he is unavailable. Thank you for being here for me on one of the most important days of my life." That made me glad I was there.

I was fairly anxious the morning of the wedding, but Kathi and I went swimming, which distracted me. I worried about having enough time to put on my tuxedo and otherwise get ready, but was dressed and at the church with plenty of time to spare. I did my duties exactly as I was instructed. At the big moment I was very worried about not stepping on Borda's gown or otherwise passing out halfway down the aisle, but I am proud to report that all went smoothly. The reception was lovely, and I managed a wonderful dance with Borda, again in place of Rick. I enjoyed a number with Kathi, Jennifer, and Shirley. I found food I could eat, and slept fine. Thus, overall I had a very nice time. More important, I did a good thing for Borda and, indirectly, Rick, in the process.

Because this expedition went so well I agreed to accompany Kathi to her family reunion a few weeks later. Things once more were fine, and I now really believed travel was a viable option for me. I therefore overcame a major source of anxiety and showed myself that maybe life overall was not as dire as I thought. I was truly on the road to recovery!

By the fall of 2006 I seemed to be returning to what Dr. Quinton always refers to as my usual "high functioning" state. In other words, ordinarily I operate at the level of a very successful professional despite my illness. I do well enough that no one suspected my condition until I publicly disclosed it several years later. This makes me a rarity among her patients, or any other psychiatrist's for that matter. I was no longer afraid of class or my students. Moreover, my memory of the cases in Torts was returning to me. When I read over them they made sense and I could begin to recall them on my feet. This was a tremendous improvement, as now I gradually could move away from the lectern rather than being frozen behind it with my book. I did not need my mantra anymore; teaching was starting again to be something that came naturally to me. Clearly my twenty years of experience were paying off once more. Indeed, I actually found myself enjoying the challenge of the teaching, the back and forth with students, aspect of my profession. Dr. Quinton, whom I see monthly, and John Turner, whom I see every other week, were a great help to me. Dr. Quinton "tweaked" my anticonvulsant/mood stabilizer, antipsychotic, anti-depressant, and antiinsomnia medications as needed. On his part, John Turner talked me through the day-to-day problems of my life. Before I could get too comfortable, however, other concerns arose that cumulatively kept me a bit out of kilter.

My diversions were multiple. Some related to school, in particular non-teaching obligations, and others had nothing to do with it. Four major Law School issues plagued my fall. In 2006-07 I had to do service as well as teach since I was working full-time. Hence, my first obligation was again working on the upper class moot court competition I had helped the Moot Court Board put on for years. Nothing really bad happened, but it was something I always found stressful, particularly after problems like I encountered with the first year arguments in 1997. Stress was something I did not need. Still, I could have handled things fine were this the only stressor out there.

The second concern was my chairing the Reinstatement and Probation Committee. Never a particularly pleasant job, one specific former student was a real problem. The former student petitioned to be reinstated to the Law School and told a pretty compelling story. The only problem was, if one looked carefully it had holes in it. As chair, I had to find out what was really afoot. I ended up playing Sherlock Holmes and digging around for information in a way the chair generally does not have to, and in fact almost *never* has to, do. This was especially problematic as everything the Committee does has to be highly confidential, so I was walking on eggshells. In the process I/the Committee was threatened with a law suit and called various uncomplimentary things to the University's central administration. I had to meet with the Law School's Acting Dean to explain what was going on without disclosing too much when he was called by his superiors and asked what was afoot. After a number of hearings the former student was finally denied relief, but by then I was nearly a basket case. I *really* did not need to be in charge of one of the nastiest reinstatement matters in memory, but you take the bad with the good. Just my luck this was not the year when the chair had relatively little to do, as at times is the case!

The final two Law School problems came to me as a faculty member in general rather than via a committee. The first involved the search for a new Dean. This long process involved interviewing candidates for the position and supposedly saying how you felt about each one during a large group meeting. I felt incredibly uncomfortable with this as I feared any negative comments would find their way back to the ear of the successful candidate and turn him or her against me should I back a losing one. Given my 2004 breakdown I was particularly paranoid about how a new Dean would treat me, and feared that if the wrong person were selected my career could be over. I had heard stories of other places where a new administration had run off someone who did not fit the mold of the desirable faculty member, and just *knew* that might happen to me. I maintained as low a profile as possible but worried a great deal about the selection.

The second general issue was very important to me and created by far the most harm of all the Law School matters. It revolved around what was called the strategic planning process. The Law School periodically has to generate a plan for its future, and this year one was due. Accordingly, the faculty went through a seemingly endless series of meetings where it addressed a number of proposals. One of these produced grave difficulties for me. But first, a little Law School history as deep background behind my problem.

For about one hundred years there were two ways to get a law degree in Louisville. The first entailed attending the Law School full time for three years, the usual period one goes to law school. It permitted the student to work up to twenty hours a week while in school. The second was a four year track, with students on it working more than twenty hours a week. The classic student under this program worked forty hours a week or so during the day and went to law school in the evening. The student did so as the student needed to work to support the student, and perhaps his or her family, when it was not economically feasible to be a standard student who did not work a regular job. Or, the student was already established in a career in banking, medicine, corporate work, or a myriad of other activities. He or she wanted a law degree to help him or her advance in his or her employment while not giving it up for the sake of a three year stint in law school. There was a steady demand for this type of legal education, although far fewer students wanted it than the traditional three year program.

From 1905 to 1950 the night students attended a separate law school, but in 1950 it merged with the Law School. After that the Law School had both a day and evening division, which generally was referred to as the Night School. Many attorneys, featuring a number of judges including Marty McDonald and his father, partners in major law firms in Louisville and elsewhere, a Pulitzer Prize winning journalist, and hundreds of ordinary people were able to be lawyers by graduating from the Night School. This latter group included people like, as noted, Kathi. She never would have been able to attend law school, meet me, and become my wife but for the Night School. Like Kathi, there were numerous Night School alumni who were eternally grateful for the opportunity it gave them to become attorneys and as a result were incredibly devoted and loyal to it.

I always was a very strong proponent of the Night School for a number of reasons. First and foremost, I liked the opportunity it gave people who wanted so badly to become attorneys that they were willing realistically to have no life for four years while they worked all day, went to school at night, and spent the rest of their time studying. That is the sort of dedicated person, I thought, who should have the chance to be a lawyer. Moreover, I found night students to be a very interesting lot. They tended to be older than day students and to have real life experience they brought to class. As a consequence, when I discussed any number of issues in Torts or Decedents' Estates I had someone in the class who was an expert on the subject because he or she worked in that area. Having someone talk knowledgeably about the point made it more real for the class and me. Next, I thought having the Night School helped further the University's public metropolitan research mission by, for example, giving non-traditional students access to a legal education. Finally, I could relate to night students as they were closer to me in age and had already had lives with marriages, children, divorces, deaths of close relatives, and other things that added to my Torts and Decedents' classes. Thus, I was an advocate for night students long before I met Kathi. After I married her, I of course had a more personal stake in the Night School considering her feelings on the subject.

Periodically the faculty would discuss closing the Night School

269

for any number of reasons. Each time the effort was defeated after the Night School alumni rallied behind their beloved program. I always loudly opposed the attempt, and was joined by a core group of other faculty who favored the Night School.

During the strategic planning process in the fall of 2006 closing the Night School again came up, and this time my colleagues were really serious about doing so. A number of different reasons undoubtedly made them feel this way, and I will not speculate about their motives. I of course opposed the plan but would have to go along with it if it won on the merits and was approved by the University's central administration. I would not like it, but if the battle were lost after a full and fair debate, that was that. I *was* concerned that the process be transparent. Then, Night School students and alumni could express their views and the administration would know the costs and benefits of what it was approving before any Rubicons were crossed. The Law School faculty who favored closure could elaborate on the benefits. I could note that the costs could include many angry Night School alumni whose donations to the Law School might dry up considering their displeasure over what had been done as well as depriving those in the community of the opportunity the Night School provided them.

The issue finally came to a head at a strategic planning meeting where the faculty tentatively voted overwhelmingly, over my strongly expressed objection, to close the Night School, or at least effectively to gut it by making it impossible any longer for students to work all day and still earn a law degree by taking classes entirely at night. The plan was for the Acting Dean to convey this sentiment to the University's President and Provost, apparently to get their concurrence so closure would be a *fait accompli* before anyone on the outside was the wiser. This I found very objectionable. If the University decided to close the Night School after full disclosure of the plan, so be it, but due process notice was essential first. Still, I would take no direct action about the matter since at this point it was not public.

What I did do was keep Kathi advised, as I do about most things affecting my life and mental health, about what the faculty was planning. As soon as she learned she wanted to rally the troops to attempt to block the action, or at least to let the President and Provost know how Night School alumni felt about it. I, however, told her she could not do so, again, as long as the plan was not public. She reluctantly agreed not to.

At a Friday afternoon strategic planning meeting I asked the Acting Dean if he had met with the President and Provost about the Night School issue. He stared up at the ceiling for several moments before looking at me and stating that he had done so that very morning. He also said the President would be coming to meet with the faculty the following week. While it was not entirely clear about what the President was coming to speak it seemed clear that the Night School's future would be on the table. This immediately worried me immensely, as the feared *fait accompli* seemed to be looming.

With this in mind, I specifically asked the Acting Dean, after he answered my initial question, whether since he had met with the President and Provost the faculty's tentative decision regarding the Night School's fate was now officially public information. After a pause, the Acting Dean said it was.

As soon as the meeting was over I called Kathi and relayed the Acting Dean's words to her. She immediately jumped into action. She composed an e-mail message to all the Night School alumni she knew. In it she related the faculty sentiment, pointed out the upcoming meeting with the President, and solicited their communicating with the President and Provost that they did not want the University to deprive future potential students situated as they had been from the opportunity to get a legal education at night. For this I came to refer to her as the "Paulette Revere"

271

of the Night School. While I did not necessarily endorse all her methods I was proud of the way she fought for that about which she felt strongly.

Her e-mail generated a veritable firestorm. The President and Provost were inundated by e-mails, faxes, and telephone calls from concerned Night School alumni. When the President met with the faculty he observed that he had gotten more e-mails about this issue than he got e-mail spam in a week. This seemed to annoy him, as he did not like to be blindsided by an academic unit's action leading to such a reaction.

Many of the messages were very angry—I best recall a very original one accusing the faculty of launching a "Pearl Harbor-style attack" on the Night School. The *Courier-Journal* published a series of articles on the Night School, including two editorials opposing its closure and paying tribute to what it offered to the public. There also were a number of letters to the editor about it. Wherever I went I faced questions about the Night School. Kathi became the heroine of her fellow Night School alumni, at the same time becoming *persona non grata* among much of the Law School faculty. She retains that status among some even today.

As one can imagine, this entire situation created incredible stress for me. It precipitated a rift between me and many of my colleagues that took a long time to mend. Indeed, I am not sure it has done so with all of them even today. It even generated a threat from one of them. He darkly hinted that many of the faculty were very angry with me because of Kathi's actions. He then bolted out of my office before I had the opportunity to respond that Kathi is her own person and that I neither control her actions nor intend to try to do so. We train our students to be effective advocates for positions in which they believe, and I was not about to interfere with Kathi's use of the advocacy skills she had learned both at the Law School and in the years thereafter. In the twenty-first century husbands do not control their wives' behavior, a principle our students, faculty, and alumni assuredly endorse.

Eventually, the Night School issue became a manic fixation for me about which I ruminated incessantly. Manic symptoms interfered with my sleep, led to increased irritability and volatility, and required Dr. Quinton to represcribe the antipsychotic from which she previously had weaned me. About this time my tardive dyskinesia mouth movements markedly increased and the strong TMJ symptoms appeared for the first time. I personally blame the painful TMJ condition on the stress of the Night School controversy. With TMJ I had to eat a soft diet, wear a dental appliance most of the time, regularly see a TMJ treatment specialist, and hurt much of the time since stress made me clench my jaw and thus set off the TMJ. At one point Dr. Quinton actually ordered me to skip a scheduled planning meeting just to reduce my stress level. Accordingly, I suffered deeply for the stand I had taken.

If the Law School matters were not enough, two other stressful issues were out there, one involving Kathi and one me. The problem with Kathi was that her employer was up for re-election and someone had filed to run against him. Hence, in addition to his regular work Judge McDonald had to campaign during every spare moment to get union endorsements, media nods, permission to erect campaign signs, etc. Kathi frequently appeared for him at candidate fora and the like when Marty had a conflicting engagement and, obviously enough, could not be two places at once. We went to church picnics while wearing campaign t-shirts in order to get his name out and had his bumper-stickers on our cars even though we had Indiana license plates and thus clearly could not vote in the Kentucky election. The kicker here was that if Marty were defeated, not only would he be out of a job but Kathi might very well be also. She assured me that another judge would hire her were Marty to lose, but I was extremely worried nonetheless. It got so bad that although I was invited to attend the election night party I had to decline as I was too stressed out to go to it. It all turned out for the best, as Marty was re-elected with fifty-five percent of the vote, but this was one more thing to weigh me down.

The last item was the aforementioned crucial, and very stressful, one of coming out of the closet and telling about my career as a legal academic with a severe mental illness. When you added this plan to the other stressors, once again, a perfect storm had arisen to push me over the edge. Like any person with bipolar disorder, I had a limited ability to control my obsession over the Night School, the moot court competition, the reinstatement case, the dean search and strategic plan, the reelection campaign, and writing the article. I lost weight to the point that my family practice physician expressed considerable concern. By the end of the semester, I was a wreck, both physically due to the TMJ and mentally. Unfortunately, in addition to all my other problems the current antipsychotic drug I was taking triggered anxiety as a side effect. Interestingly enough, I had, when all the ballots were counted, garnered excellent teaching evaluations in appellate advocacy and solid ones in Torts I.

Over the holiday break I tried to recuperate but had serious difficulties from the TMJ and severe anxiety about the new administration at the Law School and my ability to teach my spring courses. For some reason, I was more worried about teaching Torts II, which I had managed to handle the spring before, than I was Decedents' Estates, which I had not taught since the spring of 2004. Finally, Dr. Quinton put me on a new antipsychotic, Seroquel, that was supposed to deal with some of the manic symptoms I was starting to exhibit, bipolar depression, and severe anxiety. Thus fortified, I began the new semester.

I weathered the initial tempests of the spring, with both Tort II and Decedents' Estates seeming to go well, but things quickly started to unravel. I again had to take my anti-anxiety/stage fright medication before each class. I worried about making inappropriate comments, being theatrical and irrelevant, and singing when in a manic state as I went off on my aforementioned *Blazing Saddles, Titanic,* and *300* tangents in Torts II and, especially, Decedents' Estates.

The new Dean wanted to implement many changes, including some I feared might compromise my ability to continue in my career, and the strategic planning process continued to distress me. Not surprisingly, my painful TMJ symptoms and boring soft diet were a continuing issue.

Indeed, my bipolar and stress condition-induced TMJ symptoms became so severe that my jaw would "lock up." On several evenings all I could eat for dinner was pureed mashed potatoes because they required no chewing and I could eat them with a spoon without really opening my mouth. Eventually, almost every time I got engrossed in working on my article my right jaw muscle would go into spasm and set off the very painful "locking up" symptom. The only way to relieve this problem was to cease working on the article and do something else less stressful. I often refused to do that for fear of forgetting an idea if I stopped work.

My TMJ therapist recommended that I try using a microwave-heated moist heat gel appliance to warm the jaw muscle and consequently relieve the spasm. As a result I bought two of the devices, one for home and one for work. They generated some relief, although I had to be careful not to burn my face as I did on at least one occasion. Also, at work I had to make sure not to have anyone see me heating the device in the faculty microwave or applying it in my office lest I have to answer unwanted questions.

I also exhibited increased manic irritability. The fate of the Night School was a continuing source of stress as I argued excessively with some colleagues about this still unresolved point.

Sleep became more of a problem, with the ever-present danger that lack of sleep would fuel the manic symptoms. A routine annual work-plan meeting with the new Dean engendered an absolute flood of bipolar anxiety that proved to be unjustified, but a real problem nonetheless.

In her effort to assist me Dr. Quinton raised the dosage of my Seroquel, and while this helped matters to a degree it generated unpleasant side effects on the short term and fears as to permanent damage akin to that caused by the lithium on the long. These included the weight gain, elevated cholesterol levels, diabetes, sedation, dry mouth, and tardive dyskinesia Dr. Phillips and I had discussed in 2004. Every time I started to calm down about the fate of the Night School it would come up in some way and my manic response would recur. Stress, and my reaction to it, was a constant enemy, as was my tendency to catastrophise about everything.

On several occasions my manic irritability got away from me. Once it did so shortly before a Decedents' Estates session over student attendance, or rather lack thereof. Immediately before class I went in a total rage to one of the associate deans who knew about my condition. She managed to talk me down enough from my fury to teach what turned out to be a rather tense session by proposing a viable alternative to my loudly berating the class over the non-attendance problem. As it was, several student evaluations complained about my strict, and totally appropriate, attendance policy. I was following that of the Law School, and it was clearly set out in my course syllabus. Still, the reviews expressed annoyance over my action. It was unclear whether the problem was how I approached the issue or the mere fact I had the effrontery to enforce the rule. Had I not spoken with the associate dean, there would have been many protests of my screaming at the class over attendance violations. After this, Dr. Quinton again had to raise my Seroquel dosage.

She had to do the same thing once more when I had difficulty interacting with Law School staff members over my demands for support services. I got upset when they could not explain to me how to employ the Law School-norm Microsoft Word word processing program with which I was not familiar and that I was using to write the article. I loudly expressed my manic frustration when I overtly stated that the few Law School secretaries we had should know how to help the faculty in the use of Microsoft Word. Again, a perfectly justifiable belief, but thanks to my mania I probably voiced it too vociferously.

When I became increasingly obsessed with my personal crusade of finishing the article Dr. Quinton had to raise the dosage of my Seroquel even more to a dose more than double that which I took when I first started taking the drug. She did so in order to allow me to sleep more than a few hours a night, as I would wake up filled with new ideas for additions to the article. She also wanted to control my manic irritability and impatience.

Finally, by spring vacation in March, despite all the medication, I was floridly manic. For example, one night I was so obsessed with completing the article that I worked on it until 5:30 AM, slept until 10:30 AM, and then resumed work on it. As a result, Dr. Quinton again redoubled my Seroquel dosage. My mental health had deteriorated significantly. Hence I decided to cancel, for medical reasons, the compressed, and therefore stressful, summer Decedents' Estates class I earlier had agreed to teach four days a week. Instead, I just would do some research over the summer, if anything Law School-related at all—I do not have to work then, as I am on a ten month contract. Consequently, as in the summer of 2004, I had to call off a summer class in order to husband my strength for an upcoming semester.

Over spring vacation I worked manically on the article. Once I basically completed it the increased dosage of Seroquel began to take effect. Relief over not having to teach the summer Decedents'

Estates class flooded through me such that the mania started to ebb, although I still had intermittent TMJ symptoms with which to deal. Perhaps, at least for this particular episode, the worst was over. Still, I was on the higher measure of Seroquel for the foreseeable future, including a significant daily amount at 5:30 PM. Since my spring Decedents' Estates class met at 5:35 PM, I took the Seroquel immediately before going there. As my system by now fully had adjusted to it, the drug did not adversely affect my ability to teach at all. Indeed, most likely I could not be doing so without it. Still, I did wonder how many law professors take a substantial dose of a powerful psychiatric medication immediately before class. Something interesting to ponder.

As was by now all too apparent, being off lithium meant my disease was harder to manage and far more dangerous than during the lithium years. I had more mood swings and fear about my work and health prognosis. Every little stress pushed me towards mania or depression, and I constantly had to call Dr. Quinton and/or John Turner for advice as to how to handle the latest crisis. Sleep, or the lack thereof, was a constant concern lest it trigger a manic episode. With mania came impatience, irritability and a tendency to lash out at others, sometimes with justification and sometimes without it. Stress-induced TMJ became more and more of a problem. Alcohol consumption was forbidden lest it adversely interact with my various psychiatric medications and markedly increase the risk of suicide. I worried if my condition would allow me to publish on any sort of regular basis, although managing on good days to write the article was a positive sign. I constantly griped to Kathi about the numerous medications even though I realized they were necessary.

Speaking of medications, I then was on eight separate psychiatric prescription drugs in order to function as a law professor. Add to these the eight other prescriptions I was taking to deal with physical problems attributable to my disorder such as TMJ, high cholesterol, difficulty with bladder emptying and prostate functioning, anemia, anorexia, and post-surgical digestive problems and my medicine cabinet was overflowing. At least I did not have massive weight gain or heart arrhythmia like some in my support group. I learned from them that being on seven or eight psychiatric prescriptions is not at all unusual, just as constant tinkering with the drug cocktail is the norm. Indeed, the reason for frequent visits with the psychiatrist is to let him or her alter the medication regimen to deal with the concerns of the moment.

In the spring of 2007, while at times I forgot that I have a severe mental illness, the need for the next dose of Seroquel, or a side effect from it, reminded me of the bitter truth that I have, permanently, a severe, potentially disabling, and life-threatening disease. Still, I soldiered on. After all, I had no other choice, short of disability or suicide, both of which I had tried and neither of which was a particularly attractive alternative. Despite my manic interludes, I was back in the game. I had proved to myself that a law professor who suffers from severe bipolar disorder can teach, write at least the autobiographical article, and do service like anyone else in the profession. My teaching evaluations bore out their part of the equation, as they ultimately were very good in Decedents' Estates and decent in Torts II.

As the semester drew to a close, so did the writing of the first draft of the article. But that was a beginning, not an ending. While my first drafts are usually close to their final form, I still worry over them a good deal before I send them out for review. Thus, I now pored over and over roughly fifty-five pages of manuscript, including footnotes, as I edited and fine tuned. Kathi was dragooned into the matter also, as I depended on her as my associate editor. Together we labored until I finally was satisfied. Because I was so focused on having this article accepted by the *JLE*, I also had mailed out drafts to Ramsay and my father-in-law Mike for their comments in order to get additional perspective. Once I incorporated their many helpful suggestions, I went another step and sent unsolicited copies to some authorities in the field for any assistance *they* would offer. In the process, I risked totally destroying the veil of secrecy behind which I had hidden for years. I never would have contemplated doing that when in a non-manic state.

One of those to whom I wrote was Dr. Ramona L. Paetzold, a professor at the Mays Business School at Texas A&M University. Ramona, while not a law professor, is a lawyer who teaches various legal principles to business students. In 2005 she wrote an incredibly detailed and moving article about how courts and employers treat those with bipolar disorder. In it she discussed her own battles with our mutual disease. Hence, we have much in common. Ramona has an even more severe case than I do, and has lost several work years as a consequence of severe episodes. We became friends, and she offered many helpful comments on my draft. Later, in one of those coincidences no one would have believed had it not been true, we learned that Ramona is the daughter of Mike's uncle, making her Kathi's first cousin once removed. Kathi had not made the connection as Ramona's birth name was not Paetzold. All this cemented the relationship between Ramona and me.

Another person to whom I sent a draft commented that the piece needed to be much shorter, and then made a wonderful additional observation, as I recall:

"Did you know that Elyn Saks at the University of Southern California Law School has a book coming out about mental illness in legal academics?"

As I had never heard of Elyn Saks, I did not, but I fired off an e-mail to her early March 20 to investigate. Little did I know how important this person so quickly would become to me.

"I have secretly been working on an article I hope to place in the *Journal of Legal Education* about life as a law professor who suffers from a severe mental illness, in my case bipolar disorder. I understand that you are working on a book about mental illness in the Academy. Is that true, and if so what is the premise of your book (are you yourself mentally ill, if I might ask [as noted, mania can make one act or speak in a way many would consider rude or nosy], or are you addressing the issue as an outsider)? What is its status (is it ready to come out, etc.)? I can e-mail you a current draft of my article, if you'd like to see it. My illness is a secret from most of my colleagues (I've kept it a secret for 20 years), so please keep my inquiry confidential [once again, I trusted a total stranger to keep my most personal matter private]. I look forward to hearing from you."

Later that day I received a response that both thrilled and chilled me:

"How nice to hear from a fellow traveler! Your article sounds most interesting and important. My book is not so much about mental illness in the academy as about my experience of mental illness in the academy (and elsewhere!). That is, it's a memoir and not a book about others as well. The book is called 'The Center Cannot Hold: My Journey Through Madness,' and it's to be published in August of this year. My own illness is schizophrenia. I was very much 'in the closet' except with closest friends until recently; at this point most of my colleagues know about the book and about me more generally. I must say the reaction has been incredibly good. Still, I do worry about the effect of the book on people I don't know. And will it marginalize my other work? Etc. etc. I really only know one or two other law professors with serious mental illness. It would be great to connect up and learn a bit more about each other. (Do you ever get to LA?) Finally, I would be pleased to read a draft of your article. If you have an interest in my manuscript I could send it along. Good luck. What you (we) are doing is, if I may say so, brave. And I hope it helps destigmatize our illnesses."

The room swirled around me as I absorbed this message. First, I had encountered someone who apparently shared my knowledge of historical trivia and hence knew that "fellow travelers" were long-time hidden Communist sympathizers much as we were law professors who had hidden our severe mental illnesses for decades. Second, I had a potential friend with whom I could share many of my troubles and insights as they would be hers also. Third, someone had beaten me to the front of the publication queue! Was my article unneeded, so that all my emotional turmoil and effort writing it were superfluous? I eventually would come to agree they were not. Little did I know at the time that not only had I produced my most important piece of scholarship to date, I also had just started probably the most significant, and closest, friendship of my life.

23

I immediately called Professor Saks and had an extraordinarily warm conversation with this kind, gentle, and brilliant woman. We exchanged biographical information and I asked her to send me a copy of the page proofs of her book, which she did by express delivery. Between the conversation and manuscript I learned a great deal about Elyn.

Elyn R. Saks was born in Miami in 1955. Her father is a lawyer, and eventually her father and mother had an antiques business. Thus, she lacked for nothing. She was an outstanding student even when she exhibited early symptoms of schizophrenia. When time for college approached her parents wanted her to attend one in the South, so she went to Vanderbilt University. She majored in philosophy, learning ancient Greek in order to read Aristotle in his original words. She graduated as valedictorian of her class. She won a prestigious Marshall Scholarship to Oxford University, where she studied philosophy and earned a M. Litt. degree. However, her schizophrenia fully exhibited itself there. Her battle with it forced her to take four years to earn her diploma. She ultimately entered Yale Law School, where she quickly became even more acutely delusional and psychotic. She was hospitalized, and often kept in restraints, for much of the fall of 1982, one year before I was in the far more pleasant surroundings of Highland. She returned to Yale in 1983 and this time made it through. She was a member of the *Yale Law Journal* and graduated with honors in 1986, a classmate of Sam Marcosson. She somehow kept her schizophrenia under control after Yale. When I spoke with her in March 2007 she was Associate Dean for Research and Orrin B. Evans Professor of Law, Psychology, and Psychiatry and the Behavioral Sciences at the Gould School of Law at USC and Adjunct Professor of Psychiatry at the University of California, San Diego, School of Medicine.

It was great to have multiple law professors making the same point, just as it was good to have both Ramona Paetzold and me doing so. Indeed, the more the merrier: Elyn, Ramona, Kay Jamison, me, we all helped show that having a mental illness is not inconsistent with having a successful, and happy, professional and personal life.

At around this time, I hit an important life transition. One of the long-time facilitators of my support group decided to retire from her position, and I was asked to take over from her. As a result, I became facilitator. Much as at Crescent Hill, I had progressed from a bleeding hunk to a calm, consoling group leader. Nearly simultaneously Kathi took over as facilitator of the family member support group. Today both of us are on the Board of Directors and are the facilitators of the Manic-Depressive and Depressive Association of Louisville, Inc., with me serving as corporate Vice-President and Kathi as corporate Secretary. In this capacity we help those with my illness and their loved ones. It is sometimes stressful, but always rewarding, work. Kathi and I leave most meetings with the warm feeling one gets when one helps others cope with their experience with bipolar disorder.

On April 23 I mailed the article, accompanied by a lengthy and impassioned cover letter, to the editors of the *JLE*. The article was forty-six pages long. In the letter I noted that, pursuant to *JLE* requirements, I was only submitting the article to it rather than sending it to a number of journals as legal academics normally do with their works. I was putting all my eggs in one basket because I so wanted the broad dissemination of my message to law professors throughout the nation publication by the *JLE* would guarantee.

At around this time, I wrote two short articles for *Bar Briefs*, the monthly newspaper of the Louisville Bar Association. They appeared in its May and June 2007 issues. While they were not major scholarship, they were important as they were the first publications I had generated since 2001. Yet another indication I was well along my journey back from the disaster of 2004!

Now that the big article was done, I got to wait and worry until I heard back from the *JLE*. As I have noted, I do not wait well. I had no idea how long it would take to hear. I realized that, as summer was fast approaching, it might be months before the *JLE*'s editors contacted me. I ruminated over the issue with great regularity. Each daily call with Elyn would feature me bemoaning the wait. She tried to calm me, but I grew fixated with the fear that the article was too long and that the *JLE* would reject it as a result. I thus spent much of the summer on two projects: reediting the article to shorten it and writing another piece. I was increasingly grateful that I had decided not to teach Decedents' Estates, as I was under enough, mostly self-imposed, pressure without having to do so.

The reedit saw me go through the April 23 version of the article line by line and throw out everything I thought I could. I deleted chunks out of footnotes, and even whole ones. I whittled the text, using the editorial skills I had honed during years of teaching legal writing. I was very unhappy over some of what I felt I should leave out. I was determined, however, to have as barebones a version as possible so I gritted my teeth and sharpened my red pencil. Kathi watched me carefully to insure I was not falling prey to the mania of the spring once again. While I may have come close to doing so, I somehow held myself together. Finally, all the cuts generated a probably better thirty-five page version of the article. Now that the reedit was done, I had to decide how to employ it.

By this point I was in daily discussions with Elyn and/or Sam over whether to send the shorter work to the *JLE*. It was a real debate: on the one hand, if I sent it in it might cause the editors to consider me troublesome or as lacking confidence in my initial effort. Either might be seen as a sign of weakness that might lead them to rebuff me out of hand. On the other, if I did not and I later learned the *JLE* rejected me as the article was too long I would never forgive myself. What a conundrum! I tried to get Kathi, Elyn, Sam, John Turner, Dr. Quinton, or anyone to tell me what to do, but all were too smart to fall into the trap. It was my article, my baby, my essence, and it was for me to determine its fate. Finally, I threw caution to the wind and acted. I wrote a letter to the *JLE* editors in which I argued why the April 23 draft was wonderful while at the same time proffering the twenty-five per cent shorter work if they preferred it. With that done, I turned to the summer's other major activity, writing another article about a subject close to my heart: Elyn's book.

Ever since I first read the page proof of *The Center Cannot Hold: My Journey Through Madness* I was struck by the similarities between my own story and Elyn's. As I later would note, we are roughly the same age and both grew up in Florida with a dachshund in the household, did extremely well in school, were Phi Beta Kappas at the "V's" of the Southern Ivy League (Vanderbilt and Virginia), were on the law journals and graduated with honors from the Yale Law Schools of the North and South (Duke likes to think of itself as such), have been hospitalized multiple times for severe mental illness, became tenured full professors at law schools whose faculties had very little (in Elyn's case a few of her colleagues knew about her schizophrenia but kept it to themselves) or no (in mine) idea of our diseases when they awarded us that status, take antipsychotic medications that have caused us to develop tardive dyskinesia and other dangerous or unpleasant side effects, are recognized experts on important social issues, and have enduring marriages. There are differences, such as Elyn's illness prevented her from practicing law or clerking for a federal judge, but the similarities far outweigh the distinctions. Thus, while Elyn's pedigree is definitely the more sterling of the two, overall mine is not half-bad either. Anyway, as Sam said, it is not a competition. I decided to help publicize Elyn's book, and add a publication to my résumé, by writing the rave review it deserved.

Once again, I first carefully researched the issue. I went through many medical works to learn about schizophrenia and distilled my findings into the first part of my review, which I called "Surviving the Scourge of Schizophrenia: A Law Professor's Story." I talked about the stigma that exists against those with schizophrenia. I noted that they have been called "the lepers of the present day," with the leper traditionally the most stigmatized figure in society. After summarizing Elyn's memoir I turned to my special perspective on it based on my disease. I observed that while Elyn and I disagree on some things we concur on the most important, such as that the stigma against those with mental illness is evil, most so afflicted are not violent or threatening, and they can have very successful academic and professional careers. I ultimately heaped praise on what I deem to be the most important book about living with mental illness ever written.

By mid-July I had made good progress on the review and hoped to hear soon from the *JLE*. Elyn grew increasingly excited as the publication of her book neared. During our daily conversations I shared her joy at seeing all her hard work finally bear fruit. Meanwhile, since I thankfully had overcome my fear of travel the previous year I was able to make a very important journey for an extremely special occasion. As my gift to Kathi on the occasion of our tenth wedding anniversary I took her for a two week tour of the home of her ancestors, the fabled green island of Ireland. We saw and did many things, and Kathi seemed captivated by her gift. It made me very happy to show her the love and appreciation I feel for her and all the care she has so selflessly provided me over the years.

Upon our return from our trip several things happened in rapid succession. Perhaps most important to me, the *JLE* accepted my article for publication in the spring of 2008. It chose the shorter over the longer version, but that did not really bother me. All that really mattered was that the piece was going to appear where I wanted and as a result my story would reach the audience to which it was directed! The saga of my life and my battle with bipolar disorder would be told! Kathi, Elyn, Dr. Quinton, Sam, and John Turner all shared in my exhilaration at this news. Also, I completed my review of Elyn's book and mailed it out to a number of journals to see if one wished to publish it. Thus, by the start of the fall semester I already had accomplished a great deal.

The return to class felt right to me. Even more than the year before, I was comfortable while teaching. I needed neither medication nor mantra before doing so; I was completely "high functioning" once more. I fully could remember again so that I could roam around the room and never lose my place or forget that about which I was speaking. I again was where I was in 2003, an experienced and well-regarded teacher of two very important subjects, Torts and Decedents' Estates. My illness and related personal issues probably insure I never will be excessively popular, but I do my job and leave behind budding attorneys who know what they need to pass the bar examination and then practice their chosen profession. Already a generation of lawyers has benefitted from my instruction, and hopefully at least one more will do so. Of that I am justifiably proud.

Between the years 1989 and early 2008 of my ongoing service as member, and for several periods Chair, of the Reinstatement and Probation Committee I quietly advocated for students with mental and/or emotional concerns. I would explain the individual's condition to the other Committee members. They generally knew nothing about mental illness and consequently tended to discount psychiatric grounds for academic problems. I would emphasize that with proper care the affected student possibly could succeed at the Law School. I did this without ever disclosing my own disease. Still, I think I effectively advocated for, and affirmatively helped, a number of individuals who got back into school at least in part from my efforts. Time will tell the future impact of my endeavors for petitioners with similar difficulties now that I no longer have to hide my own condition.

Offers to print my review of Elyn's book reached me relatively quickly. Eventually I received a number of bids for it and I ultimately accepted the one from the most highly rated offeror. Although I had planned for the review to come out after the *JLE* article so that the article would be my "coming out" announcement, it did not work out that way. The journal putting out the review moved so rapidly that it would be in print before the end of 2007. As a result, I had to alter the mental scenario I so carefully had constructed. In December I e-mailed my colleagues, told them the review was coming out very soon, and revealed my illness to them. I also noted that the *JLE* article would be arriving in a few months.

In September I wrote a review of Elyn's book that appeared in the *Courier-Journal*. Nationally, as Elyn and I discussed daily, her memoir was received extremely favorably by numerous sources. For example, *People* magazine wrote a feature about Elyn and it, and *Time* magazine later named it one of the ten best non-fiction books of 2007. I raved about it, and received a number of favorable comments about my piece. Little did the *CJ* editors suspect what was to come a few months later.

Also early in the semester, I again supervised the upper-class moot court competition. Nothing especially memorable happened that year. However, I decided enough was enough and that I simply could no longer deal with the stress of trying to co-ordinate everything without having any real say over what was done. I bided my time until my disorder became public. Then, I asked the Dean to assign the competition to someone whose health the stress would not adversely affect. He agreed to do so. I hope that after roughly twenty years I am permanently done with working with student moot court programs.

During the fall, as my happiness over the turn life had taken grew, I felt the urge to fully return to my old friend, pre-Beethoven classical music. I had not been in a choir for some years, but I could enjoy music other than by singing in one. At first, I continually listened to the few classical cds I had in my collection. Then I proceeded to purchase many more in what became a near, if not outright, manic spending spree. At least it was fueled by elation rather than loneliness and depression as had been the case so often in the past. Music was a joy, not a way to escape from the difficulties of reality. Today I have a substantial collection of which I am quite proud and, as noted, listen to music constantly. I do so at home, in the car, and, via headphones, at school and the Y. Music is one of the great loves of my life and still helps me in times of trial as well as pleasing me when I am contented.

As knowledge of my condition gradually spread, I became something of a hot commodity for mental health advocacy and related groups. I was invited to join the Boards of Directors of both MHAKY (Mental Health America of Kentucky, formerly the Mental Health Association of Kentucky) and NAMI Louisville (the National Alliance on Mental Illness of Louisville). I accepted both invitations and thus was poised to become an advocate for those afflicted by severe mental illness.

At the end of the year, I was quite pleased at both the publication of the book review and the pending *JLE* article. 2007 had gone very well for me, with generally good teaching evaluations, ample service, and productive scholarship. 2008 seemed likely to be even better.

24

As 2008 dawned I took a very important step: I wrote a piece intended as an editorial for the *Courier-Journal* entitled "Mental Illness, Stigma, and the Person in the Office Next Door." In it I noted that when I reviewed Elyn's book in the *CJ* during the previous fall I left out an important fact—that I myself have a severe mental illness and have achieved all I have to date despite that fact. When I submitted it to the *CJ* editorial staff they were so impressed by it that they made it the feature editorial in the January 21 issue. This immediately generated a huge number of letters, e-mails, and telephone calls thanking me for going public. Many were from those who told me their own stories about dealing with the psychiatric conditions of themselves or their loved ones. They said my words helped them believe it was possible to be a success despite having a mental disorder, and also attacked the stigma that is such a terrible problem. They especially liked the closing portion of my editorial. There, I noted both that many are touched by mental illness and you never know about the mental health of your neighbors at work or home.

It was most gratifying to read the massive correspondence. It included words like: "You are one of the two best professors I had the privilege of having for class while pursuing my law degree. I am sure it took great courage to write the letter you did. I deeply admire you for that. It is only when people like you speak up and out and witness to who you are and what you have achieved while fighting the demons of mental illness that society will finally come to learn and accept that there is no more shame in mental illness than there is in a broken leg. The only shame is failing to do anything about it."; "I thought that the article was compelling and that it laid shame on those who would stigmatize someone who is ill—it was powerful—There is still far to go—but this article is one more stab at the invisible giant of stigma."; "Your story will serve as an inspiration to others who may yet need the blessing of a good example. I myself am the better for hearing it."; and "I was overwhelmed by your willingness to speak out on this still somewhat taboo subject. We've all known people who have been afflicted with mental illness, yet it seems as though it is alternatively viewed with suspicion, ignorance or fear. Hopefully, by your example, people's attitudes will continue to change and society will become more willing to learn and understand what mental illness is all about, and that it does not prevent those who suffer from it from being highly productive." I could see that I had generated the same sort of reaction as Elyn did when her book appeared. This could only be good for both me and the mental health community. Both the Boards at NAMI Louisville and MHAKY were thrilled and moved at my disclosure. Each now had on its Board a highly successful mental health consumer, the sort of example it wanted to present to the community.

While this was going on, I decided to write another article for the *Bar Briefs* specifically directed to the local legal community. It was entitled "Severe Mental Illness in the Academy: A Secret Revealed" and appeared in the February issue. This generated another flood of reaction. Former students and others, many of whom had missed the *CJ* editorial, reacted to my disclosure about my successful career and disorder. I was very moved by words like: "We used to spend our Sunday afternoons with you and others beagling many years ago. I cannot tell you what an enormous service you have provided to those who struggle with severe or even moderate mental illness. I admire your courage for speaking out. You have rendered a great service to the legal community."; and "In the words of another T.R. whom I admire, '. . . Bully for you.' Great article, if we are going to talk the talk of diversity and equality then we must, as a profession, walk the walk." In particular, it and my earlier *CJ* article moved an important public official to go public with her own experience with mental illness and stigma.

Some in the community were aware that about a year before the husband of a local circuit judge who himself was an attorney and prosecutor had committed suicide. The tragedy occurred, at least in part, because he was unwilling to seek proper treatment for his severe depression as he feared stigma. His fear was not without some justification. When one of his colleagues had gotten psychiatric help he was teased unmercifully by others in the prosecutor's office. When the judge read my *CJ* and *Bar Briefs* articles they moved her to contact me and say she would like to help in the battle against stigma. In short order she was on the Boards of MHAKY and NAMI Louisville, and therefore another prominent voice for mental health treatment.

At school, I was teaching Torts II and Decedents' Estates, which ultimately generated very good reviews in Decedents' Estates. My disclosure had an immediate and positive impact on the way students view those with a psychiatric condition. For example, for years in Decedents' Estates I have taught about the rule that someone must be mentally competent (have "testamentary capacity") to make a will. The case in the book involves a Missouri doctor who amassed a considerable estate and effectively disinherited one of his daughters. She argued that he lacked the requisite capacity when he executed his will. She offered as evidence, among other things, that he had long been diagnosed as suffering from "manic-depressive psychosis." The jury agreed with her and threw out his will. I always ask the students what they think about this, and for many semesters the students invariably agreed that someone with such a diagnosis must be incompetent to execute a will. This time, their response was much different, probably as they now knew their professor also had "manic-depressive psychosis," or at least something very similar. They agreed that someone with a mental illness could still be competent to determine the fate of his or her assets upon his or her death. I was the example for this conclusion, as they knew I have a will. If I was capable of making one—and, indeed, of teaching their class—maybe their predecessors had jumped to a conclusion too soon in deciding the capacity issue.

Every time I have taught Decedents' Estates since January 2008 students have at least said they do not think a diagnosis of a mental illness automatically equals a lack of testamentary capacity. Similarly, Torts I students apparently have altered their view on the standard of liability for those with that condition. I think the sea-change in both classes is directly attributable to students' eyes being opened by my example. That helps explain why I thought it important to go public in the first place.

By spring vacation it was time for one of the most exciting events of my life. Thanks to Elyn, the Gould School of Law at USC had invited me to speak on mental illness in legal academia and I gladly agreed to do so. Kathi and I flew to Los Angeles and checked into our hotel. Soon, Elyn and her husband Will came to meet us, and Elyn and I finally set eyes on each other. We embraced and chattered away like two old friends who had not seen one another in some time. It was wonderful to be with her.

On March 11 Kathi and I went to USC where I spoke to a large crowd on "Severe Mental Illness in the Academy: A Law Professor's Story." The audience was very receptive, and members asked a number of questions concerning my life and career. They seemed glad to know that Elyn is not unique. If there are two such legal academics out in the open, there doubtless are many more hidden in the shadows.

Once I returned to Louisville, the parade of speaking engagements began. By the end of 2008, I spoke fourteen more times to a variety of groups. These included social work students, psychology students, law students, nursing students, police officers being trained to deal with people with mental illness in crisis, NAMI audiences, psychiatric rehabilitative workers, and mental health workers. Most important to me, I again addressed the University's Department of Psychiatry. This time I spoke of my life before and in Louisville and of my ties to the Department ranging from Dr. Bell to Dr. Manishadi to Dr. Humphrey to Dr. Quinton (she went to medical school at the University and trained in psychiatry as a fellow in the Department). Dr. Bell had died shortly before my talk so I did not get to see that great and good man one last time. Dr. Manishadi could not attend (he heard me on a later date). Both Drs. Humphrey and Quinton were in the audience and listened to my many compliments of them. John Turner also was there and the subject of my highest praise. At the end of my address I was asked a number of questions, followed by a rousing ovation. Dr. Quinton was swamped with well-wishers after my speech (I think they were proud of her for doing such a good job of keeping me going). When it was all over she asked for a hug. I was happy to accommodate her request.

In all my talks I emphasize two major points: "stigma's wrong, and treatment works." That pretty much sums up my feelings—the stigma of mental illness is unjustified and wrong, and treatment of at least some with severe mental illness can be quite successful. If anyone does not believe the latter point, let him or her look no further than at Elyn and me.

I spent hundreds of hours writing, rehearsing (although she was kind enough never to complain, Kathi must have gotten sick to death proof reading and timing each practice speech to make sure it was good and took no more than the allotted amount of time), and delivering these addresses. While I had a basic talk with which to work, I tailored each oration to the particular audience to which I was speaking. One reason all were so effective, in my estimation, was the personal touch I gave to each. I later was named Mental Health Consumer of the Year by MHAKY in recognition of my mental health advocacy efforts.

Over the course of the year I got much positive feedback. It included comments like: "Thank you for your inspiring speech. While it must have been hard for you to recount the struggle you have had with your illness, your story carried a most positive message to your audience. That message is that treatment works when it is delivered to the patient and your living presence provided a living, fighting example of success." Also: "Your talk yesterday was just terrific. It is not often that someone of your stature is willing to talk publicly about their personal experience with mental illness. Many have thanked me for arranging it and have been more enthusiastic about your presentation than most any that I can recall. I believe that it was particularly powerful because it is so personal, you are so accomplished in your field, and yet you are willing to share your story despite the risks. Your work, along with that of Elyn Saks, goes a long way to reduce stigma and is a great contribution to the mental health field." Further: "As I think was evident from the students' questions, they were able to gain a great deal of knowledge from you that will benefit their professional development. While it is one thing for me to share various textbook examples or examples from my experience of working with persons who live with similar illnesses, it is a much richer learning experience for my students to hear you tell your own story. In your talk, you touched on so many topics that we will explore throughout the semester, such as, all the various medication issues and struggles that one faces when living with a serious mental disorder. Even more important than that aspect, you made it real for the students, you shared your sense of humor, and you allowed them to see the great success and full life that is possible." And: "Your presentation on the Stigma of Mental Illness was both informative and entertaining. I have received numerous comments from those in attendance about the positive impact your talk had on them and their perceptions of those suffering from mental illness. I think the personal sharing embedded in your talk made it especially powerful."

In addition to my own speaking efforts, the Dean asked me to organize a program about impaired attorneys and the bar applications for students with mental health concerns. This reopened my old, long-festering wound relating to the stigma bar examiners in states like Florida and Kentucky direct towards applicants with a psychiatric history through their many questions about such care. That this keeps students from seeking treatment they need was brought home by the anonymous e-mail I received from a third year student at the Law School. He or she said fear of the reporting requirement kept him or her from going to Alcoholics Anonymous meetings to deal with his or her drinking problem. Instead, he or she tried to handle the matter alone. An unsurprising failure successfully to do so led to an alcohol-related arrest that hurt his or her chances with the bar far more than reporting having sought help would have done.

Other Brandeis faculty have told me that they know of students whose refusal to seek psychiatric counseling is attributable to their desire to avoid the Kentucky reporting requirement. Sam has mentioned he is aware of a highly qualified graduate who would have made an outstanding Kentucky attorney who chose to leave the Commonwealth and practice elsewhere in order to avoid its inquisitional character and fitness questions. While I do not know the identities of these students I think it awful, and unenlightened, that the bar puts them in such a Hobson's choice.

I arranged a discussion session with representatives from both the Indiana and Kentucky character and fitness committees and the impaired lawyer groups from both states. I even helped pay for pizza for those who came. A large number of students attended the program, which was only partially successful as the bar officials danced around the question of what happens to an applicant with a mental illness or substance abuse problem. Finally, I took the bull by the horns and, as I recall, asked the Kentucky spokesperson what I deemed the crucial question:

"Could I be admitted to the Kentucky Bar?"

"Hmm. You have bipolar disorder, correct?"

"That's right."

"Ever been hospitalized for it?"

"Five times starting in 1980."

"When was the last one?"

"Three in 2004."

"That's four years ago. You on medication?"

"Lots."

"You take it as prescribed?"

"Always."

"You see a psychiatrist?"

"Every month."

"How about a therapist?"

"Every two weeks."

"You're holding down a regular job."

"I'd say so. I've been here since 1986."

"OK. Yes, I think you'd be admitted. You'd have to give us access to your medical records, and might be asked to appear before a committee to discuss your ability to control your disease."

"Would that group be mental health professionals?"

"Probably not."

So there was the response. I probably would be admitted after having to open my most intimate records to bar examiners and possibly to answer demeaning questions posed by questioners with no knowledge of mental health issues. This reinforced my previously noted solution, which I kept to myself: "I'll pass, and just keep my Florida Bar membership. I can train Kentucky attorneys without being one myself, and that's what I'll do."

This did not help our students who need to be licensed in Kentucky, but they will just have to deal with the Kentucky (or Indiana) bar examiners and hope for the best. I do not think what they heard from them was very reassuring. When I discussed the session with Elyn she thought it quite interesting since the California bar application asks practically nothing about the psychiatric history of applicants. She did recall that when she applied to the Connecticut bar it inquired about any history of mental health treatment, but once she truthfully and fully disclosed it she was admitted with no difficulty.

Finally, the big day arrived and the *JLE* article came out. The *JLE* editors, one of whom is a renowned constitutional law scholar on the faculty at Harvard Law School, were most generous in their comments in the "From the Editors" commentary at the beginning of the issue. About my piece, they said I had written a "riveting and extraordinary stor[y] of what happens when legal education must be conducted under extreme stress." That immediately sounded good to me. What followed made me incredibly happier: "In what is likely to be another classic on these pages, Professor James T.R. Jones courageously reveals his 'secret life' as a law professor with bi-polar disorder. Joining his friend and colleague, Professor Elyn Saks, he publicly recounts his private struggles through treatment for mental illness, all while continuing as a law professor. His story will inspire others (perhaps inaugurating a new range of 'coming out' stories) who have struggled with both mental and physical disabilities to continue to teach, write, and follow their vocational dreams and goals."

Much as I always had hoped, the article generated a spate of correspondence from law professors around the nation. One example will suffice: "I just finished reading your article. It is very moving. I applaud you for your candor and courage in writing the piece. I think it's terrific that you've shared your story. Thank you for coming forward and describing both your struggles and your successes." A number of those who responded indicated they themselves had psychiatric issues but were not willing to go public with them. One woman called me in tears when she finished the piece. I had to comfort her over the telephone and ask her to contact me sometime in writing, which she eventually did. Overall, I obviously had struck a nerve. Hopefully my effort was more than a flash in the pan, and, along with Elyn's, will engender real change in the way the legal academic profession views mental illness and those who suffer from it.

What about my own colleagues? The reactions varied from warm congratulations to dead silence. I was pleased by the kind words I had directed my way, and interested in the lack of response from others. I was not certain whether they thought it was no big deal and thus did not require comment or wished I had kept quiet about my situation. I later ran across an article by Dr. Kay Jamison where she recounted reactions to *An Unquiet Mind*: "Several colleagues made it abundantly clear that it would have been best to keep my illness private. Others were obviously embarrassed by my disclosure and appeared to have no idea what they should say or do in my presence." No one on the Brandeis Law School faculty has ever told me I should not have written my article.

Almost as soon as the *JLE* hit the street, Elyn, Sam, John Turner, Dr. Quinton, people at NAMI Louisville and MHAKY, some in my support group, and others all encouraged me to write a book for the general reading public. Kathi was willing for me to do so so long as I would not become manic in the process as I did when writing the article. I promised not to go down *that* road again. I then pondered what to do. I was unsure whether

I would have enough uninterrupted time to do the job, but then remembered I had not had a sabbatical since 1995 (the medical leave in 2004 did not count as one). If I got one I would have a whole semester off to write. When you added that to a summer either before or after the sabbatical, it would give me seven months to focus on nothing else. Suddenly the idea seemed more attractive.

When I submitted my sabbatical request the Dean, who has been incredibly supportive of me ever since he learned of my condition, immediately endorsed it and sent it to the central administration. It, in turn, approved it. Thus, I would have time to write my memoir. Now I just would have to sit down and do so, reliving, in the process, some things I would rather have kept forgotten.

Over the summer, I gave several speeches, fine-tuning my message in the process. I also began preliminary work on the book. In particular, I bought and carefully studied a paperback on how to write a memoir Elyn had recommended to me. I quickly learned there is a special art to composing an autobiography, and I tried to absorb the methodology for doing so. As I had never before written a book, this would be exploring new ground for me.

I also experienced additional medical problems, some of which turned out to be triggered by my psychiatric medications. First, I learned I was slightly anemic. Dr. Quinton, the drug guru, immediately said that was probably from a rare side effect of one of my prescriptions. My primary care doctor sent me to a hematologist who ran a battery of tests, including a very painful bone marrow biopsy. After all of them, and a series of intravenous iron infusions, he concluded the anemia was from the psychiatric medications. Surprise!

Second, I had lost considerable weight. I was happy to do so, since, as noted, a common side effect of antipsychotics is significant weight gain. At six foot two inches I was running about 165 pounds, which put me at the seventh percentile of a body mass index calculation. My primary care doctor again was concerned, but Dr. Quinton explained the symptom by saying anorexia is an uncommon side effect of one of my psychiatric medicines. This time the other physician just took her word for it. I am happy to take the pill and keep my weight under control.

Finally, my otolaryngologist discovered I had a lump on my right parotid gland, one of the salivary glands. Since my father had had cancer there, the physician was concerned about it. While he thought it was probably benign, he was not certain and said we should take it out. Accordingly, in late July I had another major surgery. I worried considerably about having this done and the possibility I had cancer like so many others in my family. Once more, the rumination that is a hallmark of my disease ran amok. When I awoke from the five hour surgery I asked Kathi:

"Is it benign?"

"Yes. I told you so."

There was a bothersome temporary result. The facial nerve runs through the parotid, and I had paralysis problems. For example, my mouth drooped on the right side and I could not close my right eye. Fortunately these turned out to only be temporary issues and in due course I regained normal control of my face. It was a sign that I really was handling my illness well that I kept myself under control and went ahead through life as I waited to regain my usual condition.

In the fall, I taught Torts I and Decedents' Estates once again. Indeed, I was handling an overload for the year, as Decedents' is a four credit hour course and I ended up with fourteen hours for the calendar year while the usual burden is twelve. Although I did not really mind doing so as there was a shortage of Decedents' teachers, it showed that I was back to normal when I could carry more than my usual share of the curriculum. The semester went extremely well, with very good evaluations. I was glad to have my normal rhythm fully in place.

I gave nine mental illness talks during the semester, including that to the Medical School Psychiatry Department. By now I was well known around Louisville, and the *Courier-Journal* frequently called me to comment on mental health issues that were in the news. I was glad to be a spokesperson for those with severe mental illness. I also continued as co-facilitator for my bipolar support group.

There was one huge event in the fall. I long had wanted to get Elyn to deliver her address in Louisville. I was able to arrange for her to speak twice in two days, once for NAMI Louisville and once at the Law School. I handled every detail of her visit. Kathi, Jane, Jennifer, Shirley, John Turner, and Dr. Quinton all were in the large audience for the NAMI Louisville speech, and I made sure they met Elyn. It was a triumph, featuring both Elyn's outstanding program and the amazing PowerPoint presentation Will created and operates. I have never seen anything that comes close to equaling the latter; even our Law School technology people were extremely impressed.

The next day Elyn spoke before a large crowd at the Law School. While the University President and Provost were unable to attend, the Vice Provost for Diversity and Equal Opportunity was there and found what she heard was, in her words, "an eye opener for me." I felt very gratified that the whole stay had gone off without a hitch. It was a major accomplishment for me, and I had executed it without unduly stirring up my disorder. Indeed, while I have staged various successful events during my life, none has gone as flawlessly as this. Another demonstration that I was "high functioning" once more.

During the fall my ideological transformation was completed. I long had been tolerant of the gay, lesbian, bisexual, and transgendered (GLBT) students at the Law School because of my libertarian approach to life and my friendship with Sam. Indeed, I go into estate planning for the GLBT community in some detail in Decedents' Estates. Once I went public with my illness my empathy with them grew exponentially. Now I had "come out of the closet" just as they had done. I became a major backer of the Lambda Law Caucus, the GLBT group at the Law School. The Lambdas, in turn, have been very supportive of me. Quite a change of direction for a formerly conservative Republican.

Even more significant was my political change of heart. As the 2008 election loomed, I carefully evaluated the platforms of the Democratic and Republican parties as they related to those with severe mental illnesses and noted the difference between them. I liked Democratic candidate Barack Obama, for whom Sam was a major supporter. I ended up with an Obama sign in my yard and an Obama bumper sticker on my car. On Election Day I took the momentous step of voting for Obama for President. A remarkable event for me to cast my ballot for a liberal Democratic African-American, the first Democratic presidential candidate for whom I ever had voted. In the process I helped him win Indiana the first time that state went for a Democratic candidate since 1964. My political conversion was complete! I shudder to imagine what my mother would think if she knew.

At a time all was going extremely well, December saw a sobering event that reminded me that I still have a severe case of my disorder. I had a brief manic outburst against a student, about which I felt horrible in retrospect. My sense of guilt, and the resulting incessant ruminations, catapulted me into the abyss of depression and despair. I abruptly decided that only suicide would make amends for what I had done and ransacked the house while searching for the key to the weapons closet in order to retrieve a permanent forty-four caliber solution to what was actually a very temporary problem. I could not locate it as Kathi, having recognized something bad was afoot, had taken the key to work with her. While at the time I was quite angry at her for doing so (I thought of her as "a little #*!%$@"), in hindsight

I realize how lucky it was that she acted as she did. Truly, I suddenly was having grave difficulty charting a safe course between the twin perils of mania and depression of my disease. Unfortunately, and quite dangerously, one can never accurately predict when that might occur.

After this incident I finally admitted to myself that things had to change. I surrendered all the projectiles for the guns to Kathi, thus rendering them harmless. She immediately got rid of the bullets, etc., so that now I have nothing other than black powder to shoot out of the guns, which remain locked in the closet. I still can use them at reenactments, but they pose no danger to me.

It is frightening that despite all my success coping with my illness I can so quickly fall prey to it and abruptly travel in a few hours from normalcy to an almost irresistible urge to end my life. It shows that I, and Kathi, must constantly be on guard against such an event.

When I told this story to my support group, the reactions were interesting:

"What? Are you kidding?"

"You're the facilitator. You can't do something like that."

"Why would you be so stupid? Couldn't you see how crazy you were thinking?"

To all of them I had one basic response:

"I have the same disease y'all have, and can act like any of the rest of you. Nobody gave me a 'get out of jail free' card. So don't be surprised if someday I get really manic or depressed, or have another breakdown that puts me in the hospital, or even kill myself. It all comes with the territory of having bipolar disorder."

No one had an answer to that.

As 2008 came to an end, I prepared for another trip to California, this one to San Diego for the AALS annual meeting in early January 2009. I had been invited to speak at two different sessions there. The first was a program about mental health issues for the law school providers of support services to students. While the first speaker on the agenda used up most of the time allotted for the session, I found it interesting that most of the audience questions were directed to me and one of my colleagues on the subject of the bar disclosure issue.

Later that day Elyn came down from USC and met me. We prepared for what was, for me, the main event of the conference. The AALS Sections on Law and Disability and Law and Mental Disability jointly sponsored a program entitled "Law Professor Narratives of Mental Illness." Elyn and I were the speakers. For the first time, we gave our respective talks back to back at the same podium. I insisted on going first, as there was no way I would appear after Elyn's PowerPoint presentation, which I operated in Will's absence. I knew when I would be licked! Our two speeches were extremely well received, so the trip was worth making. In particular, it was wonderful to see Elyn for the third time in a year.

By now, Elyn and I together had made real in-roads into how those in our profession view those with severe mental illnesses. Hopefully we shall continue doing so in the future.

25

What have I learned during my fifty-eight years on the planet regarding life in general, and with mental illness in particular? Many things. First is the effect of childhood bullying and related persecution. In my case, I acquired from it the outcast mentality and inferiority complex that afflicted me for many years, and to a small degree still does so. More seriously, it may have contributed to my developing bipolar disorder later in life. It is known that such treatment can cause mental illness to flower at some point. Like me, Ramona Paetzold reports both having been tormented and brutalized by peers as early as the first grade. It can also lead to physical problems. In me, the physiological manifestations—mainly severe ulcer disease—arose at a surprisingly young age. It did the same for Ramona. Given my mother's desire to take me for counseling as a child, psychological signs were evident as well. The mistreatment also led me to dislike children as a class of persons, not a good thing for someone who as an adult would father two such individuals. About the only positive that can be said for what I endured is that it ended when I graduated from Episcopal. For that I am grateful.

Second is my taking on, and gradually overcoming, the torture of feeling I was an outcast. Once it began in childhood, it endured for decades. For everything that reduced it, such as friendship with Andy Baker or acceptance as an Echols Scholar or a war gamer, there was a corresponding counterweight such as a derogatory comment at Episcopal or rejection by a fraternity. At Duke, my welcome inside the ivied halls was offset by my problems with the private employment process. After the wonderful year with Judge Tjoflat came the relative hell with the law firm in Jacksonville, where one could be cast aside for such reasons as the crime of winning a stupid card game while staying sober. It took a spell at Highland among those many considered insane to really feel I was where I belonged and was accepted as me. At Chicago, I was not an outcast at the Law School, although I did not fit in with the *übermensch* regular faculty. However, I fared only marginally better in the academic job market than I had with law firms. Finally, at the Brandeis School of Law I found acceptance by people I liked and respected, although I did not fully trust until I had known them for over twenty years. While I doubtless never will be incredibly popular, I was granted tenure and promoted to full professor. After that, I was pretty much left alone and would probably have toiled for the rest of my career in relative obscurity had I not chosen to go public with my story. In my private life, it took years for me to feel fit to associate with others. When I thought I had found happiness with Jane I discovered it was all an illusion. Only marriage to Kathi left me feeling truly loved, accepted, and not at risk of being used and then cast aside. After forty-four years I was finally entitled to security and satisfaction in my personal and professional life. I had won the battle against being a pariah I had fought for so many years! It may have been the bottom of the ninth inning, but a victory then is a win nonetheless.

Third, I have learned to accept certain behaviors from my mood disorder as symptomatic of it. Just as one with diabetes, hypertension, or epilepsy must deal with certain things when his or her illness actively manifests itself, I face issues when my disease becomes severe like suicidality, irritability, euphoria, and over-spending. In particular, I must contend at such times with crying, sobbing, and weeping. Initially I was completely unnerved, if not totally embarrassed, by such "unmanly" actions. While society accepts male tearfulness at times like the death of a close relative or a beloved pet, it frowns on it otherwise. I have come to understand over the years, and accept, that my disorder leaves me prone to periods of extreme emotion as expressed by crying when my moods control me. I then have no more power over my disease than the diabetic or epileptic does over his or hers when the illness rules. Thus, I should not be, and am not, ashamed sometimes to shed tears, and others, male or female, with bipolar disorder ought not to be either. Of course, for the sake of appearances, and to preserve one's privacy from the prying eyes of others, one should try to limit such actions as much as possible. Someday, when the stigma against male crying or other public displays of emotion disappears not even that need be a concern.

Fourth is the importance of an art form that diverts, and even heals, you. From my days at Virginia through the toil at Duke through the loneliness in New York City and Jacksonville and Asheville through the solitude of Chicago, music kept my spirit alive and, to a degree, put me with kindred souls. Much as the notes of the magic flute of Prince Tamino led him safely though the trials of fire and water in Mozart's *Die Zauberflöte*, so did music help me weather the tribulations of my own life. Again, once I found satisfaction with Kathi I was able to enjoy it and music on their own terms. Hopefully, for the rest of my days I will continue to take pleasure from music for the right reasons and not mainly as an escape from an unhappy existence.

Fifth is the love and affection you can share with your four legged companions, especially the lovable, yet eternally stubborn, dachshund. From childhood to middle age and beyond, the "puppy children" are always there even when all others forsake you. Occasionally, for one reason or another, you encounter a dog that transcends itself and becomes a person as important as

311

any you have known in your life. Such a being was Nutmeg. As noted, it is really true that animals help one cope with life with mental illness. I cannot imagine having survived mine without at least some of the six dachshunds with which I have been blessed since childhood.

Sixth is the importance of support groups and friends. I have benefitted greatly from two groups in particular, the divorce and bipolar assemblages in Louisville. The therapy gatherings at Highland and Wellstone, when led by a quality expert, show that encouragement in general can benefit those there regardless of their individual diagnoses. At the Law School, since 2004 Sam has been a major ally, draft reader, "outing" and writing encourager and coach, and confidant. I only wish I had told him my story years before so I could have benefitted from his concern and camaraderie before my breakdown. Similarly, Ed Render, Bob Stenger, and Ron Eades have always been great with me, quietly supportive and constantly available both before and since they learned of my disease.

Elyn is a special case. Until I contacted her in 2007 I had friends with psychiatric disorders, but not peers. Elyn is, as noted, like me in many ways. In particular, she is a tenured full professor of law with credentials as good as, if not better than, mine. After years in the same shadows as I, she went public with her story as I did with mine. We each are gross over-achievers compared to most who have either schizophrenia or bipolar disorder. It is hard to describe how great it is to know each day either I will call her or she will call me for a chat sometime in the mid to late afternoon, Louisville time. I can always find her in her office, seven days a week (I prefer to work at home as often as I can). We can, and do, discuss whatever issues either of us has. We have a unique bond as the only two law professors in the United States to publicly acknowledge having a severe mental illness. As a result, in roughly four years she has become the closest friend I have had during

312

my life. If I have a problem, or even just an idea I want to run by someone, I can do so with her, and vice versa. She has been incredibly supportive of my writing this book, shepherding me through the composition and publication process. When I want someone other than Kathi to look at my latest chapter, I need merely e-mail it to Elyn for her always insightful comments. And, of course, we have visited each other on our respective home turfs, speaking to enthusiastic audiences of law students and others, as well as together to the Academy at the AALS conference in San Diego. We make an exceptional team. I do not want to imagine what it would be like not to have Elyn available at the end of the telephone or via e-mail.

I must also mention Ramona. While we are not exactly peers, as she is not a law professor but rather a lawyer who teaches law to business students, we still have much in common. Indeed, since she has bipolar disorder she is closer to me by diagnosis than Elyn. Also, she is a pioneer, as she was the first lawyer academic to "out" herself and her illness. We are in irregular contact rather than speaking daily as I do with Elyn, but each knows the other is available if needed. In particular, we are family, albeit by marriage rather than blood (affinity versus consanguinity, in Decedents' Estates language). My wife's father's uncle's daughter is at least a kissing cousin, and thus our relationship is between that of two professional colleagues, and two relatives, with bipolar disorder.

Seventh is the need to follow the recommendations of good mental health professionals, with whom I have been extremely blessed over the years. This means seeing them regularly, taking your medications as prescribed, and going into the hospital when so advised. Many with bipolar disorder suffer the greatest harm when they forget, or decline, to do so. One of the main reasons I have been as successful as I have over the years is my refusal to stray from this path. When I did so in 1995 my action nearly proved disastrous. I trust I will never make that mistake again.

Eighth is that you truly can evolve during the course of your life. I have gone from early days as a conservative Republican, to libertarianism, to ACLU membership, to the unimaginable act of voting for Barack Obama. This has resulted from rebellion against parents, political idealism, and pragmatic support for those most likely to support me and others like me. As my own views have broadened, so has my tolerance for other unpopular sectors of society such as my friends the Lambdas at the Law School.

Ninth is that mental illness can successfully be treated to allow at least some of those who have it to lead productive and happy lives. Severe mental illness is not curable—it cannot be made to go away—but it can be managed. I have done so for over thirty years, and have a good life as a result. Indeed, I have excelled. Keeping my illness a secret for well over twenty years demonstrates that I truly do well almost all the time. When I run into problems, immediate medical treatment generally resolves them. As Kathi once said, one reason she felt safe to marry me was my generally positive prognosis and that "most of the time you seem fine." If she is satisfied with my mental health, I am in good shape. Maybe I am better off than many others in society, as I actually carefully monitor my mental health rather than ignoring difficulties like depression or the like as they do.

Tenth is the great value of having a wonderful family. Aunt Bet, Rick, Ramsay, and my mother have all helped me when I have needed their assistance. Nothing showed this better than their aid during my 1983 collapse, my divorce, my 1995 surgery and illness, and since my 2004 breakdown. I still speak with my mother and Ramsay every week.

Eleventh is the incredible importance of having a loving, supportive, knowledgeable, and caring spouse. The years I have been with Kathi have been the best of my life. She is my wife, my partner, my trainer, my editor, my friend, my hall monitor, my speech coach, my lover, my finder of lost things, my daughters' beloved stepmother, and my guardian angel. She is to me all that Will is to Elyn, if not more. She keeps an eye on me every day, and can read my every mood or thought. She feels free to call John Turner or Dr. Quinton should she think I need the intervention of one or both of them. She helped pull me out of the depths of 1996, and was with me during the meltdown in 2004. She shared every moment of fear or triumph after that event, and deserves a great deal of credit for my eventual recovery from those dark days that were, in their own way, as awful for her as they were for me. I would never have gone public without her advice and support. Perhaps most important of all, she loves me enough to have married me in 1997 after John Turner told her what she must anticipate, if not to expect, when with me. Unlike many spouses of those with bipolar disorder, she has stuck by me in sickness and in health, through crankiness and exhilaration, during mania and depression, and obviously will do so as long as we both shall live. As I have said, I have told her she better not die before me!

Finally, stigma is truly an awful thing. In my life, it has adversely affected me a number of times. Before I came to Louisville, my fear of it made me hide a major part of my life. Doing so undoubtedly contributed to my feelings of inferiority and inadequacy. Indeed, how could it fail to do so?

Once I was at the Law School my dread hurt my career, costing me money on numerous occasions and on a few nearly my job itself. As I was unwilling to disclose my illness, my superiors thought I did not publish enough as I was not working as I should. They had no clue that my problem was my bipolar depression and the drugs I took to combat it, most notably lithium. Hence, my annual raises were not as high as they could have been—at best, I would be considered to be doing a satisfactory, but not an exemplary, job. When you coupled the publication difficulty with BLS teaching evaluations, I was almost guaranteed to come up short.

In 1993, as my mood plunged upon my separation and ultimate divorce from Jane I entered a real crisis. I had tenure so my job itself was not at risk, but my wages certainly were adversely affected. My 1994 Decedents' debacle probably never would have occurred had I been forthcoming about my condition. When the evaluations were predictably bad, I sat in silence as the Dean berated me for my performance and told me my salary would suffer for three years. In 1995, after I delayed my promotion request for three years until I finally was feeling somewhat better and had produced a major article my application was slapped down due to unwritten works I could not have composed in light of my mental condition. When I was both physically and mentally devastated in the spring of 1996 from major surgery and depression I received a substandard evaluation from a Dean who thought I was being obdurate rather than desperately ill. When I appealed his decision he rebuffed me on the basis that the Decedents' evaluations from 1994 and the BLS ones in 1996 were unrelated and showed a pattern of poor performance by me, when in reality they were just two tips above the surface of the iceberg of bipolar depression that lasted from 1993 until the summer of 1996.

Even after my elevation to full professor finally was approved, I rarely received maximum pay raises on the basis that I was not doing "enough" to merit them. In reality, I probably was working harder than almost anyone on the faculty, but no one could see that because my stigma fear forced me to hide the truth.

Am I criticizing the Dean and faculty for their judgments? No, as had I been in their shoes I probably would have acted exactly as they did in order to motivate an "underperforming" colleague. Instead, I blame the fear that kept me from being open about what I faced. Since I went public about my disease I have fared far better at the hands of deans who see the full picture of my performance. Had I not been unwilling to disclose my disease for so many years, my current wages would almost certainly be much higher than they are, among the lowest among the full professors at the Law School. It is highly unfortunate that I will be paid on that basis for the rest of my career for the sake of my dread of stigma.

Between my article and this book, why have I "outed" myself after nearly twenty-eight years of secrecy? Should I risk stigma from the profession and others in addition to having students fear to take my courses or give me bad teaching evaluations on account of my disclosure? I want to demonstrate, from yet another corner, that at least some of those with severe mental illness can have full and satisfying professional and personal lives. They need not and should not endure stigma or doubt as to their ability to perform their personal or employment duties. I have shown that a law professor with a severe enough case of bipolar disorder to be hospitalized five times for it can have a life of substantial accomplishment. Indeed, I have thrived in the intellectually challenging realm of legal academics where I have matched wits with both students and colleagues. When my disorder has incapacitated me, as in 1983 and 2004, I have gradually bounced back to my usual high level of functioning. Today, both in Kentucky and nationally I am a public face of one who has prospered while living with severe mental illness. Although relatively few with mental disorders flourish as I have done, I show what is possible when you combine hard work with excellent medical care and a modicum of luck.

Every so often, some well-meaning person who knows I have bipolar disorder will note my growing irritability and volatility as mania rears its ugly head. They will tell me to calm down, take it easy, not to get so excited. Being calm and collected, however, is not in my nature. If I took things easy, I never would have achieved what I have in life. Instead, I quite likely would have ended up on permanent disability or in some menial job.

Perhaps I would have labored in one of "the three f's of food, filth, and filing" work categories into which some psychiatric rehabilitation professionals tend to peg their clients, or even the "four Fs': food, flowers, folding, and filth" as do so many people who suffer from bipolar disorder. In order to overcome the many obstacles my condition has erected for me I have had to go to extraordinary lengths to hurdle over them. Thus, I cannot afford to let up, even for one second, for fear I will lose that for which I have worked over a lifetime of pain and struggle.

When Elyn and I are together people frequently ask us for the secret of our respective success. With Elyn's concurrence, I always answer:

"First, we were lucky enough to come along when the right medications were available. Second, we were from families with money so we could get the finest medical care. Third . . ."

"You're both highly intelligent."

"Neither of us says that, but I won't argue the point."

"Is there any other reason?"

"Yes. We're each too damn stubborn to give in to our disease."

That may be the real key. Various people with a severe mental illness are very intelligent, have the money for good medical care, and take the appropriate drugs yet they do not function at our level. Maybe Elyn and Ramona and I are just too obstinate, too mulish, too pigheaded, too obdurate, too dogged, too determined, too tenacious, and too persistent to surrender to a psychiatric condition. I intend to fight bipolar disorder as long as I have a breath in my body. To date on numerous occasions I have been like the Energizer bunny—knock me down with either a physical ailment or a psychiatric illness and I may stay there for a time, but eventually I fight my way back onto my feet, ready to go on with my life as if nothing has gone wrong. If I ever lose out to my disease it will not be for a lack of trying. I am stubborn, and proud of it. For once, stubbornness is a virtue, and

I will hold onto it for all I am worth. It can provide an epitaph at the Brandeis School of Law and elsewhere I would enjoy, as it says it all: "Professor Jim Jones. He was the stubbornest S.O.B. we ever knew."

Acknowledgments

M any people contributed to this story. First, I would not be alive to tell it were it not for the mental health professionals who have cared for me over the years, including Joseph Hartman, Joanna Gaworowski, Nell Endsell, Hugh Reed, John Bell, Manoochehr Manishadi, Lounette Humphrey, Deborah Quinton, Paul Phillips, John Turner, and many additional ones whose names, but not efforts, I have forgotten. Others like Scott Jarvis, George Walton, and Frank and Joann Marx do not officially fit into that category but have contributed greatly to my mental health nonetheless.

A number of individuals were kind enough to read portions of this work, which benefitted greatly from their feedback. These include Jeanne Lurie, Ramsay Jones, Ramona Paetzold, Luke Milligan, Susan Stefan, Ariana Levinson, Will Hilyerd, Ken Kress, Tristine Rainer, Tony Arnold, The Honorable Gerald Bard Tjoflat, and Mike Murphy. Michael Waterstone, Bob Bernstein, Bruce Scott, and Fred Frese gave me valuable assistance.

Both before and after I went public with my disease those at the Brandeis School of Law helped me get where I am today, especially Laura Rothstein, Ed and Joyce Render, Barbara Thompson, Bob and Mary Ann Stenger, Enid Trucios-Haynes, Jim Chen, Ron and Lillian Eades, Sam Marcosson, Nate Lord, Russ Weaver, and Tom and Rose Blackburn. Those outside the Law School include Jerry Smith, Jan Mercer, Marykay Lievense,

Barb Hedspeth, and Buck Wiseman.

Rebecca Burke did noble service in putting this book into print; I could never have gotten through the publication process without her assistance.

My daughters Jennifer and Shirley are enormous help due to the love and support they have given me both before and after they learned about my illness.

Elyn Saks has been a wonderful friend and colleague ever since the day in 2007 we learned we are the two law professors in the nation who publicly acknowledge we have severe mental illnesses. Our daily telephone conversations are invaluable; Elyn greatly encouraged me to write this book and read numerous versions of it. Thank you, dear friend.

Last, but certainly not least, is the most essential person of all, my wife of fourteen years (and counting), Kathleen Ann Murphy Jones. I never could have endured the events of the last decade, much less written my *Journal of Legal Education* article and this book, without her. More to the point, I could not look forward to many more years of life were it not for her. She makes the sun rise for me every day, and leaves many rainbows in her wake. I wish for her what they say in her beloved ancestral homeland:

> May love and laughter light your days,
> and warm your heart and home.
> May good and faithful friends be yours,
> wherever you may roam.
> May peace and plenty bless your world
> with joy that long endures.
> May all life's passing seasons
> bring the best to you and yours!

24383965R00212

Made in the USA
Middletown, DE
23 September 2015